MW00710875

Starting and Building Your Catalog Sales Business

Starting and Building Your Catalog Sales Business

Secrets for Success in One of Today's Fastest-Growing Businesses

Herman Holtz

WILEY

John Wiley & Sons, Inc.
New York • Chichester • Brisbane • Toronto • Singapore

Library of Congress Cataloging-in-Publication Data

Holtz, Herman.
    Starting & building your catalog sales business: secrets for success in one of today's
fastest-growing buinesses / Herman Holtz.
        p.   cm.
    Includes bibliographical references.
    ISBN 0-471-50816-0
    1. Mail-order buiness.   I. Title.   II Title: Starting and building your catalog sales
business.
    HF5466.H585   1990
    658..8'72—dc20   90-30608
                                                                                    CIP

Contents

Preface

1. What Is the "Catalog Sales" Business? / 11

Catalogs and selling by mail. What is distinctive about catalog sales? What is sold by catalog? Why do customers buy via catalogs? What are the pros and cons of catalog sales? What is the catalog sales business? Must you produce you own catalog? Must you buy in quantity and maintain an inventory? Are catalog sales always conducted by mail? Where are your markets? How can you find your prospects? Can you get any kind of mailing list you want? What kinds of mailing lists are available? Summary.

2. A Few Starter Ideas / 29

A few of the many popular items sold by catalog. Advantages and disadvantages of catalog purchases. Overcoming the disadvantages of catalog purchases. Highlighting the advantages of catalog purchases. The marketing value of exclusivity and innovation. Vendors as customers. Generalization versus specialization.

3. What to Sell: Finding the Right Line / 53

Crucial importance of "buying right." Categories of merchandise. The advantages of many items. A few broad classifications. Leaders and loss leaders. The ideal item. The search for ideal items. Tips on finding items. Acceptance of change.

4. Basics of Marketing / 73

Retail store sales versus catalog sales. The impact of direct response. Is the customer always right? The role of marketing. A few definitions.

Testing conventional wisdom. Teasers and subterfuge. The fundamental sins of marketing. Serving the customer.

5. Marketing Via Catalogs and Mail / 97

Marketing as the art of persuasion. Appeal of price, both low and high. Desire to win. Appeal of belonging. Fear and greed. Demographics. Market segments, positioning, and niche marketing. Inducements. Getting reliable answers.

6. Writing Catalog Copy That Sells / 123

Communication and persuasiveness. The elements of written sales copy. Proof and promise: The heart of persuasive copy. What constitutes proof and what constitutes credibility. How much proof is needed? A few facts and myths about copy. What are you really selling?

7. The Important and Necessary Elements in the Mailing / 153

Direct mail: basic examples. The sales letter. Strategies of the direct mail presentation. Brochures. Catalog packaging. Individual business and individualized catalog copy. Information required in catalog copy. Getting help.

8. Mailing Lists: A Critical Necessity / 177

How crucial is the mailing list? The list vendors. The key functions of mailing-list management. Assessing the quality of lists. Kinds of lists. Building your own list of inquirers. Database marketing. What is a database manager? Database versus mailing lists.

9. Costing, Pricing, and Accounting / 201

Costing and pricing. Accounting for the lay person. Do you need an accountant?

10. What It Takes to Succeed / 213

The high failure rate of business. A few fundamental discussions. Marketing is business. Basic mistakes of marketing. Growth: What is it? Special sales and promotions. Conversion.

11. Financing Your Future / 229

How much money will you need? A few basic facts about financing. Debt financing. How to write a loan proposal. Financing with credit cards. Help from the government. Grants. Equity financing.

12. Miscellaneous Aids to Success / 245

Marketing without money: Using PR (public relations). Getting leads. Testing. Mail-order law.

Appendix A: Mailing List Managers and Brokers / 261

Appendix B: A Few Sources for Special Services / 263

References / 265

Index / 267

List of Figures

1–1.   The Maine Hunting Shoe® in the L. L. Bean catalog.   4

1–2.   Cover of the Bluestocking Press catalog.   15

1–3.   Cover of Tools of the Trade catalog.   16

2–1.   A page from the Inmac® catalog.   31

2–2.   A page from the Egghead Software® catalog.   33

2–3.   A page from the Electronics Boutique® Software catalog.   34

2–4.   A page from the Mission Orchards™ catalog offering express delivery.   37

2–5.   A page from the catalog of Visual Horizons.   39

2–6.   A page from the M & B Company's catalog.   40

2–7.   Two pages from the J. Peterman Company catalog.   42

3–1.   A page from Harry and David Holiday Book of Gifts.   58

4–1.   Cover of The Software Labs catalog.   75

4–2.   Page from Willow Creek's catalog.   77

4–3.   Cover page of Quill® Corporation catalog.   95

5–1.   Cover of the Tiger Software catalog with price and express shipping promised.   101

5–2.   Cover of the Simply Tops catalog with special appeal.   103

5–3.   Page from the Quill catalog using fear motivation.   106

5–4.   Page from the Quill catalog using gain motivation.   107

5–5.   Catalog page showing hair styles.   116

5–6.   Another catalog page, including order form.   117

6–1.   Price appeal copy.   129

6–2.   Another example of price appeal copy.   130

6–3.   "We've got it all."   132
6–4.   "We're the best. See us first, last, and always."   133
6–5.   Secondary benefit.   134
6–6.   Another example of secondary benefit promised.   135
6–7.   Fear motivation at work.   136
6–8.   Special features (and implied benefits).   137
6–9.   Miscellaneous approaches.   138
6–10. Some examples of "asking for action."   139
6–11. Cover of Citibank card special catalog to members.   140
7–1.   First page of typical sales letter.   157
7–2.   A "sincere" sales letter.   159
7–3.   First page of "straight" sales letter.   161
7–4.   Another "sincere" letter.   162
7–5.   Inside cover of a catalog used as a sales letter.   163
7–6.   Front cover of a monthly catalog.   167
7–7.   Typical catalog page.   168
7–8.   Typical catalog order form.   170
7–9.   Page from a catalog selling books.   171
8–1.   A list of subscribers to an industrial trade journal.   181
8–2.   A list of a different type of subscriber.   182
8–3.   A page from the Ed Burnett Consultants list catalog.   183
12–1. Typical publicity release.   248
12–2. Journalistic inverted pyramid.   250
12–3. Typical product release.   251
12–4. Basic data sought by test.   256
12–5. More sophisticated data-gathering form.   256
12–6. Sheet 1, variations of data-collection forms.   257
12–7. Sheet 2, variations of data-collection forms.   258

Preface

Cataloging is part of the mail-order industry—a major part. In fact, cataloging can be considered an industry in itself, inundating the marketplace today with over 8,000 catalogs in circulation (primarily via the mails), accounting for billions of dollars in buying and selling, and supporting a host of satellite industries such as printing, mailing list management/brokering, advertising, mailing services, advertising specialities, and publications.

Perhaps a relatively mundane mode of doing business today, catalog sales have a rather romantic history, with such historic pioneers as Sears Roebuck and Montgomery Ward. A century ago, an inspiration for the success of catalogs as a vehicle for marketing was the relative isolation of the rural areas of the country and of the farmers and others who lived there. Catalogs then served a well-defined need, and the Sears Roebuck catalog became almost a tradition; it was a rare farmhouse or other rural dwelling that did not boast a copy of that catalog at that time.

Rural isolation is hardly a consideration today. With modern automobiles and high-speed highways, the rural dwellers can reach supermarkets, shopping malls, and department stores as readily as the urbanites and suburbanites. So perhaps the practical need for and reliance on catalogs in rural areas has passed, but the habit and emotional attachment have not: Millions of people still enjoy window shopping through thick catalogs while resting in their own living rooms, and then having the merchandise they order delivered to their door, regardless of where they live. In fact, catalogers do not all rely entirely on the mail today: A customer can even go to some retail outlets, order there from the mail-order catalog, and take the merchandise home with them! Many small merchants rely on catalog shopping to sell merchandise they do not carry in stock. (In fact, the term catalog stores refers to such establishments.) There are even some old-fashioned door-to-door salespeople selling shoes, cosmetics, and sundry other products out of catalogs. There are also "party sales" and other multilevel sales activities today that rely at least partially on catalogs and order-taking for future delivery.

In fact, the diversity of what is sold by catalog today is many, many times greater than anything envisioned by Sears and Montgomery Ward a century ago. Today, catalogs offer cosmetics, medicines, foods, furniture, equipment, auto supplies, office supplies, computer supplies, housewares, hardware, tools, paints, clothing, vacation plans, insurance plans, electronic devices, appliances, gifts, greeting cards, home improvements, and almost anything else that is sold by anyone anywhere via any medium.

Some catalogs offer exclusive items, such as rare imports and other items not to be found elsewhere easily. What's more, diversity is only one of the benefits catalogs have to offer. Catalogs spell convenience and, usually, economy; those alone are powerful forces in the marketplace. Many, perhaps most, catalogs offer economies difficult to find elsewhere, even in the many large discount stores. (That is especially true in the desktop-computer field today, for example.) Economy is one of the major motivations that drive many to prefer buying by catalog: Customers expect to find prices lower in catalogs.

Catalog sales thus continue to flourish with such prominent practitioners today as Lands' End, L. L. Bean, Spiegel, Fuller Brush Company, Avon, Mary Kay, and Fingerhut, to name only a few of the many long-established, heavy hitters in this industry. Yet, as a business venture, catalog sales are also hospitable to the small venturer working from his or her home, and to the small, established business adding catalog sales to broaden their marketing base. (Bear in mind that while mail order and catalog sales have many distinctive features, they are not truly industries or businesses of themselves but are ways of doing business.)

Mail order generally attracts an estimated 2 million newcomers trying their luck at starting a home-based mail-order business. Most, of course, find that significant success is somewhat elusive and no easier to reach in mail order than in any other way of doing business. Many do not grow beyond that early start-up scope, and they either continue to indulge their mail-order efforts more as hobby than as a serious business or go on to try their hands at other ventures. Among those start-ups, however, are those who venture into catalog sales, some via one of the multilevel marketing plans, some via a franchise-like arrangement with a supplier of merchandise and catalogs, and some as entirely independent venturers.

In no field has there been a more rapid or more widespread growth of catalogers than in the desktop computer business: Just about every item relevant to the personal computer—hardware, software, accessories, supplies, and services—is available from catalogers, the majority of them relatively new to cataloging. As one writer has put it ("Mail Order Strategies," Russ Lockwood, Personal Computing, February 1989), "Unfettered by costly storefronts and high profit margins, mail order companies can sell well-known hardware and software at 40, 50 and sometimes 60 percent off list price. And many mail order companies now offer recognized private-label brands that combine high quality with low price."

The magazine conducted and reported on a survey of 65 mail-order suppliers, presenting detailed descriptions and appraisals of 10 of the suppliers surveyed. The report covered a number of factors, including both the variety of hardware and software items and the customer service and support. The service and support are especially important considerations in mail-order and catalog sales businesses because buying from a cataloger is an act of faith. The customer must trust the supplier to make good on guarantees when necessary, to repair or replace defective items promptly, and to make refunds when necessary. A reputation for trustworthiness in these respects is a valuable asset. It is, in fact, more than that: It is a necessity.

Unfortunately, the casualty rate is high, probably because it is possible to launch such a venture from one's home; it appears to be easy to start, and in a sense it it. It is possible to start with little capital and to work at it part-time, while holding down a full-time job. It is also possible for other members of the family to pitch in to help because it can be started as a home-based business. Nonetheless, it still requires a great deal of hard work and a great deal of patience; success rarely comes quickly.

Despite the high casualty rate, many do manage to grow from start-ups at their kitchen tables or in their garages and basements and become major successes in catalog sales They manage to master the many complex details of business generally and the mail-order/catalog business specifically. The pages that follow were written with the fervent hope that they will inspire and aid in the creation of a few more such successes.

HERMAN HOLTZ

Starting and Building Your Catalog Sales Business

1

What Is the "Catalog Sales" Business?

Selling by catalog is a business that can be as kind to Mom-and-Pop entrepreneurs, whether moonlighting or working at it full time, as it is to the giants in that field.

CATALOGS AND SELLING BY MAIL

Mail-order businesses reap over $100 billion annually, according to *Small Business Opportunities* magazine ("Make It in Mail Order," September, 1989). The article estimates that 100,000 companies now distribute 12 billion mail-order catalogs every year! If you find it difficult to grasp 12 billion, think of it as more than 30 million catalogs in the mail every day.

The number of catalogs in *The Catalog of Catalogs* (Edward L. Palder, Woodbine House, Kensington, Maryland, 1987) also boggles the mind. Palder's book is 457 pages long, 373 pages of which are devoted solely to listing catalogs. The back cover of this thick paperback claims to list 8,000 catalogs across 450 categories, a quantity I do not dispute. Even so, I was unable to locate a number of catalogs that I know to be widely advertised, such as those of the Specialty Merchandise Corporation, Hanover House, and Best Mailing Lists, among others. (Oddly, the author also failed to list the catalog of his own publisher, Woodbine House, which offers a copy of their catalog to readers of the *Writer's Market*.)

These comments are not intended to criticize Palder's handsome work. Quite the contrary, the author has done a magnificent job and has produced a useful reference. However, it does illustrate the enormous number of catalogs extant that even with this massive research effort, it was possible to miss a

1

number of well-known catalogs. It is interesting, too, that in checking back on his original compilation, the author found only a 4 percent "error" rate—entries no longer entirely valid because an organization had gone out of business, moved, sold out, or merged with someone else. Such a low error rate on directory listings is truly remarkable.

Palder's table of contents illustrates the almost unbelievable diversity of what is sold by mail, with 26 pages of listings, many of them subdivided. Two and one-half pages are devoted to listing items under the major heading "Arts & Crafts," for example. Some other categories with many subcategories include "Automotive Parts & Accessories," "Collectibles," "Foods," "Gardening," "Home Furnishings," "Home Improvements," and "Photography." For anyone looking for ideas for things to sell by catalog, this resource is a treasure chest.

Most catalogs are published by retailers who use them as vehicles for selling their goods by mail, such as the well-known firms of Sears Roebuck, Montgomery Ward, Fingerhut, and Spiegel. Most are therefore quite pleased to send a catalog to anyone who requests it, although some ask for a nominal fee (typically $1 or $2), and a few request an "SASE" (self-addressed stamped envelope). Those who charge for their catalogs often promise to "refund" the money with the first order (actually a credit on the first order).

WHAT IS DISTINCTIVE ABOUT CATALOG SALES?

Smart Catalog Businesses Are Smart Businesses

When the well-known and successful cosmetic seller, Avon Products, Inc., ventured into a new line with its *Family Fashions* catalog, Avon management had no idea that the new venture would cost them $4 million the first year, or that the new catalog would continue to lose money for three more years. The situation did not turn around, and the catalog venture did not become profitable, until the catalog venture's vice president of marketing, Bill Willett, was moved into the top slot. A change of management at the top—and undoubtedly the concomitant new top management emphasis on marketing with some sensible reorganization—finally made the difference. In retrospect, that is not too surprising: Emphasis on marketing is almost always beneficial, for sales success is where overall business success begins. Certainly, general business success is not possible without successful marketing.

This does not make catalog sales a different kind of business. Quite the contrary, the general verities of business apply to catalog sales or any other venture, whether conducted by mail or other means. Selling by catalog differs from other businesses only in terms of its way of doing business. In fact, catalog sales is usually a subset of both mail-order and direct-mail businesses, and it can be explained, in essence at least, within that frame of reference.

Maine-based L.L. Bean, one of the oldest and best-known catalogers, illustrates the business nature of catalog sales. When the formerly booming market for preppie fashions plummeted, Bean was caught by surprise and suffered a severe drop in revenues; a department store suffers a similar loss when caught with styles that make the public yawn widely. Bean recovered neatly, however, by going back to basics—by once again featuring all the old reliables on which it had built its business originally, such as the Maine hunting boot and other outdoor gear (see Figure 1–1).

Although smart merchandising should not be underrated, it is only part of what makes a successful catalog sales business. Taking good care of customers is no less important when selling by catalog than it is when selling face-to-face or by other means. In fact, if anything, excellent customer service is even more important because many people are fearful of buying by mail, especially for the first time, and creating customer confidence is therefore paramount in importance. Highly conscious of that, of course, one of L.L. Bean's recovery measures was the addition of toll-free telephone service for customers, a convenience that is becoming more widespread, as is the availability of fax transmissions for ordering. Convenience appeals to prospects who are prosperous enough to value convenience and comfort above economy. Further, such modern refinements as toll-free calling and fax machines also suggest the prosperity and success of the seller and so encourage customer confidence: Anything that makes you appear to be highly successful—upscale—also makes your offerings more credible and increases customer confidence.

Mail Order, Direct Mail, and Catalog Sales

The mail-order business and the direct-mail business often overlap, but the terms address two different categories of business. The *mail-order business* is a method of doing business, by which customers can purchase products (i.e., via mail order), regardless of how the products were promoted or sales were solicited. The *direct-mail business* is a means through which a vendor can promote products and solicit sales (i.e., via direct mailings to prospective customers). Clearly, a catalog sales business is likely to incorporate both

Figure 1–1. The Maine Hunting Shoe® in the L. L. Bean catalog.

strategies—soliciting business via direct mail and encouraging customers to purchase products via mail order.

Thus, the term *direct mail* refers to the *method of soliciting business* by mailing sales literature directly to prospects, using mailing lists of individuals or organizations believed to be good prospects for whatever is being sold. It is actually an advertising method by which each prospect is pursued into his or her home or office individually. It is thus aggressively "direct" and derives its name thereby. Once customers decide to purchase a product (or service), they may do so in retail stores, by mail order, or by any other means offered by the vendor. In fact, many in the direct-mail business take great pains to note their distinction from mail-order businesses.

In contrast, the distinguishing trait of *mail order* is that orders are placed by mail, and the product usually is delivered via the same channel. Sales to mail-order customers may be solicited through various methods, such as advertising in print media, on radio, and on TV. Originally, it was expected that all orders would be placed by mail and that all goods ordered would be shipped via the same medium. The trend toward using credit cards, with almost everyone having and using at least a bank card (MasterCard or Visa, usually), has led to many orders being placed by telephone, to be charged to the credit card. More recently, the fax machine has become popular and is rapidly becoming as common and widely used in business establishments as telephones, so that an increasing number of orders are being placed by fax transmission. Obviously, this broadens the definition of *mail order* to include electronic forms of communication.

Further, the definition of *delivery by mail* has broadened in recent years. Shipment of the merchandise ordered is not necessarily by parcel post, as it once was. Many people find other, private-sector delivery services more reliable and more convenient than today's U.S. Postal Service. Nonetheless, *mail order* continues to be the general term used to designate that business.

For the most part, the catalog sales business is both a direct-mail business and a mail-order business. Nonetheless, though it is based on the direct-mail approach to soliciting business through distribution of catalogs, the seller may turn to media advertising for *lead generation* (i.e., helping to compile the lists of prospects to whom he or she will mail catalogs). Moreover, some small number of catalogs may be distributed by other means than mail: Sears and others with retail outlets often make catalogs available to customers visiting their outlets, for example. Too, many catalogs are distributed at trade shows, conventions, and other such conclaves. There are even a few catalog stores, which are retail outlets that carry a limited inventory (and often have even a limited array of models on display). Sales personnel at these stores take orders from customers who examine catalogs and then wait for mail delivery of the items.

Thus, catalog sales are not always solicited via direct mail, and catalog customers do not always order from catalogs by mail. In fact, some retail outlets permit customers to purchase directly (and walk out with) the items listed in their catalogs. So perhaps the feature most distinctive of the catalog sales business is that the sales literature delivered to prospects are primarily catalogs (which does not bar the seller from sending other literature along with catalogs).

WHAT IS SOLD BY CATALOG?

An enormous variety of items can be sold by catalog, and they are. Among the many catalogs arriving at post office boxes and at home mailboxes are those offering various kinds of merchandise:

Office supplies	Fax machines and other office devices
Computers, with accessories and supplies	Vitamins
Shoes	Printing (e.g., stationery)
Clothing	Health foods
Computer software	Items for resale
Books	"Specialty" merchandise
Novelties	Jewelry
Mailing lists	Lingerie
Electronic devices	Art supplies
Automobile accessories and supplies	Type fonts

Catalog sales businesses are so numerous and varied that at least one imaginative entrepreneur has made a business of assisting catalogers to distribute their catalogs. American Parade of Catalogs® (144 S. First Street, P.O. Box 4507, Burbank, CA 91503-4507) publishes a small colored brochure that lists 145 catalogs in the 1989 issue of its mailer. Eleven of the catalogs listed are free; most cost a dollar or two; and a few run to $3, $4, and even $5. The catalogs cover a staggeringly wide variety of items—jewelry, housewares, electronics, apparel, and even catalogs of catalogs, somewhat in the manner of Palder's book.

WHY DO CUSTOMERS BUY VIA CATALOGS?

I subscribe to the *Computer Shopper*, which is called a "magazine," but it is actually more a mail-order catalog of computers and related items than it is a magazine. The majority of its 800+ 10" x 13" pages carry the advertising of many different firms that sell by mail, usually at discounted prices. It carries some excellent articles about computers, but the articles seem incidental to the many pages of advertising by mail-order suppliers of entire computers and computer parts, accessories, and supplies that dominate the publication. The publishers obviously recognize this fact: A full page in each issue is addressed to the readers under the title "A Practical Guide to Mail Order Shopping in *Computer Shopper*." This advises the reader with "Tips on Shopping," "The Law on Mail Order," and other sections, as a valuable service to readers.

When it was launched a few years ago, magazine experts predicted rapid failure for it. They failed to perceive that its appeal was not as a magazine at all, but as a vehicle for easy-chair shopping. Most readers use it (as I do) to find the best sources for their computer-related needs. Despite all the other computer magazines published today, it has virtually no competition in that regard.

A lesson can be learned here (beyond the obvious one that self-proclaimed experts are not always to be taken seriously): A great many people love to shop. They frequent modern shopping malls, and they are fond of browsing through catalogs and periodicals that have extensive advertising. Mail-order catalogs, which encourage ordering and delivering products by mail (or other convenient parcel delivery services), have their own special appeal to the buyers, as well as to the sellers. That is partly due to the convenience factor, but it is also partly due to the atmosphere of shopping at complete leisure, without any pressure to fend off the solicitous salesperson eager to make a sale or the imminent closing hour of the mall, or a spouse's complaints of, "Let's get out of here and have dinner."

WHAT ARE THE PROS AND CONS OF CATALOG SALES?

Such terms as *mail-order business, direct-mail business, catalog sales business,* and *retail sales business* describe ways of doing business; they are not specific industries or businesses per se. The first three terms describe specific alternatives to *retail sales outlets* (operating a store, showroom, or office for walk-in trade) or to *field sales forces* (having a sales force making personal and direct calls on prospects and customers). There are pros and cons to doing business in each way. A few comparisons offer a better view of what *catalog sales* means in terms of advantages and disadvantages. For example, the marketing costs are certainly not a trivial consideration among the costs and investments required for doing business.

Investments and Costs Required for Various Business Methods

A business venture of any kind requires investment, sometimes referred to colloquially as "front-end money," and sometimes referred to as "capitalization." Capitalization can vary widely, both in gross amounts and in the purposes for which it is needed: Some ventures require relatively small initial investments, while others require large investments. The nature of the needs for capital varies too, for there are several kinds of capital investment necessary, dictated by the nature of the business. A given business venture may require capital for any or all of the following:

- Equipment and fixtures
- Building renovation
- Inventory
- Operating capital

A retail store usually requires a fairly extensive investment in fixtures and equipment (carpeting, shelving, counters, display cases, registers, and other items), as well as inventory (stocks of merchandise). The amount of operating capital needed can be quite heavy too, especially if there is a payroll to meet and accounts to carry, even for a short time.

A field sales force calls directly on prospective customers, rather than inducing prospective customers to visit. This approach to sales minimizes investment in equipment and fixtures because such an enterprise can be conducted out of a warehouse or office in a low-rent district. It can even mean a relatively small amount of operating capital needed if the salespeople work strictly on commission and do not draw advances. The inventory costs can be minimized, too, if orders do not have to be delivered immediately or can be *drop-shipped* (shipped in your name by another supplier, usually the distributor or manufacturer of the item).

In terms of investment, catalog sales is similar to a field sales force operation: The catalogs serve as your sales force, calling directly on prospects via the mail. Although you do not pay commissions to salespeople when you sell by catalog, you undertake what is probably an equally high cost of getting orders. Typically, you must invest a great deal of money to win a customer by mail order or direct mail. In fact, a rule of thumb advocated by many experts in the field is to expect to spend about one-half the selling price to get the order.

That is, expect it to cost you $5 to get a $10 order. Out of the remaining $5, you still must pay for the item and for fulfillment—packing and shipping.

Unique Cost and Profit Calculations of Catalog Sales

Unfortunately, with today's high costs for everything, recouping the cost of the item, the fulfillment cost, and the overhead out of the remaining $5 can yield an impossibly low margin for the seller. The principal costs for mail order and direct mail include advertising, printing, and postage. All these costs have grown over the years, but none have soared quite as much as postage and paper. (The increases in paper costs alone are responsible for much of the great increase in printing costs.)

For the most modest direct-mail campaign and the most slender catalog, and even with donated labor (personally performing all or most of the labor yourself), you will find it difficult to get below a rock-bottom cost of $300 per 1,000 pieces mailed out. (You will probably have difficulty in getting it that low, in fact.) Even if you get a substantial return on your mailing, such as a 5 percent response rate, that means a direct-mail marketing cost of $6 per order. This is $1 more than even the conventional wisdom on per-order costs ($5 per $10 order), so the rule of thumb does not apply to small orders. Moreover, the costs to you of what you are selling (i.e., shipping, handling, and per-item costs) must be well below $4 on a $10 item for you to gain a profit.

The preceding example actually underestimates the direct-mail catalog costs because the postage costs are relatively high for mailing catalogs (depending on the size of the catalog, of course). You cannot expect to manage catalog mailings as cheaply as $300 per 1,000; your actual costs will be much higher. Because of these harsh realities, many in mail order are quick to warn newcomers that they must have an absolute minimum selling-price:cost ratio of 3:1, and even that can be risky today. A much safer margin would be 5:1 or even greater. Moreover, there are other considerations.

Not everything can be sold for three or more times its cost. Nonetheless, the example given here assumes that it is possible. The $10.00 item would cost $6.00 for the marketing via catalog and $3.33 for the item, leaving you only $.77 as a gross profit from which to deduct the costs of fulfillment (packing and shipping the order) and your overhead (including your own salary). That is quite a slender margin, even on a large mailing. What's more, even this slender margin is based on generous assumptions—that you can (a) do your mailing at a $300/1,000 pieces cost, (b) get a generous 5 percent response, and (c) buy the item for one third its selling price.

Consider another example: If you sell a $20 item, your selling costs will probably rise a bit because it is usually more difficult to get prospects to spend $20 than it is to persuade them to spend $10. At least, you must operate on that assumption. That is, to get that same 5 percent response (50 orders per 1,000 pieces mailed), you would presumably have to increase the literature you send out, incurring considerably more printing costs and possibly even higher mailing costs. Let's assume that the mailing now costs you $400 per 1,000 pieces (still quite modest) or $8 per order. But the item, at one third its selling price, costs you $6.67, leaving you $13.33 to pay related costs and earn a profit.

The basic mailing and printing costs are fairly constant, within a range, so the larger the selling price, the larger the margin of safety. Beyond the postage bulk rate available to you, the postage costs will not decline with increased volume. Nonetheless, the total volume you mail is important. The printing costs decline sharply with volume, so the unit cost for 50,000 copies is far less than it would be for 5,000 copies.

Unfortunately, the actual response rate would probably decline with increases in the price of the item offered, so it would probably be more realistic to expect a 2 or 3 percent response than an optimistic 5 percent. A 3 percent response would produce 30 orders, costing you $13.33 to get each order plus $6.67 for the merchandise. That leaves you with nothing with which to cover the other costs (e.g., overhead), so you would lose money on that.

In contrast with the preceding examples, it is possible to earn an acceptable profit with a low response rate (e.g., 1 or 2 percent) if the numbers are working for you instead of against you. Suppose that you are selling a $65 item that costs you $20. Further, suppose that your mailing costs you $500 per 1,000 pieces, and that you get a 1½ percent response. That yields 15 orders, each costing you $33.33 to win plus $20 for the item, for a gross cost of $53.33. You have $11.67 per each of the 15 items, with which to pay your overhead and chalk up a profit. Note, however, that at a 1 percent response, you would lose money. Fractions of a point in response rate can be crucial in direct mail: One-half of one percent may spell the difference between profit and loss.

Other Considerations Regarding Catalog Sales

The preceding harsh facts apply when you have only one item to sell, and the item is a one-time item, which the customer will purchase only once or twice in a lifetime. You must make your profit on that single, individual sale. Under those circumstances, there is no way to retrieve a loss from an unprofitable mailing campaign. However, given somewhat different conditions, there are ways to make a campaign pay off and produce a profit even when you only recover costs or even lose money on each sale resulting from the original mailing! There are several ways to make this happen, in fact, if you plan ahead:

- Bounceback sales
- Follow-up mailings
- Lifetime relationships with customers

Bounceback Sales

The mail-order effect known as "bounceback sales" is one way a marginal campaign can often be made to yield profits, after all. The term refers to a method of winning additional orders from customers by enclosing a customized sales solicitation with the item when you fulfill the original order. If the item is suitable for use as a gift, you might suggest buying another one as a gift, and you might offer a special discount to customers buying a second one. Usually, however, the solicitation is for a completely different item, but one that is likely to be attractive and useful to anyone who found your original offer appealing. For example, if you sold customers a camera originally, you might enclose sales literature offering special lenses, a tripod, a carrying case, or some other related item, in filling the order. Ideally, you should offer all these and more, which is itself a catalog idea!

It is not unusual to get as high as 15 or 20 percent return in bounceback orders if customer satisfaction with the original order is high and the appeal for a follow-up order is strong. Remember that the bounceback orders do not cost you any more to get, other than the few cents for the sales literature you enclose with the original order, so you make a large gross profit on bounceback orders. In fact, some catalogers deliberately employ this idea, using *loss leaders* (items on which the profit is minimal or even less than cost) to encourage sales and opportunities for bounceback orders. (This is also known as "inquiry advertising" and "lead generation.")

Follow-Up Mailings

A phenomenon in marketing is well known to most experienced marketers: Persistence pays off in marketing, as it does in most things. The salesperson who continues to call on prospects despite never getting an order in early visits increases the probability of a sale with each visit. This is not to say, of course, that every prospect will eventually become a customer; many will not. However, many will say "no" repeatedly, but they will eventually say "yes" if you persevere and pursue them long enough.

It can be speculated that many prospects are reluctant to do business with strangers, but after repeated appearances—even in the form of a direct-mail package—you begin to become a familiar face, appearing dependably at regular intervals. This almost inevitably leads to an impression of trustworthiness. Also, my own experience has taught me that many people read an appeal, intend to place an order, but procrastinate or forget to do so until subsequent mailings remind them and finally induce or stimulate them to action.

Whatever the correct explanation (and there are probably as many correct explanations as there are individual customers), each repeated mailing to a given list of customers tends to produce better results than the previous one, up to a point. Eventually, the response rate levels off and perhaps even declines slightly. Nonetheless, only repeated mailings and monitoring of the results can make possible an assessment of your list's potential for profit. (Chapter 12 discusses means for testing and evaluating a mailing campaign).

If you determine that your offer is basically a good one, it is probably a mistake to give up on it too soon (i.e., simply because the early or first mailings were disappointing). Many campaigns that start weakly finish strongly, especially with a bit of fine tuning. Mailing campaigns may be similar to military ones. One historian observed that in war and military operations, victory often goes to the more stubborn and more persistent commander—not necessarily to the better strategist or tactician or the commander who should logically have been the victor. The victor is merely the more persistent commander.

Making Sales Versus Making Customers

The preceding examples have been campaigns in which the seller is marketing a single item, as in the case of Joe Cossman selling his "Ant Farms" or Gary Dahl selling his "Pet Rocks." These are sink-or-swim marketing programs: Everything is staked on the appeal to buy some single item, usually a novel item. If the item or the presentation does not do well, there is probably no way to salvage the program.

On the other hand, many mail-order dealers offer a line of merchandise, and they do not depend on the appeal of a single item. For example, Sears and Spiegel offer an extremely broad array of general merchandise. Quill® Corporation offers a more specialized line of products and is the nation's largest mail-order supplier of a broad array of office supplies, equipment, and other business/industrial needs. Also, thousands of smaller organizations offer an array of merchandise or services, and sometimes both. For example, Crutch-field® Corporation of Charlottesville, Virginia, sells a variety of office equipment—computers, calculators, fax machines, and others—along with the related supplies, and it also lists a variety of computer services in its "Personal Office" catalog. (The company also offers a separate catalog of stereo equipment.)

Other services are also sold by catalog. For example, at least three organizations sell seminars in this manner. They mail rather slender and simple catalogs, listing a variety of seminars to be presented in different places on different dates. They list the seminars as also being available to business firms for in-house presentation to employees on a custom, contractual basis.

The principal difference between single-product entrepreneurs such as Joe Cossman and product-line organizations such as Quill® Corporation is simple: Joe Cossman concentrates on a single item and must recover his costs and make his profit on each sale of that item, whereas Quill can afford to lose money (and probably does) on a first sale to a new customer because it has many things to sell and will almost surely get repeat business from satisfied customers. Profits will result from subsequent sales.

To put this another way, Cossman makes sales, and Quill makes customers. That distinction is not intended as a value judgment: Both are legitimate ways of doing business, and each has its up and down sides. Cossman carries little or no inventory or, at worst, a simple inventory of a single item, whereas Quill must maintain a large inventory of thousands of items, with a heavy investment tied up in it. Cossman has almost no payroll to carry, whereas Quill must keep a rather large staff at work. But Cossman does not have the asset of an established business; his business is little more than whatever is in his head at the moment, so he has no major capital asset to sell. Quill is an established enterprise with a definite worth, and has—is—a major capital asset with a large book value (i.e., its market value as a saleable asset).

Following are some leading catalogers. See how many you recognize:

L'eggs	Hosiery
L.L. Bean	Outdoor goods
Fingerhut	Miscellaneous products
Lillian Vernon	Miscellaneous products
Spencer Gifts	Gift items
Avon Fashions	Clothing
Harriet Carter Gifts	Gift items
Swiss Colony	Food gifts

Figis	Food gifts
Burpee	Seeds
Wisconsin Cheeseman	Food gifts
Lands' End	Apparel

WHAT IS THE CATALOG SALES BUSINESS?

It is not easy to define the catalog sales business. Obviously, Sears, Spiegel, Crutchfield, Quill, and many other well-known firms are in the catalog business: Their catalogs are formal, ubiquitous, and well known. But what about the smaller entrepreneurs and operators, those who work from their homes and whose catalog is a typed or printed folder, sometimes not more than a single page of items offered and sent out by direct mail. Are they also in the catalog sales business?

Examples of Small Catalog Sales Businesses

Bluestocking Press and its publisher, Jane A. Williams, exemplify the small catalog sales business. Bluestocking Press sells its own and other books via a (currently) four-page catalog (see Figure 1–2), focusing on certain subject areas relevant to children, education, and work. As Williams puts it herself, her catalog focuses on "1) learning options for kids; 2) work options for kids and adults; and 3) books that promote reading and reason."

Similar, but on a larger scale, is the Ross Book Service of Miriam D. Ross. Ross publishes several book catalogs, titled generically *Tools of the Trade*. (She says that she is now changing the name of her business from "Ross Book Service" to "Tools of the Trade.") One is subtitled *Books on Business Communication*, another *Books on Graphic Design*, and a third one *Books on Working with Words*. Most of the books listed (see Figure 1–3 for an example) are publications of established, large book publishers, and the catalogs run to as many as 40 pages. She strives to make her lists as complete as possible, although she is well aware that her business would be more profitable if she winnowed the slow sellers from her lists and concentrated on the most popular titles. She observes, "There is still too much of the librarian in me."

Bob and Beverlee Reimers, of Fredericksburg, Texas, call their home-based business, "Books 'n' Bears by Mail." They issue their two catalogs in the form of 8 ½" x 13" sheets that are typed and corner-stapled. The current book

Bluestocking Press / Educational Spectrums, P.O. Box 1014, Placerville, CA 95667   (916) 621-1123

Recommended Books

The following titles are highly recommended and are being made available to you along with our own Bluestocking Press titles. You may order directly from us, Bluestocking Press, at P.O. Box 1014, Dept. ES, Placerville, CA, 95667. We never recommend (or offer for sale) any books we do not use ourselves. All books are guaranteed. If for any reason a book does not live up to your expectations please return it to us in resaleable condition within 30 days for a full refund. No questions asked. Prices and availability subject to change.

EDUCATIONAL OPTIONS and LEARNING RESOURCES

1989-90 NATIONAL DIRECTORY OF ALTERNATIVE SCHOOLS: With Sections on Foreign Schools and Resources for Home-Schoolers by the National Coalition of Alternative Community Schools (NCACS) lists approximately 500 educational alternatives in 47 states and 16 countries arranged by state and country in zip code order.
156 pages, 5 1/2 x 8 1/2, paper $12.50

ALTERNATIVES IN EDUCATION by Mark & Helen Hegener is a basic guide to what's available in education today including alternative community schools, learning cooperatives & exchanges, home schooling, organic learning, Waldorf & Montessor, correspondence schools, vocational schools, alternative colleges, apprenticeships and more.
120 pages, 5 1/2 x 8 1/2, paper $8.75

FOR THE CHILDREN'S SAKE: Foundations of Education for Home and School by Susan Schaeffer Macaulay explores educationist Charlotte Mason's (1842-1923) ideas "that children are persons who should be treated as individuals as they are introduced to the variety and richness of the world in which they live." (see *Books Children Love*)
165 pages, 5 1/2 x 8 1/2, paper $6.95

HOME SCHOOL PRIMER by Mark and Helen Hegener, editors of *Home Education Magazine*, is an introductory manual for anyone interested in home-based education. Sections address: What is home schooling? What do parents do with their children all day? Does Home Schooling Really Work? What Do Parents Teach? Legal Aspects of Home Schooling; Accountability; Curriculums; College for the Home Schooled Child; Support Groups; and Socialization. A resource section lists support groups by state, home schooling publications, children's publications, learning aids, curriculum suppliers, educational catalog suppliers, and home schooling books.
40 pages, 8 1/2 x 11, saddle stitched $6.50 ppd.

∞ ∞ ∞ ∞ ∞ ∞ ∞ ∞ ∞ ∞

THE HOME SCHOOL READER: Perspectives on Teaching & Learning by Mark and Helen Hegener. A collection of the best writing that has been published in the first five years of *Home Education Magazine*. This book presents a wide variety of perspectives on home schooling from some of the best writers in the field - answering questions on legal issues, socialization, personal experiences, selecting curriculum materials, teaching specific subjects, higher education, accountability, compulsory education, and more.
156 pages 5 1/2 x 8 1/2 $10.75

HOME SCHOOL: Taking the First Step - A program planning handbook by Borg Hendrickson. For anyone who is ready to go beyond the basics covered in *The Home School Primer* this detailed and thoroughly researched book includes state home schooling laws; national and state support groups, support services; descriptions of teaching methods/approaches; curriculum suppliers; recommended readings; periodicals for children; periodicials for educators; teaching materials, aids and information suppliers. Organized by sections: Section 1 addresses Home-Schooling Questions and Answers: Is home schooling legal? How do I deal with my local school board and local school administrators? What are my options if I'm not legally qualified to teach? Will my home-schooled children be isolated? What if my child is "exceptional"? How can I be sure my children will be motivated to learn? Will my home-schooled child be able to enter or return to public education smoothly? How do I know if I have what it takes to home teach? Sections 2 and 3 are particularly useful for those homeschoolers living in states that require them to maintain records, prepare lesson plans, statements of intent, conduct annual evaluations, etc. Section 4 is a listing of state regulations and procedures. Section 5 lists support groups and services for home schoolers, Section 6 is a gold mine of reading and periodical resources for the child learner and parent educator. The Index includes checklists, worksheets and samples. Even if you're not home schooling the resource guide in this book is invaluable. Borg Hendrickson's and Mary Prides' books combine into a formidable combination of materials for both the experienced and newcomer to home learning.

The book all parents need when deciding on the question
of home schooling.....essential for all public and academic
libraries to support questions and research.
- Library Journal 3-89
323 pages 7 x 10 perfectbound $14.95

IN THEIR OWN WAY: Discovering and Encouraging Your Child's Personal Learning Style by Thomas Armstrong, Ph.D. argues that children are individuals with distinct personal learning styles. Armstrong explains how to identify a child's personal learning style/s and how to find the most appropriate learning environment for that style. *In Their Own Way* should be the first book read by any person who cares

Figure 1–2. Cover of the Bluestocking Press Catalog.

TOOLS OF THE TRADE
Books on Business Communication

Ross Book Service
3718 Seminary Road, Alexandria, VA 22304 • (703) 823-1919

1989

$2.00

Business Management

101 of the Greatest Ideas in Management
Uris, Auren
1986 310pp
H1310 $24.95

101 Ways to Cut Your Business Insurance Costs Without Sacrificing Protection
McIntyre, William S. IV & Gibson, Jack P.
1988 190pp
H1698 $19.95
How to shop for property, liability, auto, and workers compensation insurance to get the best coverage at the best price.

The Arthur Young Business Plan Guide
Siegel, E.S. Schultz, L.A. & Ford, B.R.
1987 184pp
H1424 $22.95

Assertiveness for Managers: Learning Effective Skills for Managing People
Cawood, Diana
1988 144pp oversize
P1695 $9.95
How to handle a problem employee (or superior). The assertive way to respond to criticism. How to be yourself and still get ahead. Special concerns for women managers. How to be a 'career coach.'— with lots of examples.

Basic Accounting for the Small Business
Cornish, Clive G.
1984 186pp
P0781 $5.95

Be Your Own Boss: The Complete, Indispensable, Hands-on Guide
Shilling, Dana
1984 385pp
P0143 $8.95
Dana Shilling has worked for "Wasp, Wasp, and Token", and she prefers working for herself. Here she presents lots

of good advice and some strong opinions on starting and running your own business.

Becoming Self-Employed: First-Hand Advice from Those Who Have Done It!
Elliott, Susan
1987 153pp
P1420 $7.95

Blow Your Own Horn: How to Market Yourself and Your Career
Davidson, Jeffrey P.
1987 271pp
H0142 $16.95
It's not enough to be bright, ambitious and hard-working— the only way to ensure success these days is through self-promotion. Davidson offers many ways to build recognition, find a mentor, create networks, develop an ongoing 'internal achievements list.'

The Book of Fax: An Impartial Guide to Buying and Using Facsimile Equipment
Fishman, Daniel and King, Elliot
1988 134 pp
P1782 $12.95
Buying a fax machine is a complicated decision, because the technology is complicated. This brief book will help you decide between a $300 and a $3000 machine, whether to buy the new PC fax boards, whether to lease or buy. It also covers fax 'etiquette', how to avoid fax junk mail, how to integrate with other business machines.

Building United Judgement: A Handbook for Consensus Decision Making
Avery, Michel et al
1981 124pp
P0141 $10.95
Reaching consensus is an alternative to majority vote. This handbook explores methodology from the viewpoint of social change activism, useful to all.

Building Your Business Plan: A Step-by-Step Approach
McLaughlin, Harold J.
1985 297pp
H0180 $24.95

Business Etiquette Today
Dunckel, Jacqueline
1987 107pp
P0706 $7.95
In succinct, easy to read form, here are all the basics for advancement on the job. Helpful to the executive who needs a refresher, invaluable to the beginner. Notes the difference between business (non-sexist) and social manners, and advises on their respective uses.

Business Plans That Win $$$: Lessons from the MIT Enterprise Forum
Rich, Stanley R. and Gumpert, David
1987 220pp
P0179 $8.95
'Studying this book can win you not only investment dollars, but also higher profits from a better run company.'— *Christian Science Monitor.*

Creating the Successful Business Plan for New Ventures
Hosmer, LaRue and Guiles, Roger
1985 212pp
H0171 $21.95

Subject Index

Business Management 1
Consulting 4
Business Writing 5
Speaking, Listening,
  & Presentations 7
Marketing 10
Direct Marketing 11
Advertising 13
Public Relations
  & Publicity 16
Corporate Image
  & Logos 18

Two other *Tools of the Trade* editions available from Ross Book Service provide information on available books in areas of:

■ Graphics – $2.00
■ Working with Words – $3.00

Figure 1–3. Cover of *Tools of the Trade* catalog.

list is three pages long, and the current bear list is five pages long, with text and halftone illustrations of the stuffed bears.

Carol's Creations, of Iowa City, Iowa, is the home-based business of Carol Krob. Krob is a professional needlework designer, and she markets her line of kits and patterns through her own mail-order catalog, a 5" x 8 ½" black-and-white publication of 32 pages, in which she describes and illustrates her products. She says that except for the photography and printing, she produces the catalog herself in what she refers to as a "'low-tech' operation" that has produced good results for her.

Definition of Catalog Sales Businesses

In the final analysis, the definition of catalog sales appears to be far more a matter of kind than of degree. Any entrepreneur offering a variety of standardized goods and/or services described in a mailer and listed at standardized prices, may be said to be in the catalog sales business. It is thus a business that anyone—or almost anyone—can enter with a relatively small investment.

For this book, however, that broad a definition stretches so far as to invalidate the real concept. I therefore arbitrarily rule out borderline catalog sales and confine these discussions to enterprises based on the concept of a mail-order catalog as a bound publication of at least a few pages, devoted primarily to products, with or without related services. It is possible to start on a small scale, with modest investment, as a full- or part-time enterprise, selling by mail and/or other media, and based in one's home or elsewhere.

MUST YOU PRODUCE YOUR OWN CATALOG?

Prohibitive Costs of Slick Catalogs

The cost of producing any catalog in quantity, even a simple one, is high. Aside from the costs for printing and binding is the great cost and labor of preparation. The cost of producing one of the elaborate, multicolored catalogs of a Sears or a Spiegel is prohibitively high for the average small business. (Printed reproduction of color photographs requires a printing method known as "process color," including three or four negatives of each colored page—depending on whether you use the three- or the four-color process—and an equivalent number of press runs. That becomes prohibitively expensive for any but a major catalog-distribution campaign.)

Were the production of full-color catalogs a requisite for catalog sales, few other than Sears, Montgomery Ward, Spiegel, and other large firms could afford to enter the field. Fortunately, it is not a requirement. There are other ways for the "little guy" to enter the catalog sales business and even send out a slick and expensive colored catalog with his or her own name on it. In fact, many relatively large catalog sales enterprises do not produce their own catalogs and could not afford to do so, at least not without substantial assistance from manufacturers, wholesalers, franchisers, and/or others who subsidize or otherwise support the efforts of the smaller organizations. In fact, many firms wholesale merchandise and supply catalogs that can be imprinted with the retailers' names.

Wholesale Companies That Produce Catalogs for Retailers

National Publications, Inc., of San Diego, California, sells over 100 "opportunity books" via catalogs, according to proprietor and chief executive David Bendah. The company offers to establish dealers and to supply its catalogs, either blank or imprinted with the dealer's name and address, at prices beginning at 15 cents per catalog for 500 copies, with the unit price declining to 10 cents at 5,000 or more copies. Bendah even offers to sell reproducible copy to any dealers who prefer to print their own imprinted catalogs.

Specialty Merchandise Corporation (SMC), of Chatsworth, California, is a wholesaler of inexpensive "specialty" merchandise (e.g., clocks, cameras, cutlery, jewelry, lamps, and other such items), many of them inexpensive imports from the far East. It sells only to its dealers, whom it refers to as "Associate Members." It advertises widely in periodicals, especially "opportunity magazines," soliciting new dealers. Those who sign up with the firm can buy their multicolor catalogs and get a series of manuals and other items to guide them in selling the company's merchandise, which they buy for as little as one third the company's advertised list price.

Another supplier of what they describe as "beautiful gift catalogs" is Mail Order Associates, Inc., of Montvale, New Jersey, who also advertise widely in periodicals, seeking new "associates." Still another supplier of catalogs is Merlite Industries, of New York City, a jewelry merchandiser whose advertisements in magazines pursue both retail customers (to whom wholesale prices are promised) and dealers, to whom it will supply catalogs and the promise of an opportunity to earn profits.

Still others—only a few others—are the Lotions & Lace Company, of

Riverside, California, supplier of what the company advertises as exotic lingerie; the Anka Company, Inc., of Warwick, Rhode Island, a supplier of jewelry, which furnishes catalogs to anyone who wishes to become a dealer; Anchor Specialties Co., of North Providence, Rhode Island, supplier of a line of belt buckles, belts, and other specialty jewelry items; Cook Bros., Inc., of Chicago, which supplies general merchandise; and Mason Shoe Mfg. Co., of Chippewa Falls, Wisconsin, a long-time seller of shoes by catalog.

MUST YOU BUY IN QUANTITY AND MAINTAIN AN INVENTORY?

Many of those wholesalers and manufacturers who supply catalogs expect dealers to buy in quantity and to stock their merchandise, so selling to dealers is their chief objective. On the other hand, many will drop-ship goods for dealers, although at a lesser discount than that offered to dealers who maintain an inventory. Premier Publishers, Inc., of Fort Worth, Texas, supplies catalogs listing the company's many books, and it offers to drop-ship for dealers. (The dealer supplies a shipping label, with the customer's name and address, and the publisher ships the book under that label.) In fact, it also sells a widely distributed publication titled *American Drop-Shippers Directory*, which lists many sources of merchandise that a dealer may have drop-shipped. Of course, a publication of this type must be revised periodically, and the publisher advertised the 16th edition in 1989.

Pros and Cons of Building and Keeping an Inventory

It is possible to come up with many arguments, pro and con, both for building a large inventory of your own and for relying on drop-shipping. Maintaining your own inventory gives you much better control over product availability, cost increases, and promptness in filling orders (you have little control when you depend on drop-shipping). It gives you a higher markup, sometimes an exceptionally good markup when you make an exceptionally good buy. However, it also gives you no protection against the chance of being stuck with a large number of an item that *bombed*—failed to attract buyers. (Of course you have no way of knowing which products will yield only 100 sales and which will yield sales of 20,000 or more.) Bill Willett, of what is now Avon Fashions, believes that inventory management is one of the keys to success in catalog sales.

Inventory Management

Saying that inventory management explains success versus failure is easy. Defining inventory management is more difficult, and explaining it is even more difficult. Certainly, success in inventory management is not entirely a matter of method and discipline; it is also a matter of luck: Few, if any, are wise enough always to know how well a new item will sell (i.e., How will the fickle public react to new items?). Many, if not most, of those marvelous "special sales" in which merchandise is sold at a fraction of the original list price are the result of missed guesses of customer reaction to a new item. Miniskirts were a huge success; maxiskirts were marginal, at best, and maxicoats were in a class with Nehru jackets.

Ideally, in managing inventory, you ought to be able to buy a modest starting inventory and then either buy more or buy no more at all, as the results of your marketing dictates your need. Unfortunately, it doesn't usually work out that way. If the item catches on and sells well, the original supplier is swamped with orders and either may not be able to supply more when you need it or may only be willing to supply more at a higher price, which makes a profit impossible for you. That's why you gamble on your judgment (or perhaps others' judgment) that the item will sell well, and you order enough to meet anticipated demand. For that reason, try to establish more than one source of supply for each item, especially new ones, and buy large quantities only if you have no alternative. In any case, wisdom in buying is, indeed, a key to success in catalog sales, but it is more so with some items (e.g., fashion-dependent items) than with others (established staples).

ARE CATALOG SALES ALWAYS CONDUCTED BY MAIL?

The clear implication has been that all or nearly all catalog sales ventures are mail-order ventures. That is implicit not only in the preceding paragraphs and pages, but also in the descriptions offered by catalog suppliers, many of whom refer to the mail-order business in connection with using their catalogs and selling their merchandise. No doubt, a very large proportion of all catalog sales are made by mailing catalogs as the centerpiece of a direct-mail package and by taking orders via mail and telephone. Not all catalog sales, however, involve mail order or direct mail. The "catalog store" mentioned earlier in this chapter illustrates only one of several novel ways in which catalogs can serve as the centerpiece of effective and successful sales programs.

Merchandise "Party Sales"

Selling catalog merchandise by mail is probably the most logical and sound way to sell books, specialty items, and many other mundane products. Some kinds of catalog items, however—often the more exotic items—can be sold equally effectively—perhaps even more effectively—by means other than mail. Some suppliers of merchandise lines and catalogs suggest "party sales," for example. This is a method whereby the dealer invites a few friends to a "party" (social gathering) in his or her home, where he or she demonstrates the merchandise, distributes catalogs, and takes orders, with advance payment or deposits, the merchandise to be delivered a few days later.

The dealer also tries to recruit from among those at the party prospective hosts or hostesses for similar sales parties in their homes, for which they will get some free merchandise as a gift and/or earn a commission on everything sold there. The dealer will distribute catalogs and make the presentations. However, the dealer always tries to make two sales at these events: The dealer not only sells merchandise to attendees, but also tries to sign up attendees as new hosts or hostesses for future parties. That is a necessity to keep the sales program going.

High-grade kitchenware—pots and pans—has been sold this way. Also, many other kinds of merchandise, especially the higher priced exotic and luxury items, such as lingerie, jewelry, and cosmetics, are well suited to party selling. This type of selling—merchandise parties—appears to be both more favored by and more effective with women than with men, so it tends to be used most often in selling items that appeal to women.

Other Nontraditional Modes of Catalog Sales

Party sales and catalog stores are not the only alternatives to mail order for catalog sales; there are many others, such as the following few.

Fund Raising.　In fund-raising campaigns—selling merchandise to benefit some worthy nonprofit cause (e.g., a church or a high school team)—the seller can approach individuals (a) directly and in person at their homes and offices, (b) by telephone, and (c) at gatherings. In each case, customers are invited to browse through the catalogs and make selections.

Flea Markets.　This is similar to selling at gatherings, except that this selling is definitely done for personal profit rather than for fund raising. The vendor must have a booth or a table, and it is usually helpful to have some merchandise on display.

Wagon Jobbing. This involves selling merchandise from a vehicle, such as a van or truck, and it can be conducted as part of a flea market or independently at random. However, if it is a catalog sales business, it depends on the catalog for most of the orders, even if inventory is carried and orders can be filled on the spot.

Route Sales. This is door-to-door selling, but it may involve calling on people in offices and other places of employment, either instead of or in addition to calling on people at home. This method is, in fact, a well-established (many years old) means of selling Fuller Brush, Avon, Mary Kay, Raleigh, and many other product lines. The salesperson leaves catalogs and then calls back later for follow-up, although individuals can order by mail or by telephone in the meanwhile.

Brochures and Catalogs as Adjunct Sales Strategies

You can use any or all of these approaches in place of or in addition to mail order. You may find your own unique way of creating and using catalogs as a sales tool. Many years ago, when I sold Fuller Brush products for a time, the Fuller Brush Company did not yet have a catalog of their many products, but had many small brochures. I prepared for each day's work by stamping my name and telephone number on all the product brochures and assembling them into thick bundles, thereby improvising my own catalog! I stuffed one of my homemade catalogs into the mail slot of every home where I did not get an answer to my knock. I soon began to get more than a few orders by telephone at home every night. (I was in catalog sales before knowing there was such a business!)

WHERE ARE YOUR MARKETS?

Despite all the viable market alternatives that many catalog sellers use profitably, the major emphasis and the bulk of catalog sales are still focused on mail order, and it is thus necessarily the main focus of this book. As Quill® Corporation head Jack Miller puts it, "there is no faster, more direct, more viable way of getting to market." He points out, as the U.S. Small Business Administration and others have, that 97 percent of our 13–14 million businesses are *small businesses* (having fewer than 100 employees). That raises another question: Is the catalog sales market based more on sales to individual consumers or on sales to businesses?

The answer is, of course, that it depends on the nature of the product line sold. Of course, if you sell office supplies or advertising novelties, the bulk of your trade is going to be to businesses, and if you sell vitamins or cosmetics, you are going to deal primarily with individual consumers as private citizens. Some lines, however, such as computers and related items, enjoy a substantial sales potential in both market spheres.

HOW CAN YOU FIND YOUR PROSPECTS?

In my opinion, marketing is by far the single most important activity in any business venture. Without marketing success, there is no business, so nothing else is really of great consequence if marketing is not successful. Improvised or casual marketing is not often effective; to be effective, marketing must be planned carefully and thoroughly and carried out in the same manner. Marketing begins by identifying either what you will sell or to whom you will sell. For this discussion, I assume that you have decided what you wish to sell, so it remains to identify your best prospects.

The general definitions are pretty obvious. In most cases, you know immediately whether your products are going to be used mostly in work settings and other business environments or used only privately and personally. You usually know whether men or women—or both—are going to be your prospects. You often can judge easily such other qualifications as whether your prospects must be home owners (such as for selling a product that only a home owner is likely to purchase) and whether they are blue-collar or white-collar workers (e.g., if you are selling leather briefcases or hard hats). However, even these broad categories do not adequately draw a profile of your best prospects.

You will realize your need for narrow and sharply defined profiles of ideal prospects when you set out to rent mailing lists. (Note that you *rent* them, usually for a one-time use; you don't buy them. This is discussed in more detail in Chapter 8.) The mailing-list brokers you investigate will each send you a catalog (yes, they, too, are in the catalog sales business!), and you will suddenly realize that you can and must choose from an enormous variety of mailing lists.

Do you want to mail to accountants? If so, what kind of accountants? You will find lists of accountants subclassified in many ways, such as the following small sample:

Accountants who are . . .
  in education and government
  in industry
  in accounting firms
  certified public accountants (CPAs)
  owners and partners
  internal auditors
  wholesalers of accounting machines
  self-employed
  tax specialists
  women

Do you want to mail to executives? If so, what kinds of executives? Here are just a few of the categories:

Executives who are . . .
  in advertising
  in banking
  branch managers
  in broadcasting
  chief executive officers
  chief financial officers
  senior vice presidents
  general managers
  in manufacturing
  in marketing

You can get lists of teachers classified by the subjects they teach and the grades they teach; physicians classified by their medical specialties and the kinds of geographical areas in which they practice; executives classified by their personal names and titles or by the kinds of businesses and industries that employ them; individuals by where they live and how often they buy by mail, how much they spent the last time they bought by mail, or what they bought by mail; and by dozens of other classifications. You can get lists of subscribers to various periodicals; customers of various large businesses; homeowners or apartment renters; those who recently bought a home or those who recently sold one; persons living in specified locations or persons who do not live in specified locations. The variety of choices grows steadily as information technology grows.

Perhaps you are interested in odd and unusual lists, such as the nearly 250,000 members of the Doris Day Animal League, the 8,000 individuals who made a donation to the Dull Knife Memorial College on the Northern Cheyenne Reservation, the 70,000 known habitual writers of bad checks, or the 18,000 men who bought books on how to meet women.

The choices you can have are almost unlimited today because computers and related technology have made this possible. They have made the collection of so much data possible—inevitable, in fact—and they have made it possible to sort those huge banks of names according to many categories and subcategories. You can draw almost any kind of desired profile you wish. The down side of this limitless availability is that you must decide just what you want because your mailing list is critically important to your success. The best marketing proposition can fail for no other reason than that the mailing list used was not right for the campaign.

CAN YOU GET ANY KIND OF MAILING LIST YOU WANT?

Not everyone rents mailing lists. Three kinds of mailers do not rent others' mailing lists: (1) Well-established mailers have built their own lists and thus have more than enough "house" lists (lists they own) for their needs. (2) A few mailers cannot find the kinds of lists they want and must compile and build their own lists. (3) A very few mailers could rent suitable existing lists, but they simply prefer to build their own lists for one reason or another. For example, some object to the cost of renting lists, some are convinced that they wind up with even better lists when they build their own, and some believe that it simply makes better business and economic sense to build their own lists from scratch, despite some drawbacks in so doing.

The inability of some to find the kind of rental lists they want may seem strange. In the face of the enormous array of mailing lists that the list brokers can offer, the natural assumption is that you can get any kind of list you want, regardless of your needs and demands. That is simply not true. You cannot get some lists because there has not been enough demand for such lists, or for some other reason, the lists do not exist. (In fact, the prospects' names exist on rental lists, but the brokers do not have them coded into categories that make possible their retrieval for you. This will probably be clearer in Chapter 8, "Mailing Lists: A Critical Necessity.")

For example, I wanted mailing lists of organizations that wrote proposals regularly in pursuit of government contracts or that wanted to learn how to pursue and win government contracts. These certainly would include defense-related companies (developers and manufacturers of weapons systems of all kinds), firms that support the government's space programs, and many of the other high-tech companies. In addition, the list would include many companies that provide a wide array of computer equipment, supplies, and services, as well as many companies that develop training programs or that write technical manuals. Further, not all of my prospects would be commercial and industrial companies; nonprofit organizations, associations, labor unions, hospitals, universities, and other kinds of organizations also pursue government contracts, and I wanted their names on my lists.

Thus, the extent of my list seemed daunting. However, not all high-tech companies, labor unions, universities, and others do pursue government contracts. I would want only those that did, indeed, pursue government contracts. No available list offered the breadth and the specificity I needed. To use rented lists, I would have to mail to all high-tech companies, labor unions, universities, hospitals, and others. I would pay both for list rentals and for the mailing costs on lists of which not more than 2 or 3 out of 10 were even prospects for me, so 80 percent of my effort and dollars would be wasted. I could not afford to mail eight times the number I should normally have to mail, so my campaign would probably falter and perhaps turn out a total loss. That is, if I could afford to mail to 15,000 names, and I used lists that were only 20 percent right for me, I was effectively mailing to only 3,000 names. For that reason, I decided to compile my own lists. It proved a wise decision.

WHAT KINDS OF MAILING LISTS ARE AVAILABLE?

Most of the lists offered by list brokers are not actually the property of the brokers; instead, they belong to organizations that entrust them to a "list management firm," which then rents out the list and takes a commission for doing so. (These firms are list managers to those whose lists they manage and market on a commission basis, and they are brokers or vendors to the customers who pay for the rental of the lists.)

Response Lists.   Allegedly, the best lists are the customer lists of a mail-order firm (e.g., L. L. Bean), the subscribers to a magazine (e.g., *Ladies Home Journal*), or other such lists of known kinds of respondents, called "response lists." Response lists comprise those customers who have responded to sales appeals in some way.

Compiled Lists.   By comparison, *compiled lists* are "cold" lists, in that it is not known whether those listed have responded warmly to any sales appeal. Their common characteristics are membership in an organization or an occupation or some other demographically determined grouping. Although views regarding the value of these has changed a little, they are still rated far below the response lists in esteem value. Lists can be compiled from many sources: Telephone directories, membership lists, advertising, and information appearing in various publications, to name a few sources. Names pulled out of membership lists and telephone directories are *cold* indeed—names about which you know almost nothing. However, that is not necessarily the case for all compiled lists. In my own case, I compiled the bulk of my lists of government contractors and would-be contractors from help-wanted advertising placed by the organizations in major newspapers. Knowing the field as well as I did, I was able to judge easily from the advertising which companies were most suitable for my needs. I also was able to get some useful short lists from other sources, including some publications and other documents available from government agencies (e.g., a list of contractors available from the U.S. Navy at the time).

Names obtained from many membership lists are not entirely cold. For example, if you get the membership list of the American Psychological Association, for example, you know quite a bit about those whose names appear on that list. Also, many directories of members furnish other information so that you can subclassify the list.

Customer Lists.   Of course, everyone who buys from you, regardless of what list the name was on originally, has become a customer, and the name should be then transferred to the most valuable list of all mailing lists: your customer list. Those are the names you now own, no matter where they came from, and you are entitled to use them again and again as your own property. You thus get a double benefit every time you sell to someone for the first time because you acquire another name for that prized customer list.

Inquiry Lists.   Another way to build your lists is via inquiry advertising. Inquiry advertising is discussed at greater length in Chapters 1 and 8, but it merits a brief note here. Briefly, it consists of running small, low-cost advertisements designed specifically to attract inquiries from prospective customers, thereby building mailing lists. More than one catalog mailer uses this as a primary way of building mailing lists, and for many, this is a favored way of building lists.

SUMMARY

All the foregoing was intended to orient persons who are new to the field, and to set the scene for all readers. Earlier in this chapter, I pointed out that mail order, direct mail, and catalog sales are not specific industries or businesses in themselves (although there are some "wholesalers" whose real business appears to be selling their catalogs to naive new dealers). Instead, they are ways of doing business. That is, these terms describe ways of reaching and presenting sales offers to prospects and of completing sales transactions thereby. The point bears repeating, for it reveals another important difference between selling by mail and selling out of a retail establishment: In mail order, you don't sit and wait for prospects to come to you; you go out to them.

Bear in mind that people act in their own interest. Prospects buy from you only when they perceive that act to be in their own interest. Order-takers wait for prospects to form that perception spontaneously and entirely of their own volition; marketers help prospects form that perception by advertising and other presentations. Simply mailing catalogs is not enough. You must give the prospects reasons—motivate them—to browse through the catalog and to be induced to buy some of the items listed therein. Inducement to buy is, after all, the true objective of the entire effort, and it is thus the true objective of all the pages that have gone before and that follow this one.

2

A Few Starter Ideas

The success of the free enterprise system stems largely from the genius of thousands of innovative entrepreneurs. The catalog sales business can boast its own share of such clever and imaginative people.

A FEW OF THE MANY POPULAR ITEMS SOLD BY CATALOG

Many catalogers are exclusively in catalog sales enterprises, although some may be marketing more than one catalog (i.e., more than one line of merchandise). Others are in cataloging as adjuncts to their main enterprises. In fact, Freeman F. Gosden, Jr., an experienced direct-mail specialist, says in his book *Direct Marketing Success* (John Wiley & Sons, 1985) that stores and catalogs "go together" because the two ventures—store retailing and direct mail—are mutually supportive in a number of ways: sharing many costs, selling off remainders or surplus, and otherwise lending each other strengths.

The facts appear to bear out the idea. Many department stores and other retailers add catalog departments to their retailing operations. For example, Staples, an office supplies discounter with 27 retail outlets and a catalog for walk-in shoppers, has recently decided to create another catalog for mail-order shoppers. Staples management insists that it does not plan to use direct-mail cataloging except incidentally as a convenience for its customers. Nonetheless, Staples is creating a special catalog for the purpose—for the convenience of those who wish to order by mail or telephone and have merchandise shipped to them—and obviously Staples will not turn their noses up at any new or additional business that results.

It works both ways: Some businesses have added retail stores to what were originally catalog or mail-order operations. Sears and Montgomery Ward are two outstanding and well-known examples of organizations who are heavyweights in both catalog and retail-store operations.

For some retailers, catalog sales have been life preservers. Horn & Hardart, for example, the restaurant people best known for their Automats in New York and Philadelphia, where they started over 100 years ago, fell on hard times in 1972, during the modern era of fast food and other changes in the restaurant business. To revive the faltering company, Horn & Hardart turned to catalog sales. Horn & Hardart (H&H, as it was popularly known to its patrons for many years) acquired Hanover (a catalog sales business) as a subsidiary, with the 3 catalogs Hanover published at the time (grown to 23 today). In fact, Hanover's Chief, Jack Rosenfeld, has been quoted recently by Phyllis Weinberg, writing in *Catalog Business* ("Can Jack Rosenfeld End the Heartburn at Horn & Hardart?" November 1989) as predicting that H&H will not even be in the restaurant business a few years from now. (Currently, H&H still operates Automats, the Bojangles chicken restaurants, and several Burger King franchises.)

This kind of diversification is really not surprising, for there are few kinds of merchandise that cannot be and are not sold by catalog; even many perishable items are sold that way today. Almost anything that can be sold by any means can be and is sold by catalog, including services of many kinds. Gifts, foods, drugs, novelties, toys, advertising specialties, vitamins, computers, office supplies, software programs, art supplies, lingerie, outdoor items, sporting goods, perfumes, cosmetics, stamps, coins, books, magazine subscriptions, seminars, business plans, record albums, tape cassettes, sheet music, correspondence courses, mailing lists, shoes, garments, haberdashery, hand tools, power tools, small appliances, large appliances, leather goods, furniture, housewares, jewelry, towels and linens, stationery, printing services, writing services, illustrating and drafting services, printed specialties, greeting cards, closeouts and surplus, coins, antiques, and plumbing fixtures are just a few of the items that can be and are sold by catalog through mail order and direct mail. (It would probably be easier to compile a list of items that are not sold by mail or that are impractical candidates for catalog sales.)

The enormous success of the personal computer has spawned many catalogs devoted to selling computers and a wide array of accessories and supplies. The Inmac® Personal Computer Catalog is among the leaders in this field and mails an attractive catalog (see Figure 2-1) with many full-color illustrations of the large number of products offered.

Another kind of product that lends itself well to catalog selling is computer software. One company, Egghead Software®, sells their products (mostly software, but also a few hardware items and computer books) by

Figure 2–1. A page from the Inmac® catalog.

catalog and across the counter in a chain of retail stores. Their catalogs are light-hearted (see Figure 2–2) and busy with good humor. Electronics Boutique® also sells software by catalog (Figure 2–3), but a bit more soberly.

ADVANTAGES AND DISADVANTAGES OF CATALOG PURCHASES

An ample number of examples has proven that almost everything that can be sold at all can be sold profitably by mail generally and via catalogs especially. Still, some items are better for cataloging—easier to sell via catalog—than others are. The suitability of certain items has a special importance when you are starting a catalog enterprise and need to have as many things going your way as possible to build your base and become firmly established. As a first clue to determining the most suitable items for catalog sales, consider what factors inhibit or promote people's decisions to become catalog customers.

Buying by mail has advantages and disadvantages, as perceived by the customer. It's important to face these squarely and to understand them—from the customer's viewpoint—to develop a workable marketing strategy for cataloging. First, consider the apparent disadvantages.

Why People Hesitate to Buy by Mail-Order Catalog

One immediately apparent disadvantage is the delay: In the typical case, buying by mail means waiting for the merchandise, often a week or more. For some, this is mere inconvenience and minor annoyance. For many, however, no matter how long the delay in deciding to buy something, once the decision is made, the object must be obtained immediately. The desire must be gratified at once, and that is a powerful motivation for many. (For example, the prospect of driving away immediately in my first new automobile played a large role in influencing me to buy it when I did, despite the several years I had yearned for a new one but put off buying it for a variety of practical reasons.)

A second drawback that some customers see is that they do not have the opportunity to examine the item directly. They must rely on illustrations, descriptive language, and written promises of benefits and other attractive qualities. That gives some customers considerable pause when the item is expensive and the seller is unknown.

A third disadvantage is the inconvenience and expense of returning an item that is unsatisfactory for any reason. The customer must then go to considerable trouble to pack up the item and to ship it back by some means.

Figure 2–2. A page from the Egghead Software® catalog.

Figure 2–3. A page from the *Electronics Boutique® Software* catalog.

Moreover, if the item is one that the customer has had to assemble, he or she must now disassemble it, a distasteful and irksome task at best. In some cases, the seller insists that if returned, the item must be repacked in the original carton. That results in the inconvenience of storing the original packing materials for a time, perhaps for the entire guarantee period. If the item is to be replaced, the customer must wait again—a double wait this time, for it takes time for the returned item to reach its destination and for the seller to ship out a replacement. Even if it is returned for refund, there is the additional wait for a refund or a credit slip.

Still another disadvantage perceived by many is that of doing business with an unknown, or relatively unknown, organization. Even the most trusting customers are somewhat hesitant to order major items from and rely on the guarantees of unknown firms located hundreds of miles away.

Why People Choose to Buy via Mail-Order Catalog

There is a flip side to much of this: Although buying by mail represents an inconvenience to some, it is a great convenience to others. It is a convenience in that the customer does not have to leave home or office to shop, to place the order, and to receive delivery. A customer can shop—browse through a catalog—and make purchases while relaxed in an easy chair with a cup of coffee!

Other possible advantages to buying by mail (and by catalog) vary with the marketing strategies employed by the cataloger. That is, you, as the cataloger and mail-order seller, can create and make customers aware of those advantages through what and how you elect to sell—the conditions of the sales. The advantages you can thus create for and offer to your prospective customers represent two strategic approaches: (1) Some strategies offset—or even eliminate—some or all of the disadvantages described, and (2) some strategies offer special benefits not normally offered or made available to customers through other retail channels. Those two approaches should be considered when deciding both what you will sell by catalog (and mail order) and the conditions under which you sell.

OVERCOMING THE DISADVANTAGES OF CATALOG PURCHASES

Immediate Delivery.   Sears, Montgomery Ward, J. C. Penney, and any others who run joint retail store and catalog sales operations can and do overcome the disadvantage of forcing the customer to wait at least several days for delivery by making it possible for customers to place catalog/mail orders at the sellers' in-store mail-order counters and receive immediate delivery on the premises by picking the items up at the warehouse entrance. If the catalog price is slightly lower than the over-the-counter price (as it usually is), the customer thus gets a price advantage for the slight inconvenience of going to the mail-order counter to make the transaction and to the warehouse to accept delivery. And the customer can usually visit the display counters and examine the items before ordering them, overcoming another drawback to catalog/mail-order buying.

Speedy Delivery.   Of course, not all catalogers can offer these conveniences and enjoy the best of both worlds because most do not have the dual retailing capability; instead, they deal entirely by mail, telephone, and shipping services. Many catalogers have overcome the inconvenience of delay by offering overnight delivery via the many express services—Federal Express, United Parcel Service, Express Mail, Purolator, and others available today. Those selling inexpensive items are forced to charge extra for express delivery, as the Mission Orchards™ catalog sheet of Figure 2–4 explains, but those who are selling only "big tag" items usually do not charge extra for the convenience of express delivery but absorb it as part of the overhead, the cost of doing business by mail and catalog.

Easy Return.   Most request that returned items be packed in the original materials and even suggest to customers the wisdom of saving the packing materials until they are satisfied that all is well with their purchase, but not all insist that repacking in the original container is an absolute requirement for return. In fact, many catalogers today endear themselves to customers by enclosing forms and instructions to make it easy to return items that are not satisfactory for any reason, and many make arrangements to have the items picked up, and they pay the shipping costs on returns, as well. (Some ask the customer to call first and get a return-authorization number to speed things up.)

HIGHLIGHTING THE ADVANTAGES OF CATALOG PURCHASES

Many catalogers must nullify the disadvantages of catalog purchasing by offering compensating advantages in buying by mail and catalog. There are many such means, most important among them being low prices and the

Federal Express delivery available!
Do you want your gift to get there immediately? Did you wait til the last minute? For just an additional $7.50, your gift will be shipped within 3-5 days to assure delivery of your gift in plenty of time for the holidays. Orders with Federal Express delivery are guaranteed delivery by Christmas when received before December 18. Later orders may still arrive on time.

Shopping with Mission Orchards™ is easy.
IT'S CONVENIENT—shop in the comfort of your own home, whenever you want. You'll avoid holiday crowds and waiting in long lines.

COUNT ON US—we've been shipping gifts for over 50 years. Your order receives our closest attention and is promptly acknowledged.

COMPLETE GIFT SERVICE—all gifts are carefully and attractively packaged and include your personal greetings. Most importantly, your gifts are shipped on time.

OUR GUARANTEE—your complete satisfaction is guaranteed. If for any reason you are not happy, let us know and we'll make it right.

Invasion of the Giant Pears
Large as can be, these humongous Crown Comice™ pears are the kings of the crop! Friends and family will be delighted when they open this more-than-generous gift of three (gasp) really HUGE pears, each nestled in its own straw basket. They're just as juicy, sweet, and delicious as our regular sized gift pears. The only difference is, they take longer to eat!
Net wt. 2 1/2 lbs.
Gift 7 $12.95

Cinnamon Raisin Twists
Enjoy mouth-watering home-baked flavor! These gourmet delights are made from rich buttermilk pastry formed into graceful crescents and loaded with plump, juicy, cinnamon-spiced raisins. They are handmade in small batches, and 100% pure and natural with absolutely no additives or preservatives. Individually cupped for serving and arranged in an elegant gift tin.
Net wt. 1 lb., 4 ozs.
Gift 332 $24.95

Figure 2–4. A page from the Mission Orchards™ catalog offering express delivery.

judicious choice of items to sell, especially in the early phases of the venture, when the main objective is or ought to be the creation of satisfied customers who will return to buy again and again.

Reduced prices are important in a successful catalog launch because catalog shoppers tend to expect some price advantages in shopping by mail. (The popular notion is that mail order and catalogs offer items more cheaply than other retail channels.) Nonetheless, the kind of items offered is probably the more important of the two key advantages.

The two, prices and kinds of items, are not unrelated. Overhead costs are or should be considerably lower for catalogers than for retail stores, and are thus an immediate influence for lower prices. Handling items on which markup is traditionally high, such as cosmetics, drugs, and vitamins, is another avenue that ought to enable the cataloger to offer lower selling prices.

Catalogs and mail order also offer additional appeal: The customer assumes that the seller will always be able to provide the right sizes, colors, and other such individual specifications and preferences, something that is not always the case when buying across the counter, especially in the case of special sale offerings. Even when the cataloger is out of stock for a given size or color, there is a better possibility that the catalog customer can be persuaded to wait for back-ordering the item than is the case in face-to-face selling.

THE MARKETING VALUE OF EXCLUSIVITY AND INNOVATION

Examples of Exclusive Catalog Offerings

It is decidedly advantageous to sell items not readily available in other retail channels, so exclusivity and innovation are major marketing strategies. Many catalogs offering books employ and exemplify the exclusivity strategy, for in many cases, all or most of the books listed in booksellers' catalogs are unavailable in most bookstores. Many are, in fact, highly specialized technical or business books that most bookstores—other than those located in downtown business districts and on college campuses—normally do not stock or stock only in a limited way.

One firm, Visual Horizons® of Rochester, New York, fields a catalog they title "Powerful Presentations™," with the notation on the cover, "Your source for hard-to-find presentation tools." The catalog then offers a variety of supplies, equipment, and fixtures for creating and delivering presentations of many kinds. Figure 2–5 illustrates just a few of the items offered.

The M & B Company presents what it titles a "Bargain Catalog," in which might be listed almost any kind of merchandise. It is a catalog printed quite inexpensively in black ink on newsprint. The company somewhat novelly uses its catalog as a resource for finding items to sell, as illustrated in Figure 2–6 (page 2 of the catalog).

There are various ways to offer items not readily available elsewhere. One very common way is to handle a line of products that are common commodities (e.g., cosmetics, vitamins, food specialties, linens, writing instruments, paper goods, and computer programs) for a manufacturer whose name

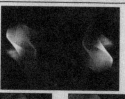

Figure 2–5. A page from the catalog of Visual Horizons®.

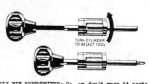

ANTIQUE SILVER DOLLARS

Authentic old real silver dollars. The real Mccoy ! The most beautifully designed silver dollar in the history of our country and the most popular collector coin. Sure to appreciate in value over the years. All are dated between 1878 and 1899. Being about 1½ inches in diameter and very thick, the heavy weight makes them even "feel" valuable ! They are allready one of the most sought after collector coins today, so get yours early while supply lasts. We offer them in three states of condition:

#0420 Morgan Silver Dollar in High Grade condition. These are beauties with very little wear. Very high detail. $19.50 ea.

#0421 Morgan Silver Dollar- Medium Grade. A little more worn than above but still very nice.................... $14.50 ea.

#0422 Morgan Silver Dollar- Worn around rims but everything still readable $ 9.95

"HOW TO REPAIR YOUR OWN 35 MM CAMERA" Book- by Cermak. 224 pages. Shows all the tricks to fixing your SLR. Origionally $8.95. #0322. Each ... $ 4.40

"THE IMAGINARY PHOTO MUSEUM" Book- Over 450 photos from 1836 to date- all classics ! Beautiful high quality prints. 270 pages. A collectors item made to sell for $19.95 each and may be worth more now- we don't know. We got a good deal on them so you do too. #0323. Each .... $ 4.75

SIX-BIT SCREWDRIVER: No, we don't mean it costs 6 bits ! Its just about the handiest screwdriver imaginable. It has 3 different sizes of flat tips, 2 different sizes of phillips tips, and 1 pointed tip (awl). Its easier and faster to change bits than to pick up a different screwdriver if you were using an old fashioned set of separate pieces. All the tips are contained in a drum magazine located on the shaft of this tool. To change, you just pull back the handle, rotate the drum to the desired bit, and push the handle forward again. Its facinating to watch each bit disappear into the drum and a new one come out. A whole change takes about 3 seconds. Whats more, you can hold the drum and shaft firmly in one hand, and turn the handle independently with the other hand- giving you more leverage than is possible with an old fashioned screwdriver. Its ruggedly built. The handle is unbreakable plastic and everything else is steel. Heavy duty hardened tips cant fall out or get lost. #0317. Each ... $ 7.70

WANTED

Your Product or Surplus to sell in

Our Catalogs

We are interested in purchasing your product. Whether its something you manufacture, something you import, or a surplus item you wish to clear out- we are interested.

Please send us a complete description, picture, drawing, etc.- full information on the item(s) you have for our consideration. A sample of your product(s) is of immense help- and required before a final decision can be made as to whether or not to purchase your product and sell it in our catalogs. Samples can not be returned unless accompanied by adequate return shipping, but its to your benifit to let us keep the sample because often we can not use the item right away- but later on when catalog space is available, or when another product becomes available that compliments your product, we can just get your sample out and make a decision on the spot and immediately contact you for purchase arrangements.

We are interested in just about anything- from crafts to surplus to electronic devices in price ranges from a few cents to a couple hundred dollars each item.

If you have something you would like to offer to us for sale we would be delighted to receive and evaluate your product(s). Please send them by UPS or through the post office to the following address: PURCHASING DEPARTMENT
M & B COMPANY
205 WINDMILL RIDGE RD
CHRISTIANSBURG, VA 24073

Figure 2–6. A page from the M & B Company's catalog.

is not well known. (Such lines are often not well known simply because they do not advertise heavily, which is one reason they are often offered at much lower prices than nationally advertised brands, although this is not universally true.)

Clearly, you can sell almost anything you wish to sell, even services, via mail order and catalogs. It is important to be price competitive, but exclusivity and innovation are probably more important as cataloging strategies. Exclusivity is always an important marketing strategy. The very ability to claim exclusivity, such as "sole supplier of Magic Cosmetics," carries weight with many people, despite the fact that they have never heard of Magic Cosmetics.

Innovative Ideas for Catalog Sales

A catalog that is quite different in appearance generally and yet entirely businesslike is that of The J. Peterman Company of Lexington, Kentucky. The catalog offers quality apparel, much of it quite distinctive and not readily available elsewhere. The featured item, "The J. Peterman Coat," is illustrated in Figure 2–7, along with the terms and conditions of sale, stated simply, clearly, and completely.

A couple who renovated and restored an old house ran into great difficulties finding plumbing fixtures, door knobs, hinges, hooks, bannisters, mantels, andirons, fire screens, sash weights, sconces, chandeliers, and sundry other items that were of a nature and in the styles of an era past, which were necessary to restore the house to its original style and decor. As a result of their many adventures in finding sources for such items, they decided to start a catalog business listing and offering such hard-to-find items for the benefit of others seeking to restore old houses, and they built a successful direct-mail business as a result.

One of the catalogs listed in the American Parade of Catalogs brochure is titled *Free Government Money!*, and it lists a variety of government programs. Another is *The World's Best Catalogs*, which lists other catalogs. Still another title is *Gifts from Uncle Sam*, which lists items that can be bought directly from the government and from the government's own catalogs.

In this era of rapid air transportation and other advanced technology, resourceful merchants have built successful catalog operations selling highly perishable items such as steaks and sea food, shipping them frozen (or even live and on ice, in the case of lobsters from some suppliers) by air express. Catalogs advertising such specialties as these have joined the ranks of the many

The J. Peterman Coat.

Classic horseman's duster protects you, your rump, your saddle and your legs down to the ankles.
Because it's cut very long to do the job, it's unintentionally very flattering. With or without a horse.
Although I live in horse country, I wear this coat for other reasons. Because they don't make Duesenbergs anymore.

J. Peterman

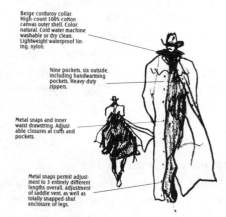

Beige corduroy collar. High-count 100% cotton canvas outer shell. Color: natural. Cold water machine washable or dry clean. Lightweight waterproof lining, nylon.

Nine pockets, six outside, including handwarming pockets. Heavy-duty zippers.

Metal snaps and inner waist drawstring. Adjustable closures at cuffs and pockets.

Metal snaps permit adjustment to 3 entirely different lengths overall, adjustment of saddle vent, as well as totally snapped-shut enclosure of legs.

Men's and women's sizes: XXS, XS, S, M, L, XL, XXL. Include your height, weight, dress or jacket size, shirt neck and sleeve size and waist size when ordering.

Price: $184. We pay shipping.

Care:
If you want to shrink the duster (lengthwise) 1 to 2 inches, cold water wash in machine, air dry. Otherwise, stretch while still damp to maintain length. Or dry clean. Use "Spray 'n Wash" on stubborn stains.

Prices in Owners Manual No. 4 guaranteed through March 1, 1990.

How to order

(Order form between pages 26-27.)

1. Write us, or even quicker, call us toll free at 800-231-7341 (or 606-268-2006 from inside Kentucky or from London, Montreal, etc.).

Be assured that when you call, you will not find us rushed, perfunctory or rude.

The fact is we are waiting for you to call. We are glad when you do. The more questions you ask, the better.

After a while, we get to know our customers by name and also know what they like and what they don't.

2. PHONE HOURS.
8 AM to 10 PM (EST) weekdays and weekends

3. SIZES.
To advise you of best size, we prefer to have as much of the following information as possible and relevant: your height, your weight (don't worry, some of us weigh more than you ever dreamed of), dress or jacket size, shirt neck size and shirt sleeve length, and waist size.

4. CREDIT CARDS.
Visa, MasterCard, American Express.

5. SHIPPING CHARGES.
None, inside U.S. and none for Hawaii or Alaska either. We pay all normal shipping charges and we've never understood what "handling" means and we don't charge for it.

6. Federal Express 2nd day air, only $6.50 to each shipment address in U.S., Hawaii and Alaska. For international destinations, call for additional charges.

Absolute Satisfaction

Anything less, and you get your money back. Period.
The J. Peterman Company
2444 Palumbo Drive
Lexington, Kentucky 40509

© 1989 The J. Peterman Company

Figure 2–7. Two pages from the J. Peterman Company catalog.

other catalogs offering food items—fruit, cheeses, candies, and other delicacies, especially those suitable as gifts.

One enterprising individual started a catalog selling a kind of homemade correspondence course: He searched out what he thought were suitable how-to-do-it books on subjects he thought many people would wish to learn and bought a large quantity of each. He then took them to a local print shop to have the spines sheared off by the paper guillotine such shops use, giving him a set of loose pages. He made a lesson of each chapter and wrote tests based on and using the end-of-chapter quizzes. He then bound the lessons in looseleaf form. He had a set of correspondence courses for little more than the cost of the books (which he bought at wholesale prices, of course) and his own time and labor. He had no problems with the copyright owners because he did not reproduce anything but used the books themselves, which were his property to do with as he wished, as long as he did not plagiarize them! He thus produced correspondence courses of good quality at a fraction of the cost that would have been necessary to write new correspondence courses. He could thus offer correspondence courses at a fraction of what most correspondence schools charge. It's a clever scheme that anyone can emulate quite easily to create almost any kind of course desired—any course on a subject for which a good-quality how-to-do-it book has been published and is available in quantity.

Some people have trouble buying clothing items because they need odd sizes. The average shoe store does not carry a size 12 AAA-width shoe in any of its many styles because there are not enough individuals in any location with that odd foot size. A cataloger, however, who is not restricted to any given area, can sell across the entire continent—across the entire world, for that matter—wherever the mails reach. Customers with odd size requirements for shoes or other items welcome the cataloger who can satisfy their special requirements. Several sellers of shoes do their business entirely by catalog, mailing catalogs directly to individuals but also supplying independent salespeople who sell door to door with samples and catalogs. Some such salespeople specialize even further. For example, one may specialize in work shoes and sell by calling on gasoline service stations, garages, factories, construction sites, and other such places where workers want heavy-duty shoes or special safety shoes. They usually sell from catalogs, although they may have samples or demonstration models with them. They can usually arrange to deliver the shoes themselves (probably a good idea from the marketing viewpoint) or to have them drop-shipped directly to the customers.

Many successful catalog ventures are built on the basis of satisfying those special needs that can only be accommodated profitably by marketing on a large scale, such as nationally. For the small businessperson, the method for large-scale marketing is by mail and catalog, which is available to all sellers, large and small. Seek out any special needs that are not satisfied locally, and devise the means for satisfying them by mail or other such means, and you probably have a sound strategy for a catalog venture. In addition to the limitless possibilities of exclusive and innovative merchandise, catalogs and mail order offer still more opportunities in this modern sophisticated and complex world.

VENDORS AS CUSTOMERS

There are a few special situations and special opportunities of which you should be aware. While you are probably aware (as is the general public) of merchandise catalogs, you may not be not as aware of service catalogs, especially those in which the cataloger's income does not derive from sales of the services listed therein. In fact, this kind of catalog venture is quite a special opportunity to create a profitable catalog business with zero investment for inventory (i.e., as inventory is used in the usual sense). The principal investment for this kind of catalog business is for advertising and printing, and both (especially the latter) can be done modestly. A bit of preamble will help to explain this concept.

Most catalogs are supplied free of charge to those who want them, although today's high costs have impelled some catalogers to charge a small price, usually refundable with the first order and imposed more to discourage children and curiosity seekers than to recover costs. Thus, most catalogers do not derive their income directly from the sale of their catalogs to those who purchase from the catalogs. Instead, most catalogers generate income by selling the merchandise offered in the catalog to the readers of the catalog.

However, a whole class of catalog businesses not only receive no income from the recipients and readers of the catalog, but they also receive no income from those who request and buy what is advertised therein. Instead, these businesses derive their income from those whose products or services are listed, for those individuals pay to be listed. In fact, many might not consider this a catalog at all, but rather a directory. However, the source of the cataloger's income does not change the catalog's basic nature: It is still a catalog that lists many items, often with ample illustrations of what is offered for sale. It is suitable for shopping—browsing through—from the comfort of a chair, which also qualifies it eminently well as a catalog. One example of such a publication comes immediately to mind: the real estate catalog or directory found so often in major metropolitan areas.

Americans have become a highly mobile people in modern times. There is a constant flow of transient residents in and out of most metropolitan areas. These transients have been transferred in or out of the area by their employers, or they come and go for other reasons. In fact, in some areas (e.g., New York, Miami, Los Angeles, San Francisco, Denver, Chicago, Washington, DC, and other cities), there are many more residents who came from other places than there are natives who were born in the area. (Natives of some places, such as New York, Miami, Los Angeles, and Washington, DC, appear to be rare indeed.)

Finding a place to live in these circumstances is almost always a problem for newcomers. Meanwhile, either those who leave are trying to sell a house or their landlords are looking for new tenants to replace them. Therefore, many entrepreneurs in these areas publish catalogs of houses for sale and apartments for rent in the area. The catalogs are generally furnished free of charge, with help-yourself stacks placed in strategic locations. Real estate brokers and others who list their homes and apartments pay for the privilege of being listed, which produces the income to the publisher. In many cases, the publisher charges a standard fee for a simple listing, with higher rates for expanded listings and advertising space available to those who wish more than a simple listing. (In some cases, minimal listings are free to everyone, and the income to the publisher derives entirely from the charges for expanded notices and advertising.)

There are other cases where the catalog/directory may (or may not) be furnished free of charge to the reader, but where the income to the publisher derives chiefly or solely from those whose goods or services are listed. For example, a government employee in the Washington, DC, area started a publication of this general type (in his spare time), but he added his own twist to the idea. He calls his publication *The Want Ad*, and he sells it wherever newspapers and magazines are sold. He runs classified advertisements offering items of all kinds for sale, free of charge to individuals selling personal property. Those who get free advertising in this manner agree to pay the publisher 10 percent of the proceeds from whatever they are selling. This is the primary source of income from this venture. Originally a simple typewritten sheet in newsletter format, reproduced by a simple spirit duplicator, *The Want Ad* is today a full-blown monthly magazine, listing thousands of items for sale and carrying commercial advertising as well, furnishing additional income to the publisher.

There are also a number of publishers of directories listing consultants and their services. Usually, the consultant is charged for a listing but, as in the case of the real estate directory, the publisher also sells advertising space for any who want it. The publisher then sells or gives the publication to business people who have use for such a directory. (Selling it at a nominal price is probably the best strategy because it confers some value on the directory, while not inhibiting its sale.)

The directory/catalog idea has wide application, and it has been used in many similar applications to create directories of speakers, seminar presenters, financial counselors and brokers, and many others who pay to be listed and who may pay an additional, special fee for advertising. (The operator of a lecture bureau, for example, would do well to provide a catalog/directory of speakers, trainers, and seminar presenters to clients and prospective clients, and many speakers would gladly pay to be listed in such a publication.) It should be noted, also, that the sale of advertising space in such publications need not be confined to those whose listings appear therein. There are almost always satellite interests, people with something to sell to readers. Those who sell or rent furniture, for example, would find it worthwhile to advertise in the real estate directory, as might automobile dealers, interior decorators, and others.

Here are a few other examples of where and how this basic idea has been or can be used in listing sources and supplies of services and goods:

- Jobs available, including overseas jobs, always a popular idea, especially with young, single people
- Tours, travel, and related services
- Discount, surplus, and closeout dealers/sources/sales
- Flea markets, fairs, trade shows, conventions
- Used automobiles wanted and for sale
- Used computers and related equipment—printers, modems, and so on
- Franchises and other business opportunities
- Health food specialties
- Multilevel marketing (MLM) propositions (there are now enough to merit a catalog or directory)
- Drop-shippers: manufacturers and distributors willing to drop-ship for dealers and thus eager to enlist more dealers

GENERALIZATION VERSUS SPECIALIZATION

Specialization as a Matter of Degree

In cataloging, as in any other venture, you can generalize, or you can specialize. The terms *generalization* and *specialization* should be considered relative terms, not absolute ones: There are many degrees of specialization. The cataloger who sells frozen premium steaks only—sirloins, club steaks, shell steaks, porterhouses, tenderloins, and others—is very specialized in terms of product. If, in addition, the cataloger is offering the product only as a premium to sales professionals (as some sellers of such items do), she or he is specializing to an even greater degree. (He or she may, however, be offering this premium item to corporate buyers, rather than to sellers, as still another avenue of specialization.) Similar specialists include the seller of live lobster and other shellfish or the cataloger who sells a broad variety of gift-packaged food items, such as cheeses, jams, jellies, fruits, and related items. *Generalization* and *specialization* become meaningful only with elaboration—explanation of how and where the business is specialized. Some applications of the catalog sales idea are so specialized, novel, and innovative as to be a bit startling. The real trick in marketing is to judge the optimal point between the broad and the specialized market. That is part of what makes marketing much more art than science.

Specialized Applications for Nonprofit Organizations

Catalogs and catalog sales may be specialized in many ways, even in terms of whether the purpose or application of cataloging is a business (i.e., profit-making) venture. Public radio and TV, for example, depend on traditional fund-raising methods—donations by individuals and organizations—to finance their programming and operation. However, the imaginative minds of Minnesota's Public Radio and the Prairie Home Companion show produced a fund-raising catalog of T-shirts, cassettes, and record albums connected with the guests of Garrison Keillor's show there, or that the idea should have been picked up by and been successful for a public TV station in Minnesota.

Public television and radio are not the only nonprofit organizations to use catalogs in fund raising. Museums, art galleries, churches, and others have done so frequently, and they will probably do so more often in the future, now that they have seen how successful such fund-raising methods can be. There are advantages in nonprofit operation, one of which is a great reduction in postage costs. (Postage is one of the major costs of all direct-mail and mail-order operations.)

Pros and Cons of Specialization

There is nothing inherently meritorious about either generalization or specialization in a catalog effort. The key is to offer the customer a wide assortment of choices, of course, but the choices can be either specialized or generalized; there are pluses and minuses with each approach. Obviously, a catalog should have a clear focus both in defining the class or line of goods offered and in explaining the inclusion of those goods within one catalog. The Quill® Corporation catalog exemplifies a generalized catalog, and the Global® Computer Supplies catalog typifies a specialized one.

The Quill® Corporation catalog offers a broad variety of office and industrial supplies, and it has grown steadily to include office furniture, fixtures, full-blown desktop computers, and many related items. (The company was started by its president, Jack Miller, in the basement of his home and has been growing steadily since.) In fact, Quill now publishes several catalogs, which also grow steadily larger and more elaborate. Periodically, I get a slender catalog supplementing Quill's main, semiannual catalog and its monthly catalog of special sale items, which features computer-related items.

Despite this great breadth, because Quill focuses on general office and industrial supplies, its line of computer-related goods is limited by comparison with the catalogs of organizations specializing in computers. The most recent Global catalog, for example, includes 148 pages totally devoted to goods related to computers. The catalog mostly features items for desktop computers, but it also includes a few supplies that might be of interest to the owners of larger computers.

If you are looking for the computer supplies that every owner or operator of a desktop computer must have—printer ribbons (for the most common printers), floppy diskettes, and paper, for example—you are likely to find them in both catalogs. However, if you are looking for items to build your own local area network (LAN—used to interconnect several computers in an office), for plotter pens, or for bulk supplies for making your own cables, you are much more likely to find them in the Global catalog. Moreover—and this is significant, too—even if some of these appear in the Quill catalog, you are likely to find a much greater assortment from which to choose in the Global catalog. The message is plain enough: It is very difficult, perhaps impossible, to be both a generalist and a specialist, although many try to be both. (In some industries, this is accomplished by setting up separate divisions or companies; in cataloging, it is usually accomplished by establishing separate catalogs. Some catalog companies do publish a half-dozen or more catalogs, in fact.)

That brings up another point: There are always trade-offs—giving up one thing to get another thing. The appeal of a generalized catalog is "one-stop shopping." The buyer may be able to satisfy all or at least many needs with a single order placed via a single catalog. That is attractive to a great many busy people. However, the choice of goods offered in any given line is likely to be much greater when shopping in several more specialized catalogs. Shopping in a generalized catalog with its unavoidably limited line of goods in any given kind of item may mean compromises, making do with something that is not *exactly* what the customer wants.

Business-to-Business Versus Business-to-Consumers

The Quill catalog is directed primarily to businesses, probably to small businesses more than to large ones, although individual consumers get the catalogs too and place their orders, and Quill is large enough to service large accounts. The Global catalog is also directed primarily to businesses, again probably more to small businesses than to large ones, but the nature of modern computers is such that a great many individual consumers operate computers as a hobby or as a tool for managing a hobby. Therefore, probably a respectably large percentage of those who browse through and buy from Global do so as private citizens and individual consumers. Despite the many exceptions, however, both Global and Quill recognize small businesses as their primary audience. In launching your catalog, you must decide which is your primary audience or target group—businesses or individual consumers. (With today's surge in offices and businesses at home, the distinction is becoming blurred.) The differences in each audience's buying habits and patterns must be considered when planning a catalog operation.

Organizations for which buying is a major, ongoing function (such as a manufacturing firm that must buy many off-the-shelf parts and components or a major department store) usually employ one or more professional buyers or purchasing agents, for whom buying is a full-time job. Purchasing agents usually keep a large supply of catalogs; they are a major tool of the professional buyer's trade. The purchasing agent is concerned with several things, including

(a) finding exactly the right item as rapidly as possible, (b) getting good service, (c) receiving prompt and dependable delivery, and (d) getting highly competitive prices.

To a degree, the same criteria may also be applied by the average business executive who buys only occasionally for his or her firm. The executive, however, is often shopping for an item without knowing exactly what the item is or what the right price is. He or she may therefore glance through several catalogs, seeking and getting a hurried and limited education by making comparisons. Most people do exactly this when shopping for furniture, clothes, or any other kind of goods about which the buyer is inexpert.

The average consumer buying something for personal use, on the other hand, may enjoy shopping (browsing) through catalogs that offer a wide variety of items in a given line (e.g., a lingerie catalog, rather than a general garment catalog). The browsing itself may be a pleasant pastime for some individuals and adds a value to large, multicolored catalogs on that basis alone. Aside from the several foregoing considerations in deciding to what degree you ought to specialize with your catalog, the most practical consideration is market size.

Market Size as an Important Factor in Specialization

The significant factor that influences (or that should influence) the degree of specialization is market size. This is primarily a factor that constrains the maximum degree of specialization. That is, before you launch a catalog (or a venture of any kind, for that matter), you must sensibly determine the size of the market for whatever you contemplate offering.

Unfortunately, there are no precise or scientific methods for doing this, much less methods for arriving at estimates of what constitutes a profitable market size. However, a few rough guides are available, based mostly on commonsense practicality. You might use the following method, adapting it to your own situation as best you can. (You should be very conservative in order to minimize your risk, by providing yourself a large margin for error.)

1. Make a middle-of-the-road estimate of the average order size you can expect from your catalog distribution. After you have become established to some degree and have some experience to guide your estimates, modify this estimate accordingly.
2. Project an average gross profit based on that first estimate.
3. Calculate your probable overhead costs for start-up operations.

4. Estimate the number of orders you need, on the basis of that first estimate, to produce enough gross profit to pay all estimated costs and produce at least a break-even result.

5. Estimate the number of catalogs you must mail to get that number of orders, allowing yourself a conservative 2 or 3 percent response, at most. (Try to establish a break-even point at 1 percent, if at all possible.)

6. Profile the demographics—what kinds of prospects you must target to match the foregoing factors.

The number of catalogs you must mail (Item 5) refers to the *market size*. If you have decided that you must mail 25,000 catalogs and follow up with a repeat mailing to the same prospects every other month, you know that you must find mailing lists (or other means) to reach 25,000 prospects whom you believe to be the right ones for your offers. You must therefore not specialize so much that you cannot find 25,000 likely prospects. Even then, to be properly conservative and allow yourself an adequate margin for error—and that is itself an important thing to do—you would probably do well to settle for nothing less than a market about double the minimum that your calculations deduced. Remember always that these are guesses at best and are properly colored by your fondest wishes and so are probably not nearly as conservative as they ought to be.

Bear in mind that even with very conservative figures, you are not likely to make a profit the first year, and you might not even achieve a break-even before the second year. That is to be expected as the norm, although there are exceptions. The exceptions are truly exceptional, however, and it is almost suicidal, from a business viewpoint, to base your plans on the expectation of turning profits immediately. In that respect, cataloging is subject to the same verities of business that other ventures are, and the next chapter explores these.

3

What to Sell: Finding the Right Line

More money is lost in mail order from poor product selection than in any other way.

Cecil C. Hoge, Sr.
(From M*ail Order Moonlighting*, Ten Speed Press, Berkeley, CA 1976)

CRUCIAL IMPORTANCE OF "BUYING RIGHT"

Businesses generally emphasize the art of marketing—how to make sales and create customers. That makes good sense: The major purpose of business is to make sales and create customers. There is certainly no shortage of books, periodicals, training programs, college courses, seminars, and lectures devoted to the methodologies of success in marketing and selling. Joe Girard, Zig Ziglar, Peter Drucker, Dottie Walters, Frank Boettger, and the late Elmer Wheeler, to name only a few of the many who merit inclusion in that elite company, became famous names because they were outstandingly successful salespersons and writers on the subject of success in selling: They lectured and wrote voluminously to teach the rest of us how to sell as effectively as they did.

Despite the importance of sales skills, there is more to success in marketing than superior "sellership" (if I may coin a nonsexist term). There is superior "buyership" too. Buyership is important enough to have become a career specialty. Large companies who buy extensively usually have at least one individual who is designated the company's purchasing agent and who is responsible for all purchasing. Those who sell a variety of merchandise—large department stores, for example—have a number of buyers, usually one for each department, because they recognize the need for special experience and knowledge in buying merchandise that is to be resold. Buyers must buy the right merchandise at the right time and at the right price in order for the business to resell it profitably.

That truth applies to cataloging as much as it does to any other business that buys and sells merchandise. That is, there is no question that product selection plays a large role in success and failure; you must manage to buy the right merchandise for your catalog. Nonetheless, there are no inherently "good" or "bad" catalog items. Catalog items are only good or bad in terms of how well they sell in a given instance. The entire subject merits lengthy discussion, for in selling a line of commodities, shrewd buying can be and often is as important to success as is effective selling. Product selection was discussed briefly in the preceding chapter, primarily in terms of examples and starter ideas, but it is far too important a topic to be dismissed that quickly. It merits a chapter all its own, perhaps especially so in this book because catalog sales usually mean that an entire line of products is involved.

PREDICTION OF SUCCESSFUL ITEMS

The product line undoubtedly is or can easily become the Achilles heel of any mail-order venture, especially a catalog venture: Catalog sales depend on the inherent appeal of the items. Even the best presentation and the shrewdest and best conceived marketing strategies often can not save a line of products that nobody wants. Sometimes, effective marketing can make marginally appealing items succeed in a modestly profitable catalog promotion. There are also cases, however, where even the cleverest marketing schemes cannot quite pull it off, and the differences between success and failure are often unpredictable.

Perhaps the hula hoop would have been a failure six months earlier or the mood ring a total flop two years later. We don't know; the reaction of the public is simply not that predictable. Who can say whether the public will want to buy yo-yos, hula hoops, mood rings, pet rocks, or air ionizers? The first three of these were huge successes, although they were popular fads for only a short time, and they then settled back to become staples that did not move particularly well but are still being sold. Air ionizers never did really catch on; few people were convinced that ionizing their air was especially important.

On the other hand, some items, such as handheld electronic calculators, videocassette recorders, and desktop computers, each caught on quickly and developed a permanent market of substantial proportions. If these examples prove nothing else, they prove that predictions are always chancy; no one knows how the public will react to most new items. Who would have predicted, for example, that hundreds of thousands of people would each pay $4 for a large pebble in a wooden "cage" (the "Pet Rock") just to get a chuckle? Or that hula hoops would sell to children and adults alike as fast as manufacturers could make them—but only for about six weeks, after which they dropped dead or nearly so?

This does not mean that all attempt at prediction is worthless. Sensible businesspeople can learn from experience (their own and that of others), analyzing it, rationalizing it, and making predictions based on it. Experience-based knowledge improves the batting average in predicting success—the probability of being right—but it does not and cannot make such prediction a science. Even with experience-based knowledge, no one can be certain of always accurately predicting human reactions to a specific stimulus in a given situation. It is thus never safe to commit fully to a marketing campaign (to "roll out") without testing it. Testing allows businesspeople to learn something about probabilities, if not certainties.

CATEGORIES OF MERCHANDISE

General Versus Specialized Markets

Hula hoops, handheld calculators, pet rocks, and videocassette recorders are items that appeal to almost everyone, if they appeal to anyone. That is, the discussion in this chapter so far has referred only to the general market for consumer goods. The general market consists of the bulk of the population—that great, undivided middle class. There are many kinds of items you may offer in a catalog sent out to that great middle class that represents most of us as private citizens. However, you may recall from Chapter 2 that the general market isn't always the appropriate one for a given item or line of merchandise. In a great many catalogs, the items offered appeal primarily to certain specialized groups and classes of individuals and must be sent out to the appropriate group or individual.

Low-Risk Versus High-Risk Items

There is still another division of product types to consider, which might be characterized as "low-risk" and "high-risk" items. You may decide to stick with items of a type that are so widely accepted and used that they are regarded as necessities—vitamins, ball point pens, copier paper, shoes, and other commodities. Everybody uses these items and a great many people sell them. Your marketing problem here is not so much to persuade people to buy these items as it is to persuade them to buy the items from you. These items may also be specialties, such as computer paper and printer ribbons, which are widely accepted and used within the specialized market.

You may, however, opt to sell new and different items—perhaps novelties, apparel of new and innovative styles, new types of household gadgets, and other items that are more or less exclusive. Such items hold out the possibility of unusual success, but they also may fall flat in the marketplace. These high-risk items present a totally different marketing problem. Again, these items may appeal to general markets (such as household gadgets) or to specialized ones (such as unique display tools for seminar presenters).

IMPORTANCE OF SUITABLE MATCHES

Matching the Product and the Prospect

Regardless of the category of merchandise, you must consider how to make a suitable match: the right market for the product or the right product for the market, where the term *market* refers to the individuals addressed as prospects. "Poor product selection" thus becomes a relative idea, when viewed with this in mind. Product selection usually applies only with respect to some projected audience or chosen market for the item or line of items. The product that is a poor choice for a given market may be excellent for another market. Obviously, lipstick and other female-oriented cosmetics should be advertised to women and not to men (though there are now many male-oriented cosmetics). Nonetheless, in many cases, the issues of market selection are not nearly as clear, although they are no less important.

For example, when I was a consultant, I sold how-to-do-it information and help in writing proposals and winning government contracts. One of my early problems in doing so was finding the best market for my help. After many trials and many errors, I discovered that those companies who specialized in providing computer services to government agencies were one of my best markets, taken as a class. Given the enormous number and variety of companies doing business with government agencies, there was no way I could have predicted that. Many of my mailings were unsuccessful or only marginal successes because they went out to markets that appeared logically to be right, but that proved not to be.

Matching the Catalog's "Character," Its Purpose, and Its Prospects

The prospects addressed are not the sole consideration, either; the *purpose* to which the catalog is addressed, its *character*, is also a consideration that can make a difference in the appropriateness of the catalog, its products, and the prospective buyers. Consider the items exhibited in Figure 3–1, a page from the Harry and David Holiday Book of Gifts. Would you normally spend $69.95 for a smoked ham for your table, even a fancy one? Or an equal sum for two smoked salmon fillets? Not likely. Few people would spend that much to buy such items for the dinner table. But this is not an ordinary smoked ham or an ordinary situation. This is a *gift* item, especially chosen and packaged as a gift, and what's more, this is a holiday item.

A gift catalog operates under a different set of rules than other catalogs. You can offer assortments of merchandise that would be otherwise incompatible. If you sold office supplies in your catalog, you might have expensive fountain pens and brief cases. In any other single catalog, you would not usually include household appliances, specialties of personal apparel, *and* expensive fancy food items. In a gift catalog, however, these all become compatible with each other because they are all suitable as gifts. That makes a difference—a large difference in making otherwise dissimilar items completely compatible with each other.

Not everyone so characterizes their catalogs, although some have a general or standard catalog and one or more special catalogs, designed especially for special occasions, such as the Christmas holiday season, winter sports, or summertime. The following list of catalogs and titles illustrates how some are so characterized, while others are not:

Housewarming Sale, John Wanamaker

James River Traders Winter Sale

L.L. Bean® Christmas 1989

Scully & Scully, Inc.

D'Elegante of California Western Fashion

Country Curtains®

The Spirit of Tradition Holiday 1989, Carroll Reed

"Select Customers Only" Edition, Willow Creek

Christmas Elegance, The Bombay Company

Holiday Catalog 1989: Introducing Five New Systems, CompuAdd

FINE FEASTING MADE EASY

SPIRAL SLICED HAM

Pre-sliced and ready to serve! Our marvelous 7- to 8-pound ham is honey-cured and fully smoked, then glazed with a tasty blend of brown sugar, *more* honey, and maple syrup. Unique spiral slicing means no waste — your *best* choice for sandwiches or serve-yourself buffets!

Item No. 346 . . . $5995

SMOKED HAM

Lean, tender 10- to 13-pound prime whole hams, individually sugar-cured, then smoked to rosy perfection over a slow hickory fire. Fully cooked and ready to enjoy. Harry's glaze recipe included.

Item No. 381 . . . $6995

All Smokehouse items are available November 1 to April 30 to all 50 states.

SMOKED SALMON

What makes ours so special? First, we use only fresh-caught sockeye salmon from the cold, clear waters of the Pacific Northwest. Then each fillet is boned by hand, seasoned with savory herbs and spices, and custom-smoked over native alder. Unlike lox, our salmon is firm and fully cooked. We ship each fillet in a special vacuum pouch that keeps it moist and flavorful without preservatives — needs no refrigeration until opened. Makes a memorable delicacy for a holiday buffet . . . better order one for yourself, too! Net wt. 1 lb. 4 oz.

Item No. 380 . . . $3995

SPECIAL OFFERS

Two Smoked Salmon Fillets
to One Address Net wt. 2 lbs. 8 oz.
Item No. 385 . . . $6995

NEW • Two 8-ounce Salmon Fillets
to One Address Net wt. 1 lb.
Item No. 657 . . . $3795

NEW • SALMON PLATTER
Eye-Catching Glassware from Italy.

Chill well before setting it out, and this handsome frosted-glass server will keep salmon, hors d'oeuvres or pâté cooler . . . longer. Useful for warm dishes, too. Makes meals more appetizing . . . entertaining more elegant. *Sine qua non* for fancy seafood buffets! Measures about 19½ x 7¾ inches. Dishwasher safe.

Item No. 450 . . . $2495

26

Figure 3–1. A page from *Harry and David Hoiliday Book of Gifts.*

Winter 1989, Domestications

James Avery Craftsman® Christmas, 1989

Wireless® Fall/Winter 1989: A Gift Catalog for Fans and Friends

Selective Software

Jazzertogs® Fit is It! Fall '89 Fashions and Accessories

Harry and David Holiday Book of Gifts

Introducing Holiday '89, Chadwick's of Boston, Ltd.

The "Great Deal" Catalog, Damark

Aussie Connection, Fall/Winter/1989

Owner's Manual No. 4, The J. Peterman Company

Mission Orchards™ Holiday Catalogue 1989

The Software Labs TSL Catalog

You can see that few of these give the reader much of a hint regarding what to expect to find inside, much less provide motivation to read any. You might well surmise what to expect in a Sears, an L.L. Bean, or a Spiegel catalog simply because they are so well known, but what could you surmise about a *J. Smith Winter Catalog?* Imagine that all of these listed catalogs had arrived at your house one morning. Which would tempt you most to begin browsing?

Advance Commitments: The Power of Product–Prospect Match

Because the linkage between product and prospect is so strong, it is possible to be committed to one by virtue of advance commitment to the other. That is, if your market is already defined for you—if, for example, you are already committed to certain specific mailing lists for some reason—you must select products that are suitable for the market represented by those lists. And of course the reverse is true: If you are committed in advance to some given line of products you must find the right mailing lists—select prospects who are suitable.

Chapter 8's discussion of mailing lists shows that this consideration is not lost on the professional direct-mail specialist, who tends to study this in terms of the suitability or effectiveness of the mailing lists for the marketing campaign. In fact, list brokers talk increasingly in terms of databases, rather than mailing lists. Databases offer an order of magnitude greater definition of what and who the lists represent, providing important demographic data about the list. That helps greatly because it provides far more insight into what and who those prospects are. Even with those powerful tools, however, the problem remains to properly match products with markets, as represented by the mailing lists (or by the databases the lists represent).

THE ADVANTAGES OF MANY ITEMS

Many mail-order ventures, successful and unsuccessful, are based on a single item. This simplifies the venture in many ways, but it also increases the burden on that single item by making it entirely a go/no-go proposition. Because the customer has no alternative choices, you have all your money on one horse, greatly increasing your risk. You don't even have the possibility of bounceback orders, in most cases (unless what you sell is consumable or a good gift item, which then creates some possibility of follow-up orders). In this respect, catalog sales offer advantages in proportion to the number and variety of items offered in your catalog. The probability that prospects—readers of your catalog—will find something of interest is certainly proportional to the number and variety of items in your catalog. Still, you must specialize to some degree as a practical necessity, or you cannot *target* your mailings to a selected market that you have identified as being right for your purposes.

The number and variety of possible items you may carry is almost limitless, of course, even within some clearly identified class or group. Mail-order enthusiasts are fond of saying that anything can be sold by mail. Nonetheless, most would admit that many products are not suitable candidates for mail-order marketing. Still, many more items *can* be sold by mail than cannot be sold that way.

A FEW BROAD CLASSIFICATIONS

There is no certain method for even estimating how well a particular item will sell. Customers find all kinds of items attractive for all kinds of reasons. Hot sellers can be costly or cheap, beautiful or ugly, useful or useless, and the life of an item as a salable product can be eternal or fleeting, a staple or a fad. Despite the lack of a goof-proof method for judging items for their salability, it is at least possible to do some logical analysis in judging and comparing items. First, sort out the possibilities by whatever classifications and categories are helpful in judging the suitability of the items. Here are some tentative classes and categories, for example, with brief discussions of each:

Absolute Exclusivity.   This, the quality of being unavailable else-where, is a virtue that has been mentioned before and is mentioned again later in these pages. Many believe that this is almost a first requirement for a good mail-order item and handle only items that offer them this advantage. Exclusiv-ity is an advantage, of course, provided that the item has appeal. However, if the customer is not attracted to the item, exclusivity will not make it a success. Still, exclusivity is an excellent argument for buying by catalog if the item can be made attractive enough, and it is certainly a great help in marketing a catalog item.

Even so, exclusivity is not necessarily an absolute quality: There are degrees of exclusivity, and in many cases the items can offer relative or virtual exclusivity (as discussed previously—in Chapter 2), conferring on you the same marketing advantages that absolute exclusivity does.

Relative Exclusivity.   Convenience is a great motivator; there is ample evidence that many consumers prize convenience above price and other considerations. Therefore, if the item you offer is available elsewhere, but not in every drug store and supermarket, that is exclusivity for many consum-ers. If, for example, consumers discover that you list an item that they otherwise would have to get from an office-supplies emporium, they will often find it more convenient to order from you than to search out that special store. An important point to make here is that the customer's perception is all important. Therefore, if the customer sees your offer as representing exclusivity, that is good enough.

Broad Selection.   Another kind of virtual exclusivity is represented by an unusually broad selection of some item. Hobbyists and enthusiasts are always on the alert for and interested in adding to their collections. Dyed-in-the-wool pipe smokers, for example, often tend to have wide varieties of pipes and to take great pride in their collections, which are never complete. Such en-thusiasts will often find the assortment of pipes at the local tobacconist or pipe shop disappointingly meager. If you can offer a more complete selection and assortment, you are likely to win their hearts. You can gain many prospective and loyal customers if you can feature some truly unusual or rare pipes, preferably some that have been imported from some exotic places.

Heavy Discounts.   Many mail-order ventures are based on offering items at extraordinary discounts. The discounts may be possible because heavy volume makes slender profit margins workable, because the dealer is selling surplus and closeouts, or for any other reason. In these cases, the discounts offer a degree of exclusivity and an argument for buying from you.

Practicality.   There are practical considerations, at least two to consider immediately: (1) price, and (2) transportation. In terms of motivating customers to buy via mail order, bear in mind the caution with which people spend large sums of money. It would therefore be quite difficult normally to persuade a customer to buy a Steinway piano or a Maserati automobile by mail. These items also present problems of order fulfillment—getting the merchandise to the customer. It would not be easy to ship 2,000-pound items to individual customers, although it might work for certain business-to-business ventures. It might also be impractical to ship a delicate tropical flower from its home in the Amazon to a customer in Antarctica.

Markup.   Markup, which affects your ability to offer highly competitive prices, must be a consideration. If you are at the end of a long chain of distributors where the manufacturer, distributor, wholesaler, and perhaps even other middlemen have each marked up the original manufacturing costs to take their own profits, there is probably not enough margin left for you to offer an attractive price and still gain an acceptable gross profit. That leads you to look for opportunities to buy items from primary sources or at least sources close to the primary source. You need that to gain some latitude in pricing and profit. (Ideally, you manufacture the item yourself or buy directly from the manufacturer at deep discounts.)

Primary Markets: Businesses Versus Individual Consumers.
Relatively few items are exclusively business-to-business or individual consumer items. Most are *primarily* one or the other, but they are not entirely so unless you follow a policy of selling "strictly wholesale" or some equally restrictive practice. The average consumer might wish to buy a wholesale quantity of computer paper, trash bags, or other such item, and the corporate buyer might decide to use a catalog to buy a fountain pen as a gift for someone. Relatively few catalogs are strictly or exclusively business-to-business or consumer oriented. Many, probably most catalogers mail catalogs to and encourage any and all sales from any and all customers, regardless of whether their primary market is business-to-business or to individual consumers.

Despite the need for flexibility, you do have to decide which is your primary market: Indecision as to whom you are addressing as your main prospective customer is almost always deadly and destroys the impact of your sales message. Decide in advance that you can't have it both ways, at least not unless you launch two different catalogs, as some sellers do. For example, some sellers—Sears is one—have created a special "home office" catalog in recognition of the impact of that recent trend. These catalogs offer the same things they offer in their main catalogs, but they focus on those items most suitable for the home-based office. The catalog is clearly addressed to the owner of a home office to identify it unmistakably for what it is.

Big-Tag Versus Small-Tag Items.   It is possible to offer both big-tag and small-tag items in the same catalog, although it is not desirable psychologically—from the viewpoint of marketing strategy—to do so. You might, for example, offer jewelry ranging from $5 costume jewelry to diamond pendants. Still, one or the other is usually featured as the main theme or typifier of the line, with the other purely supplemental to round out the line. Mailing a catalog devoted to high-priced jewelry to a list of middle- or lower-income citizens is not smart marketing. Lists and items must be compatible with each other.

LEADERS AND LOSS LEADERS

In the days before word processing, when my chief writing instrument was a Selectric® typewriter, I was attracted to a mail-order office supplies cataloger principally because it offered Selectric-type ribbons at less than one-half the price I was forced to pay locally at office supplies stores. As a professional writer, I used up those one-time carbon ribbons rather rapidly, so the expense for ribbons was a bit more than incidental. In addition, while I was getting my ribbons at good prices, I ordered all the other office supplies I needed.

　　I don't know whether that supplier offered the ribbons as a loss leader to attract customers or not. He may have gained a full markup profit from those ribbons and it was thus a leader but not a loss leader. Nonetheless, he featured the item in his advertising enough to suggest that he understood its appeal and how it attracted such buyers as me. In any case, it illustrates the value of a leader in attracting the right type of buyer, the type who will buy many other items from you. That is, it illustrates the value of a leader that is representative of the line generally.

　　In fact, this supplier also illustrates the way in which a supplier can build customer loyalty through long association: Although I converted long ago to a computer and printer, and thus never use Selectric® ribbons anymore, I still have a certain fondness for this supplier and still order things occasionally from him to keep my account active.

Another point ought to be made: The line of items must have some kind of coherence, a theme or thread that binds it all together. That theme must be defined in terms of the market, which means the class of buyers. Office supplies and shoes do not belong together in the same catalog, for example. Yes, it is possible that the executive buying office supplies may be attracted to the offer of shoes, but the possibility is unlikely and the offer is also likely to jar the executive browsing through an office-necessities catalog. It may, in fact, be destructive in its effects as a distractor. If you want to sell both shoes and office necessities, do so in two different catalogs and in two different mailings, even if you mail them to the same list.

One example of using two catalogs for the same market is a projected new jewelry catalog by the Edgar B. Furniture Plantation, which reports about one sale for every seven of the $15 four-color furniture catalogs it sends in response to requests, with an average sale of about $3,000. The new catalog will offer the E. Broyhill Jewelry Collection to Edgar B. furniture customers, and the company estimates an average jewelry sale of $2,500. Company officials see nothing incongruous in offering the jewelry line to their furniture customers. In fact, they see their furniture customers as good prospects for the jewelry line because the typical or average purchase in both cases is large enough to mandate a joint husband–wife agreement in most cases. Moreover, because furniture buyers usually make purchases only infrequently, Edgar B. officials perceive the jewelry catalog mailings as a good means for keeping their furniture image fresh and for renewing it regularly.

Do you think that their plan shows sound reasoning? Will it work out as projected? Or is the projection simply wishful thinking? No one can be sure at this point. Only experience will tell. Presumably, Edgar B. will not roll out a full-fledged campaign without test mailings to find out how well their idea works.

THE IDEAL ITEM

The following list reviews the various considerations discussed here and extrapolates from the discussions to describe the six key features of the perfect mail-order item:

1. It is totally exclusive. You control it completely.
2. You manufacture it. That makes it both totally exclusive and totally under your own control.
3. It costs a small fraction of the typical market price for comparative and competitive items; you can mark it up many times its cost and still be

highly competitive. (It also makes it easy to find or create an attractive leader item.)

4. It has almost universal appeal: Everyone or almost everyone in your target market can make good use of it and is likely to want it.
5. It requires extremely little investment in inventory—almost none.
6. It is easy and inexpensive to ship.

Of course, this list should not pertain only to a single item, but rather to each item in a catalog's product line. Catalog sales is a mail-order business that inevitably requires the offer of enough items—a line of items—to constitute a catalog, even one of modest proportions. So the word item is used strictly in a rhetorical sense and actually represents an entire line of items.

THE SEARCH FOR IDEAL ITEMS

In the search for items, you have four options in conducting your search:

1. You can decide to create your own line by manufacturing the items, as in the cases of publishing a series of small reports, creating correspondence courses from how-to-do-it books, or making craft items.
2. You can search for a single line, such as a line of jewelry and cosmetics all available to you from a single source.
3. You can build and assemble your own line by finding numerous sources.
4. You can use a combination of options 1, 2, and 3.

The Complete Line

Taking on a single, complete line has its pros and cons, as most things do. Here are some of the advantages of such an arrangement: For one thing, it simplifies many things for you. You may be able to get high-quality, ready-made catalogs inexpensively, imprinted with your own name. The primary source may also be able to furnish you with other sales materials and to help you in various ways. If the brand name is well known, you may find sales resistance far less than with an unknown line. Finally, you may also be able to have your orders filled by the primary source so that you will not need to have a shipping department or to carry an inventory.

There are drawbacks too, however. You will almost surely have less control over your business, especially over what you offer your customers, in return for the benefits. You may have to sign an agreement that bars you from carrying any other merchandise, at least anything competitive, for example. You may also be forced to agree to stick to the supplier's suggested prices and offer only those sales authorized. You may be required to buy a minimum starting inventory of merchandise and catalogs. You may find yourself at the mercy of your supplier, sometimes unable to get your orders filled promptly, even if you carry an inventory of your own. You may find that you have little or no control of your source of supply on a grand scale, even to the extent of being suddenly cut off from your source for any of many reasons. Moreover, if you are required to buy a starting inventory, you may find that required starting inventory includes a large number of slow-moving items that will take you forever to sell off, while they take up valuable space.

In short, if you do wish to consider handling a complete line available from a single supplier, be aware of these and possibly other hazards, and take at least the following precautions. Investigate more than one source of supply of a complete line, preferably as many as a half-dozen or more. Get all the details from each. Compare costs, selling prices, terms, and requirements, laying them all out on paper so that you can compare them. Ask for sales figures to determine which items in the line sell briskly, which slowly, and which are the "dogs" and sell hardly at all. (If you have a computer and know how to use it, set all the data up in a relational database management program or, better yet, a spreadsheet program, which will simplify the job of making the comparisons and analyses and will actually prepare reports for you.) This will provide you an excellent education in what you can and cannot expect and will also help you decide whether this is the way for you to go.

Building Your Own Line

The obvious major advantage of building your own line is that you control the items you sell. You buy and sell as you wish, and you can still have many items drop-shipped, if you prefer. You can take advantage of special opportunities, offer loss leaders if and as you wish, drop items you don't want, and take on new items when you wish to.

The down side is that you will have to create your own catalog and sales literature, but even that is not necessarily a great burden, for even when buying items individually, you can get help from manufacturers. In many cases, they can supply brochures and other sales literature, which you can then use as original copy from which to assemble a catalog. You will pay to have it printed, of course, but you will not have to shoulder all of the expense of preparing the copy for the printer. In fact, many manufacturers can and will supply camera-ready (i.e., typeset and ready for the printer) originals for your use.

If you pursue this route, you need not start out with a complete line; few even attempt to do so, unless they are already selling the line via some other method and decide to add mail order to their marketing system. You can start with a few items, a partial line, and add to it slowly, as you grow.

The Search Is Endless

The search, for most, is never-ending. Nothing lasts forever, and nowadays, many products reach obsolescence quite rapidly as they are either improved or replaced. Hardly anyone buys gummed labels anymore, for example, because it has become so easy to buy the far more convenient labels that do not need moistening but are simply peeled off their backing and pressed to the envelope or package. If you have an early model Selectric typewriter you may have trouble finding ribbons for it because the later models used a much-improved ribbon cassette that was quite different. New products and changes in existing products take place with increasing frequency today. However, if you sell office products generally or computer products especially, you will have to remain especially alert for changes—both product and price changes—which come about so frequently as to be almost continuous in that field.

In addition to product replacements and improvements, completely new products appear constantly. One was the introduction of the press-on labels, tape, and notes that have a special adhesive that hold the item well but permit it to be peeled off without damage. Another revolution occurred when office copiers put a large dent in the carbon-paper business, and the expiration of the original Xerox® patents opened the field to competitive manufacturers of copying machines. The still-growing popularity of personal computers, with their efficient, high-speed printers, and especially the advent of the laser printer (offspring and hybrid of the laser and the office copier), have caused the sale of typewriters to slump.

There are also changes in styles, and if you are in jewelry, clothing, or anything else that is subject to style preferences, you must be sensitive to new styles that become popular, as well as those that do not. You cannot market successfully in such lines without that awareness of and sensitivity to style trends.

Life in most businesses and certainly in most catalog businesses therefore requires a constant search for the newest and the best items to add to the line or to replace something in the line. You must also search for special items and special opportunities. If you are alert, you will come across opportunities to make special purchases: a surplus lot, a closeout of a lot of factory seconds, an inventory of someone going out of business or in desperate need of cash, the first copies of a new invention, and other such deals.

The late Joe Karbo, a highly successful mail-order merchant, once bought an entire surplus lot—allegedly, a "warehouseful"—of those little devices that are installed in a front door to see who is there before opening the door, and he sold the entire lot profitably to individual customers through mail order. Mail-order guru Joe Cossman discovered a young man who built ant farms as a hobby, and he sold a great many ant farms by mail order. Many catalogers, in fact, specialize in selling only merchandise they have bought up in large lots at greatly reduced prices so that they can undersell the normal market in those kinds of items.

One merchant conducted weekend auctions as "Butch's Auction Sales" in Langhorne, Pennsylvania (I never knew him by any other name than Butch!). He spent the weekdays traveling about to the sources of merchandise he could find, driving a large covered truck, and loading into it the various discount and surplus lots of general merchandise he bought, which he resold on Friday and Saturday evenings. He could, of course, easily have filled catalog pages with descriptions of those items, had he chosen to sell that way.

TIPS ON FINDING ITEMS

In retailing, wisdom in buying is often even more important than genius in selling. That is certainly as true in cataloging as it is in any other business. Wisdom is not an accident; it results from deliberate effort, and it relies on knowledge. Still, there is such a thing as accidental discovery or *serendipity*, sometimes defined as "discovering something you didn't know you were looking for"! The well-known product labeled Adolph's Meat Tenderizer came into being because two young World War II veterans were alert for business opportunities. They happened to eat in a restaurant in which the chef was using papaya extract to tenderize tough cuts of meat, and they were curious enough and aggressive enough to investigate the phenomenon of an inexpensive steak that was as tender as a costly one. They then showed the imagination and resourcefulness to create the commercial product. The Chef's name was Adolph, and the two men chose to pay him for the use of his name because he had actually discovered the product. They began to market it, building a highly successful business.

Other products have come about by similar serendipity, accidental but propitious discoveries resulting from the alertness of the individuals involved. (It has been said that "fortune favors the prepared mind.") The vulcanizing of rubber, Cream of Wheat®, and floating soap (Ivory®), are three such examples, although there are many more. Serendipity results from being constantly alert for and ready to recognize and seize opportunities resulting from such fortunate circumstances. (If you do this consciously for a time, before long your subconscious will take over and do it for you without conscious effort.)

Nonetheless, although an alert mental state will produce unanticipated opportunities, the success of a business cannot depend on serendipity or other accidental discovery. Nor will new ideas and news of new products be forced on you by good fortune. To have such good things happen with even a slight degree of regularity, you must make deliberate, conscious, organized efforts. You must have specific and reliable methods or plans for finding new and better products to sell. You need, in short, an actual regimen of activity that will help you make such discoveries on a regular basis. You must have an almost continuous parade of new ideas to review so that you can select a few that will be of use. In this modern age, it is easily possible to do this.

The first approach to setting up a regimen of continuous research into the discovery of new-product information and ideas is reading; you must make time for this. A number of publications, regularly published periodicals, will help you in this, and a selection is listed in the References section of this book. Review all of these and choose those that you think are the best and most useful to read regularly. (I try to read all of them regularly.) Read them and respond to the advertisers in them who appear to have useful products and ideas to offer. Ask to be put on those advertisers' mailing lists for all new announcements, and take the time to read the announcements that begin to arrive in your morning mail. (The morning you are "too busy" to read the mail may be—and by "Murphy's Law" will be—the morning you will miss an important opportunity.) Learn that there is now no such thing as "junk mail" for you; all mail is worth opening for at least a quick perusal for that diamond that pops up occasionally.

Search out other manufacturers of the types of products that you wish to sell. Spend some time in your public library finding those manufacturers. There are at least a half-dozen useful guides. (See the listings of industrial directories, such as the Facts on File *Directory of Major Public Corporations* and the *Thomas Register*, which lists and describes industrial corporations, and send them your request to have them put your name on their mailing list for new-product announcements.)

Read the popular periodicals (found on newsstands) where you can find announcements and advertisements of new products that might be of interest to you. Read magazines for homemakers if you sell kitchen products, for example, and magazines for do-it-yourself enthusiasts if you sell tools and related gadgets.

There are many conventions and trade shows held every year, many of them relevant to the manufacture and distribution of products that are of direct interest to you. Make it your business to learn which are the trade shows of interest to you in terms of manufacturing and distributing products of the type you sell, and attend them. You will see new products and will learn of planned new products there, and you will make many valuable contacts if you stop and talk to exhibitors and visitors. You will collect armfuls of useful literature to carry back to your office and to add to your database. You will also get many samples of new products, and these will be useful too. And you will leave your card with a great many exhibitors and visitors, which will result in more mail, some of which will be quite useful to you.

Join associations that are relevant to your business interests. There are many of these. Become active (and thus well known) in these, and you will find many information items of interest coming your way as a result. (See Appendix B, "A Few Sources for Special Services," for listings of some of these associations.)

ACCEPTANCE OF CHANGE

Intellectual rigor mortis is a well-known hazard in the business world. It is easy to become so comfortable in the familiar routine of what we have been doing or in what we have come to believe is the ultimate truth that we close our minds to anything and everything that is even slightly antithetical to those notions. We must all overcome that all-too-human tendency to resist change. We—you—must not only accept change, but actually even welcome it.

What that means in practical terms is that you must be ready to make changes in what you sell and/or in how you sell. You may find, as many do, that some new and different line you try sells more briskly, is more profitable, or is less trouble to handle than the line you have been selling. Some entrepreneurs resist making changes; perhaps they perceive their pride at stake in defending their earlier business judgment and see change as admission of error. From a pure business viewpoint, however, change is wiser. Try to develop that viewpoint and not permit misplaced pride to interfere with sound business judgment and a wise business decision. Also, the earlier business decision may indeed have been sound (e.g., Selectric typewriter ribbons), but changes in circumstances require changes in your business.

Implementing this means adding an occasional new item to your offerings experimentally. If it proves to be a winner, move on and add other, related new items. Change of this kind is not unprecedented by any means: Many businesses find greater success in other lines than those in which they started, and many wind up in far different ventures than their original ones. U.S. Industries, a rather large conglomerate of many small-to-medium-sized companies in consumer goods, started life a century ago as the U.S. Pressed Steel Car Company, founded by the fabled Diamond Jim Brady in the heyday of the railroads, to manufacture railroad cars. The Fuller Brush Company still retains its original name, but brushes are only part of the varied line of household and personal products it offers today. In fact, it is a rare (and often dying) company that is still offering the products it offered a decade or two ago. The pace of change rarely permits products to survive that long.

Finally, do join at least one marketing or direct-mail association, and become acquainted with your contemporary catalogers. Some starter lists of these kinds of associations is supplied in Appendix B.

4

Basics of Marketing

Millions of items are sold every day via many kinds of media. Nonetheless, certain basic verities apply to each and every sale made in this bewildering milieu.

RETAIL STORE SALES VERSUS CATALOG SALES

The item that did not sell well on a retail counter is not likely to prove more attractive to prospective customers merely because it appears in a multicolored catalog. The basic laws of marketing do not change with different methods or media for marketing. Yet it is not uncommon that an item does indeed sell much better when listed in a catalog than when it was offered on a retail counter in stores. Why is this?

One reason this happens quite often is because few salespeople working in retail stores today make a real effort to sell the goods in their departments and on their counters or are even trained and qualified to do so. The sad truth is that most department store salespeople are clerks, not sales professionals. In fact, to quite a large degree, customers in stores, especially department stores, sell themselves; the sales clerks play a passive role: They merely answer questions (as best they can), accept payment, and bag the merchandise before handing it over to the customers. In the majority of sales situations today, the clerks do not even get the merchandise for the customer or assist the customer in getting the merchandise: The customer selects the merchandise and takes it to the counter to complete the transaction. Service is a definite casualty of the times;

73

it has all but ceased to exist, except in its modern form of "self-service," with minimal and often reluctant assistance from untrained and uncaring sales-people.

Catalog sales marketing breaks this pattern of indifference and self-service when it is done well. The copy in the catalog serves the prospective customer by explaining and describing the items listed and the benefits they deliver, through illustrations, through appropriate sales arguments, through price information, and through guidance in how to order the items. The catalog seller provides more service than the in-store retailer in many other ways, such as by having the merchandise packaged and delivered directly to the customer's home or office. The chief difference, or the factor that makes the difference, is that the catalog offers a sales presentation, making a distinct effort to sell by providing useful information and relevant sales arguments, whereas a great many retail clerks do not go beyond being pleasant and responding to direct questions—that is, if they know their merchandise and are able to answer questions.

Figure 4–1, the cover of the catalog of The Software Labs (TSL), of Los Angeles, illustrates this. What the company sells with this catalog is a service, although it ships a product to customers, because The Software Labs does not own the product it ships. It is an unusual situation: The product involved is known as *shareware*. It is computer software distributed without charge, but copyrighted by the originator. Users are asked to try it and to pay a fee if they like it and wish to continue using it. The owners of the software forbid its sale by anyone else, while encouraging others to distribute it. The charges made by The Software Labs (and others in the same business) are for the service of copying the programs onto floppy disks and shipping them. The customers are still expected to pay the owners of the programs on the honor system—voluntarily, that is, if they decide to keep and use any of the programs. (The instructions are included with the programs and include the owner's suggested price.)

The cover copy makes the prices clear, offers a bonus as an inducement, provides a brief preview of the hundreds of programs listed and described in greater detail in the pages to follow. There is no need for or utility in illustrating most software, and so the catalog is quite simple and straightforward. Prices are the same for all disks, so there is no need to mention price in the individual program descriptions that appear later. Note that the sales arguments on the cover reflect a clear consciousness that the offeror is not offering anything unique, but that TSL has ample competition: There are others in the same business, all with access to and offering the same programs. The sales arguments must therefore be to the effect that TSL service in selecting and

The Software Labs

COPYRIGHT (C) WINTER 1989

TSL CATALOG
FEATURING DETAILED PROGRAM DESCRIPTIONS

300 NEW PROGRAMS

VIRUSCAN	Total Proven Virus Protection
ACTIVE LIFE	Hottest New Activity Scheduler
ELECTRONIC ALMANAC	Hundreds of Almanac Features
COLLEGE PROBE	Select the Best College
HelpPerfect	WordPerfect's Best New Utility
NEWSPACE	Newest Hard Disk Space Saver
POWER DESK	Best DeskTop Organizer Office System
FREIGHT+	Complete UPS Shipping System
TRIP PLANNER	Computerized U.S. Road Map

SPECIAL LIMITED OFFER

5 FREE DISKS

SEE INSIDE FOR DETAILS

*Affordable Software for
IBM and Compatible Computers*

LABORATORY
CERTIFIED virus FREE

Only $3⁴⁹ per disk
$2⁹⁹ each for 10 or more

Plus

LOADS of GREAT NEW PROGRAMS

Graphics	Business
Database	Household
Word Processing	Utilities
Printing	Games
Spreadsheet	Education
Communications	and Much More

The Software Labs
3767 OVERLAND AV. #112
LOS ANGELES, CA 90034

**ORDER TOLL FREE
1-800-359-9998**

Figure 4–1. Cover of The Software Labs catalog.

providing free shareware programs is somehow better than others' services in doing the same thing. Thus, the sales arguments are not urging to buy and try shareware programs—there is an assumption that the reader will want those programs—but to buy shareware programs from TSL rather than from anybody else. One argument on the cover suggests that superiority by stressing that 300 of the programs offered are *NEW.* (They hope that the reader will infer that competitors' offerings do not include those new programs.) Another argument offered is "Laboratory Certified Virus Free."

The TSL catalog has several pages of front matter inside the cover, offering helpful information and explanations that should be of interest to all readers, but especially to those who are not expert computerists. The paragraph titles of the front matter are carefully designed to continue to present sales arguments. Following are the paragraph titles appearing on the first page of the catalog's front matter:

Our program descriptions are much longer and more complete.

Only the highest quality programs.

More programs per disk.

Latest program updates.

Every program fully tested. No viruses, no Trojan horses.

What you see is what you get!

The Willow Creek catalog, of Minocqua, Wisconsin, illustrates this also. (See Figure 4–2.) Note that the copy presenting *The Derrydale Cookbooks of Fish and Game* presents arguments for them, identifying them as "'must have'" books, describing their history, and authenticating the reputation of the author of the recipes, with enough detail to be almost equivalent to a browse through the book.

The benefits are mutual: The customer is given information that helps guide him or her to the right choices, while the merchant benefits because customers are being served and selling is going on.

With respect to selling, there are other ways of looking at the advantages of catalog selling. Whereas selling across the counter is principally passive, waiting for customers to approach, direct mail in general is an aggressive way of doing business: It is based on seeking out and pursuing customers individually. Catalogs offer a method for shopping to people who have little time, opportunity, energy, or desire to go out and browse through malls and department stores. Many of these people truly welcome the easy-chair shop-

THE DERRYDALE COOKBOOKS OF FISH AND GAME

These are "must have" books for anyone who prepares fish and game recipes. Originally published in 1937, *The Derrydale Game Cook Book* and *The Derrydale Fish Cook Book* were only available as very limited editions. Today, however, this fascinating pair of books has been re-released for the enjoyment of wild game and fish epicures everywhere. Here are hundreds of Master Chef L. P. DeGouy's world famous recipes for a great variety of dishes, from moose to mule deer and whitetail; from terrapin to crayfish, and even from muskrat to moor hen. Each book contains recipes for an appetizing assembly of marinades, sauces, stuffing, garnishings and beverages, including information on selecting and serving wines to accompany each course of a meal.

DERRYDALE GAME COOK BOOK *440 recipes / 6 x 9¼" / 308 pages* **$25.00**

DERRYDALE FISH COOK BOOK *475 recipes / 6 x 9¼" / 330 pages* **$25.00**

TWO-VOLUME HARDBOUND SET *915 recipes* **$45.00**

NEW ENGLAND GROUSE SHOOTING

BOOK AND ACCOMPANYING
PEN AND INK SKETCHES

Here is a very special offer for grouse hunters, William Harnden foster's classic book, *New England Grouse Shooting*, reproduced identically to the long sold-out 1942 original edition. Also, and a collection of six of the author's pen and ink sketches handsomely printed on heavy tan paper, 10 x 13" in size, contained in a beautiful portfolio and each suitable for framing. **Originally priced at $50 per set, the six sketches may now be purchased along with this superbly illustrated volume of grouse hunting literature for a total price of $55.**

   📖 BOOK............................ **$45.00**
   6 PEN & INK SKETCHES.. **$50.00**
   BOOK & SKETCH SET **$55.00**

Figure 4–2. Page from Willow Creek's catalog.

ping of browsing through catalogs and are therefore quite willing forego the help of store clerks, even when that help is substantial and useful.

THE IMPACT OF DIRECT RESPONSE

Direct mail is one of a class of marketing methods known as *direct response* marketing. That term refers entirely to marketing by seeking out prospects and making sales appeals directly to them (as in the case of salespeople calling on prospects in person), rather than waiting for prospects to seek out the seller. Retail stores do advertise in quest of customers, but that is not direct-response marketing and rarely does any substantial selling of itself—nor is that usually its purpose. The primary purpose of media advertising by stores is usually to create traffic in the store, to bring shoppers in to visit and possibly to investigate special sales offers made in advertising. Once in the store, it is reasoned, many will find things they wish to buy.

Mail order, as defined by those who distinguish it from direct mail, is analogous; it is largely passive, such as advertising in the media—newspapers, magazines, radio, and TV. Prospects may or may not even notice the advertising and become interested. Direct response, on the other hand, involves identifying specific prospects and pursuing them directly, asking for orders. It means door-to-door selling, mailing sales literature to individuals on specific lists, calling people on the telephone, addressing them in groups (e.g., at seminars), and other means for pursuing prospective customers identified either as individuals or by classes.

The means for identifying prospects (by classes or as individuals) has some significance of its own as a variable, for there are two general categories of direct-response marketing, depending primarily on the size of the item being sold. Selling truly big-tag items—an automobile, a house, a yacht, a business, a construction contract, or a training course—usually requires lengthy formal or semiformal presentations and normally more than one presentation, often several, in fact. Selling a big-tag item is not a "one-call business." It is impracticable to make such efforts on a random basis; you might not make more than one sale a month and perhaps not even that if you depend on chance to bring you face-to-face with a good prospect. To make marketing such items a practicable proposition, you must *qualify* your prospects: Make sure they are truly interested and are able to buy if they wish to, before you invest the time and effort in the presentation or the series of presentations. It is here that the meaning of "one call" becomes clear: Before you decide that any given individual represents a serious possibility of a sale, you *prospect* to develop sales *leads*. That is a process of narrowing a large group of general prospects down to a small group of serious prospects in whom to invest serious marketing efforts.

Even so, to make this work for you, the prospecting for sales leads must be done with a group or class of people suitable for the purpose. You would not, for example, ordinarily choose a group of refinery workers as prospects for buying into an expensive tax shelter program. You would try to identify and reach a group of people with high incomes and therefore large tax obligations, as the first step in prospecting for leads.

The other method for direct-response marketing is pursuing and presenting your sales appeal to a class or group of prospects, rather than to individually identified prospects, chosen carefully for their qualifications as probable serious prospects for what you are selling. That is, you do hope to start getting orders as a direct result of getting your catalogs into the hands of prospects, because the average order is not large enough to justify extended efforts to close each sale. Even so, there is an analogous situation: Catalogs of high quality can be quite costly, even when printed in large quantity, and there are also the high costs of postage, mailing lists, labor, and sometimes even media advertising in getting the catalogs out. You therefore prospect at least to the extent that you choose the classes of people in whose hands you place the catalogs, whether it is by mail or by other means.

In general, selling is—and must be by definition—a dynamic activity, not a passive one. Selling, however, is not all there is to marketing, although it is the objective of marketing and the end goal of business generally. However, if if selling is the business of getting orders, and the objective of business is creating customers, as management expert Peter Drucker puts it, marketing is all the preparatory and support work that makes it possible to get orders: It includes the decisions regarding what orders to pursue and how to pursue them, among other things. Selling involves almost nothing but getting orders; marketing involves almost everything about the enterprise that is directly and indirectly connected with and preliminary or preparatory to getting orders.

In addition to selling, there is also the matter of creating customers, which is not necessarily the automatic result of getting orders. In fact, the conventional wisdom is that the first sale to someone new creates only a buyer; a conversion is now necessary to make the buyer a customer: The buyer who returns to buy again is a customer. In many cases, especially in direct-response marketing, profitable operation depends on making customers.

IS THE CUSTOMER ALWAYS RIGHT?

"The customer is always right" is an old platitude that was especially honored during the great economic depression of the 1930s, when businesses were failing at record rates and many that survived barely did so. Another platitude of the era expressed the thought that you cannot win a dispute with a customer—that is, winning the dispute usually means losing the customer.

Consider this: Conventional direct-mail wisdom has it that you must expect to spend, on average, about one half the total sale to win that sale. That is, you will be likely to spend $10 to get a $20 sale. Or, put just a bit differently, it will cost you $10 to make a customer. That first sale may easily represent a loss, so that only continued business with that customer produces profits. Keeping that customer means follow-up sales that cost you a bit of postage and that may mean thousands of dollars in future business. Losing that customer means spending $10 to find another. The moral should be plain enough: It is almost always far cheaper to keep a customer than to find a new one. That is what always makes the customer right. The customer is the only reason for keeping your doors open.

Here is a good way to lose a customer: I received a catalog in the mail, which listed a speakerphone that attracted me. I called the 800 number furnished and ordered one. It arrived more quickly than I expected, only a few days later, and I was so delighted with it that I called and ordered two more, also allowing myself to be sold a membership in their customer's club. Three weeks passed and not a sign of anything. I called the 800 number, the only one I could find in the catalog or in the invoice sent me, and was told that no one could help me there; I would have to call customer service at another number furnished me. I tried, and the number was wrong; there was no such number. Unwilling to go through the drill of the 800 number and two or three referrals to other people, I wrote a letter of complaint to the manager whose name appeared in the catalog with a sidebar story of the marvelous service they offered. I would have accepted their apology, even at this point, but no one ever responded, and of course they will never hear from me again.

On the other hand, I ordered a keyboard from a mail-order house, and they sent me the wrong one, although I had taken great pains to specify the one I wanted. In response to my call, the company shipped me the right one by express service without waiting for the return of the one they had sent me originally, and they arranged to have UPS pick up the original one. That is what converts casual buyers to customers. It's more important than bargain prices *and* free gifts.

THE ROLE OF MARKETING

The Premises

A business is launched and organized to sell something. Depending on what it is you wish to sell, you can sell from a sidewalk stand, a pushcart, a truck, an automobile, a warehouse, a retail store of your own, a concession in someone else's retail store, a booth in a farmer's market, a table in a flea market, your own home, by mail order, by telephone, by door-to-door soliciting, and even by other means and media. There are almost innumerable possibilities and options. But you always base your approach on certain premises. These should not be (although they often are, unfortunately) entirely arbitrary ones, but they ought to be based on certain estimates made on some reasonable basis and on resulting decisions, including these four basic ones:

1. What you are going to sell
2. To whom you are going to sell it
3. How you are going to reach those to whom you plan to sell
4. What will influence those to whom you hope to sell

That sounds pretty simple, even obvious. One would assume that everyone contemplating a business venture has considered these basic questions, formally or informally, and has planned accordingly. That is itself an unwarranted assumption: Too often, beginning entrepreneurs are incredibly casual in defining their premises, and they consequently do not make analyses. Instead, they make assumptions, which are not quite the same thing and can lead to disastrous results. Let us suppose, for example, that you have decided to sell cosmetics. Here are just a few first questions that beg for *carefully considered* answers:

- Will you sell a complete line of cosmetics or only certain special cosmetics?
- If the line is to be specialized, what are the special items?
- If the line is to be complete and comprehensive, will you handle more than one brand or label? If so, which ones? If a specialized line, which brands or labels?
- Will you sell high-priced lines, medium-priced lines, or economy-priced lines?

Once you have devised answers to these questions and answered that first question (what you are going to sell), you can address that second question of to whom you are going to sell. Obviously you can't address that question properly without having answered the first one, for the customers for certain items (e.g., high-priced cosmetics) are not the customers for others (e.g., economy-priced cosmetics).

You could, of course, go at this in reverse by deciding first who your prospects are to be (e.g., blue-collar workers, white-collar workers, show-business people, executives), and then choosing the line of cosmetics that would be most appropriate to that class of prospective customers.

Obviously (I hope), the two—prospects and products—are interdependent and must be matched for compatibility. You are not likely to run a successful bargain-counter catalog (i.e., offer unknown brands and low-priced, possibly surplus or discounted goods) to an upscale, affluent prospect, or the best-known and most expensive goods to struggling workers. (Are there exceptions? Yes, there are exceptions, but a business is usually built on the rule and not the exceptions.)

Does all this sound absurdly basic and obvious, and so hardly worth discussing? It is dismaying, in fact, to learn that this is not at all obvious to newcomers to the business world. Many beginning entrepreneurs have not thought along these lines before investing their savings and risking their futures in business ventures—catalog and otherwise. It is not due to lack of intelligence; it is lack of experience.

Note that these analyses and decisions are considered absolutely basic necessities before a business venture can be launched on a practical and sensible basis. Note also, however, that these are the same absolute requirements for the establishment of a sensible marketing plan. It is almost impossible to separate the needs of a business generally from the needs of a marketing plan; they are almost synonymous. (Even nonprofit ventures are organized to "sell" something, whether it is subscriptions, memberships, votes, or donations of time, effort, and/or money, so what they do is indeed also marketing.)

Now that you have decided what to sell and to whom to sell it, you must make yet another decision and decide how you will reach those prospective customers and solicit their orders. And in this case, because you are presumed to have decided in advance that you would make your presentations via catalogs, the question is really one of how you will get your catalogs into the hands of those who are good prospects. In fact, depending on your grand strategy, the question may be one of how you can persuade your prospects to request copies of your catalog.

That can be the most difficult question to answer, and it is not unrelated to the first two questions for at least two reasons that often make the questions interrelated considerations:

1. If there are great difficulties in the way of reaching those you consider to be the right prospects for your product, you may be forced to consider changing the product.
2. If it proves that there are simply not enough of the right prospects for what you offer (i.e., the market is too small to be profitable), you must consider modifying the answer to the first question: what you will sell.

It's worthwhile to look at these problems a bit more closely because these problems sometimes lie at the heart of success or failure in catalog sales.

Are Your Premises Valid?

Suppose that you have decided to sell an exceptionally expensive line of cosmetics. The line is so expensive that even the upwardly mobile prospects who often are motivated to spend more than they can truly afford must be ruled out as prospects. Obviously, in such circumstances, you must assume that the bulk of your customers for the line must come from the wealthier classes of society. You must therefore find some means for reaching that class of prospects with your catalog.

Suppose that you cannot find a means for doing so. Perhaps no mailing-list broker is able to offer you the precise lists you want, and you cannot find a practicable alternative for compiling or otherwise acquiring a suitable list. If you cannot find some means for solving the problem, you already have marketing difficulties, and you may have to modify something in your approach. (Perhaps the line is simply not really suitable for catalog sales.)

It is possible that you may be in error about who and what are your best prospects for the line; it may well be that many middle-class women would be willing to pay the price you ask for your line. Adopting that premise and testing it—testing of premises is necessary, too, and that is discussed in the next subsection—is a possible alternative. (Testing often reveals that "known" facts are not so!)

On the other hand you may find that you can reach that projected market easily enough, but another problem appears: The market is far smaller than you had assumed it would be. It is, in fact, far too small to support your venture:

There are simply not enough customer prospects of the type you have projected. At this point, you have at least two options available, and they are or ought to be clear enough here:

1. Drop the line and assume another.
2. Broaden the line to include items that will appeal to other classes of prospects so that you can broaden your market.

Verifying Premises

To some degree, it requires a balancing act to maintain enough of a degree of specialization to attract customers and provide a marketing focus, while still being broad enough to support the venture. Testing is essential, for you start with a set of premises, premises as to what you should sell, to whom, how you will reach your prospects, what you require to succeed, and what you may reasonably expect in response and in length of time to achieve that response, but you must recognize that these premises are all tentative and unproven, so they may turn out to be false premises. You need to be prepared for that. More than one business disaster has overtaken the individual who stubbornly ignored accumulating evidence that the original premises were false, thereby committing business suicide while trying to avoid admitting to error.

It's a common problem: No one likes to admit being wrong. The solution is absurdly simple also: Never polarize your position by stubbornly insisting, even to yourself, that your premises are right. Instead, assume from the beginning that your premises are probably wrong or at least only tentative because they are only guesses dignified by the terms *estimate* and *premise*— guesses with a college degree, as some might put it—and you must work to refine them into something much more reliable.

Talking to Customers

Unfortunately, it never occurs to all-too-many businesspeople to search for the right product or service by asking the customers what they want. Lands' End is now a successful cataloger selling apparel. However, the owner started his business by selling equipment and hardware for sailboats. ("Getting Customers to Love You," Patricia Sellers, *Fortune*, March 13, 1989.) It was the customers who ordered the change, when they wrote to owner Gary Comer and inquired about sources for foul-weather gear, and Comer began to sell garments, soon discovering that it was a far better line for him than the hardware he had started with.

That was fortuitous: Comer's customers wrote him, of their own volition, giving him a clue. It is, of course, to his credit that he was alert enough to pursue the matter and follow it up. It was pure serendipity, a chance occurrence. However, it is not necessary to rely on chance; the message is plain enough: Do everything you can to encourage feedback from your customers and then read the letters they send you. (See the discussion of "Serving the Customer" at the end of this chapter.)

There is also another way to find out about the salability of products: testing. Testing is discussed in Chapter 12 in some depth and in another connection, but it is a more or less direct way of asking customers what they want. Offer alternatives, and measure the results. Customers tell you by how they respond to your offers what they really want. Although more detailed discussion of testing is reserved for Chapter 12, some limited coverage of the subject is merited here.

Testing

Most professionals in mail order and direct mail do a great deal of testing before they "roll out" by running test advertisements and mailings. As a result of tests, they may (a) drop the campaign, (b) roll out immediately, (c) make some changes and test again, or (d) make some changes and then roll out. Probably, they do one of the last two things, depending on how far removed from the facts the tests proved their premises to be.

The immediate question is what should be tested. If you read the popular literature on the subject of mail order and direct mail, you might get some misleading ideas about this. You might be led to believe that the tests should concern color of paper and inks used in the literature, the value of including a postage-paid response envelope, the motivational effect of a gift or bonus, and other such matters. If you read even more extensively and explore the reports, you will find that in one case, two-color printing produced a 0.03 percent improvement in response or that postage-paid envelopes appear to increase response, on the average, by as much as 0.1 percent.

Such results can be misleading. First of all, such statistics are significant only with very large mailings. A mailing of 1,000,000 pieces, with a response of 2 percent produces 20,000 orders. A 0.03 percent improvement in that response means 200,300 orders, or an extra 300 orders. That can mean, in turn, more than a few thousand dollars increase in income, and so it is not at all insignificant. (With a $50 average order size, that is $15,000, a substantial amount of money.) But suppose you are one of the little guys, and your entire campaign involves a mailing of 25,000, at most. That 0.03 percent improvement means an increase of seven or eight orders (7.5 orders, mathematically), hardly an earth-shaking event. Even at a $50 average-order size, it is a difference of not more than $400 in a total sales volume of $25,000. That extra $400, if it does actually materialize (statistical evidence is no guarantee of actual results!) may not even pay for the extra cost of the refinement. That factor, known as "economy of scale," works only for the large numbers, not for the small ones, and so the statistics are often not at all significant for the smaller effort.

Aside from this, more important is what such tests overlook or ignore, and often what they overlook or ignore is simply this: the pulling power of the basic message and the item. That is, the first things that ought to be tested are whether the item you are selling appeals to many of the people you address and whether your specific message is highly motivating. If you cannot get prospects interested in what you are selling, the other things don't matter anyway, do they?

In short, there is a priority of importance and a rank order of logic in testing. Whether red or black ink is more motivating is not significant if the prospect is not the least bit interested in the offer to begin with, and so it is most definitely a second- or third-order test. The important tests are, therefore, tests of the validity of the basic premises: The items offered, the prospects to whom offered, and the appeal of the offer. Only when you have verified somehow that you have an offer that is at least minimally likely to generate active interest does it begin to make sense to start worrying about and testing the second-order items that may make your venture just a bit more profitable. Otherwise the testing falls into that same class of logic as that of West Hollywood, Florida, whose citizens voted to reject the incorporation of West Hollywood as a community, while in the same balloting they elected a mayor—that is, a mayor who had no community over which to preside!

A FEW DEFINITIONS

The mail-order business, like most others, has its own jargon, with some terms that are well understood and that have essentially the same meaning for everyone who uses them. As in most fields, however, there are also some terms that mean different things to different people. To avoid misunderstandings arising out of such differences, here are a few basic terms that will be used here occasionally, with the definitions that apply in this book and probably also apply elsewhere:

Offer. Some people use the term *offer* to refer to the item offered for sale and the terms under which the offeror will sell (e.g., the price and inducements, if any, such as discounts, bonuses, or other windfalls promised to buyers). As I use the term, however, it refers to the benefit, or what the item is promised to *do* for the buyer.

That is, if you are selling a line of cosmetics, you do not sell cosmetics per se; you sell glamour, sex appeal, beauty, attractiveness to the opposite sex, or some similar benefit. *That*—the promise of glamour, sex appeal, beauty, attractiveness—is your offer because that is why prospects buy your product when they do. They buy it because (a) they want the benefit you offer, and (b) they believe that you (your product) can and will deliver that benefit. However, some prospects will be moved by the offer of glamour, some by the offer of sex appeal, some by the offer of beauty, and some by the offer of attractiveness to the opposite sex. I have my own opinion as to which of these is likely to be the most effective offer, and perhaps you do too, but testing may prove us both wrong. Test results are far more reliable than either of our opinions. You might even argue that these are all the same things, and that only the words are different, but that is also a point to be tested: What *words* are most effective in motivating prospects to buy? You must test both the ideas and the words, but probably the idea first and the words second. (The test of the words is whether they convey the idea to the reader.)

Proof. There are a number of ways to "prove" that you can and will deliver on the promise—that buying the product will produce the benefit. Logical arguments, testimonials, photographic evidence, and sworn statements are only a few. Proof, however, is whatever the *prospect* will accept as proof and nothing else; what you and I think is irrelevant here. Again, only testing can indicate what most prospects will find most convincing and persuasive.

Proposition. What some call "the offer," I call "the proposition": the conditions required and/or considerations offered to consummate the sale. That could include a special discount price, a bonus gift, a free trial, a money-back no-questions-asked guarantee, credit-card convenience, a toll-free number, or other special motivators.

TESTING CONVENTIONAL WISDOM

Mail order has its own share of myths, fables, and conventional wisdom, some of which may be valid. More accurately, probably, much of the conventional wisdom offers general rules for practices that may be true in some circumstances, but not in all. Zealots then tend to turn a single, case-sensitive for-instance into an absolute rule that has all the moral authority of religious belief! Those beliefs are also premises that you must test for validity in your own application. To accept them as absolutes is foolish, as experience after experience has proven.

Despite the cabalistic jargon of the expert professionals in direct mail and cataloging, not everything is explainable by the conventional wisdom of the field. What many people call "common sense" or "horse sense" is often the key to truth here, as elsewhere. The ultimate or specific truth is generally reached through testing, but that common sense is a prime source of inspiration for the testing, suggesting what ought to be tested. Following are a few examples.

The Guarantee

The guarantee is one such case. Many dealers in mail order are firmly convinced that an unconditional money-back guarantee is an absolute must in any mail-order proposition. This is a legacy from Montgomery Ward, who introduced this [then] radical idea in a much earlier and much different era, when merchants gave few guarantees of any kind and an unconditional guarantee was pure heresy.

Today, we have much different conditions. Nonetheless, many dealers today take it for granted that the prospect will mistrust any offer that does not include such a written guarantee, and they take pains to make that guarantee as prominent as possible. My experience led me to a different conclusion, especially after witnessing the large number of mail-order propositions that were so "loud" in their trumpeting of such guarantees that it seemed as though it was the guarantee, rather than the merchandise, that they were selling. They appeared to be actually desperate to be believed and trusted in their appeals: They were all but begging the customer to return the merchandise and demand a refund.

I was selling a kind of product that the customer could return for a refund and yet get and keep the benefit: I sold information, and the customer who acquired the information had no further need for the paper on which the information appeared. (He or she could, in fact, easily make copies of the information, if necessary.) It seemed suicidal to beg the customer to send the merchandise back for a no-questions-asked full refund! Did such an approach not imply a lack of confidence in one's merchandise and offer? Would it not be better to work at building the customer's faith in the offer?

I consequently began to test sending my literature out with firm information supporting my promises and proofs, but sans any mention of a guarantee. I would honor returned items and refund the purchase price, if the merchandise was returned in salable condition, but I made no mention of it in my literature, leaving it to my readers to infer a guarantee. Evidently, they did so, for my returns (which were not many to begin with) fell off to nearly zero and, as far as I could determine, my sales were not affected at all.

I still believe that most mail-order dealers make too much of the guarantee. It is likely that the guarantee is important and needed for most kinds of merchandise, but I believe it to have a negative effect when it is made with such emphasis and repetition that it appears to be challenging the reader or, at best, implying reservations about the quality of the merchandise and the customer's approval.

It is sufficient, I believe, simply to state the conditions of the guarantee quietly, in a businesslike manner. At the least, it is worth testing to get real evidence, instead of popular belief, to validate or invalidate the premise. We are, in fact, no longer in that time when there were few guarantees and *caveat emptor* (let the buyer beware) was the order. Today, most people assume that everything they buy bears a guarantee (as it does by federal law in mail order today), so the exhortation to return unsatisfactory merchandise may be more harmful than beneficial.

Return Envelopes

Conventional wisdom also pertains to other items and is solemnly dictated to newcomers in mail order as a dictate from on high. One of these concerns the necessity for a return envelope. Supposedly, the inclusion of a return envelope in a direct-mail package ensures a higher response rate and is thus a must in the package. However, the conventional wisdom appears to ignore the fact that not all cases are equal.

If your mail is sent primarily to individuals in their homes, the return envelope is probably a great aid, especially if it is postage-paid envelope. A great many people will procrastinate sending in an order and many never get around to doing it at all because they don't have an envelope and stamp easily at hand. On the other hand, if you mail to business addresses, you will find a different situation entirely. I was surprised to learn how rarely orders arrived in my return envelopes. People in business offices almost automatically enclose their order in one of their own business envelopes and drop it into their outgoing mail baskets, and it is then routed through someone who affixes postage and sends it on its way.

Other "Rules" of Conventional Wisdom

Two- and three-color printing costs money, usually a great deal more than one-color (black ink) printing. Special papers cost a great deal more than ordinary offset paper. Nonetheless, these and many other approaches are supposed to increase response, and perhaps they do. But perhaps they don't. What is true for one case is not always true for the next one. Also, what is true in general is not necessarily true for a specific case, such as your own. All cases are worth testing, if you have the slightest doubt.

The guarantee, the return envelope, and the colors of ink and kinds of paper are peripheral items, however, and should be tested, if at all, only after you have put the major—first priority—items to the test. The items identified or labeled here as *offer*, *proof*, and *proposition*, are the principal factors in most cases, and only testing can reveal the truth about how they are or are not working for you. When I was still a novice in mail order, I asked a self-professed expert in the field to examine literature I had printed to sell a book I had written and was publishing myself. I was preparing to mail that literature. The expert denounced the literature soundly, guaranteeing me a disastrous failure. However, with a substantial investment already made in printing, and with boxes of the literature stacked in my office, I decided to gamble the postage, so I rolled out my humble little campaign, mailing the literature and crossing my fingers. Fortunately, the literature did do the job, and I had a highly successful campaign.

Does this say that the expert was all wrong? Not at all; he was quite right, as far as conventional wisdom goes: The literature was crude and logically should have bombed. However, business, mail order or other, is always a gamble, like show-biz: When you depend on public approval, no one knows for sure what will fly like an eagle and what will sink like a stone. Even testing is not 100 percent reliable, but it is more reliable than hunches and expert opinions. In my own experience, my limited and inexpert testing had led me to believe in this package I was consigning to the mails, shaken as I was by the expert's denunciation.

Some entrepreneurs even test an offer for an item that does not yet exist. The case of the late Joe Karbo is classic. He conceived the idea of writing and selling a book to be titled *The Lazy Man's Way to Riches*, but he decided to test the idea before he wrote the book! He was sure he could write it in a few days, if necessary, and so he launched some test advertising, using the proposed book title as the headline for his advertisements. Had he gotten only a few orders, he would have returned the money with his apology. Instead, he got an encouraging response, and so he wrote the little 70-page paperback book and proceeded to sell a reported 600,000+ copies at $10 each.

Karbo was not a follower, a slave to tradition and conventional wisdom. He was a trail blazer, an innovator. He has had many imitators, people who still emulate his style, his ideas, his techniques, and, as best they can, his most successful product, his little book that brought in over $6 million. Though most of us are followers and not trail blazers, there have been others cut from the same mold as Joe Karbo. Joe Cossman is one of those.

Joe Cossman, seller of ant farms and many other successful items, also believes firmly in testing, and he urges all listeners to do as he does, risking a limited amount of money in tests before committing yourself. Originally, in seminars that he gave in the 1960s and 1970s on the subject of entrepreneurship (especially via mail order), he stated that he limited himself to a $500 investment to test a new product's salability before committing himself to it, but of course there have been many years of inflation since then, so that figure must be multiplied several times for today's economy. Nonetheless, the principle still holds.

TEASERS AND SUBTERFUGE

Enticing the Addressee

I get direct-mail packages in every morning's mail, often including catalogs. It's inevitable that both my personal name and my corporate name (and a few humorous variants of each) find their way onto many mailing lists, from which they each proliferate further. This results in a torrent of literature that visits my post office box and my residence mailbox every morning. As most busy people do, I throw most of it away immediately (but reluctantly, for I would like to keep it, but cannot for practical reasons). I do, however, always give it a swift glance to determine whether it is "junk mail" to me or something more important. In that brief glance, a second or two, I decide whether any of the mail is worth opening to see what is inside. There are almost always a few pieces that command me to have a look at what is inside. The distressing thing is that despite my special interest in all direct-mail packages—far greater than that of the average recipient—so few of the packages can arrest my attention for more than a few seconds, much less induce me to want to see what is inside the envelope.

A great many packages of literature are discarded without being opened.

If you want confirmation of that, visit any busy post office and look at what is in the trash barrels in the post office lobbies. (One mail-order entrepreneur made a regular practice of doing this, salvaging many of the discarded packages to study at his leisure in order to evaluate what does and does not work. You can get quite an education in mail order this way.)

The inventive brains of the mail-order experts come up with many ideas to trick or persuade recipients of mail-order sales literature to open the envelope and read what is inside. They do so with messages printed on the outside of the envelope: "envelope copy" or "teaser copy." Some, however, trick the reader.

Tricking the Addressee

Most people soon learn to identify advertising mail as such, even when there are no direct clues, such as teaser copy on the exterior of the envelope. The clues include bulk mail indicia and bulk mail stamps, labels with codes, envelopes bulging with inserts, and many others.

Methods that attempt to trick addressees into believing the envelope to contain important information include preprinting such words as "Personal," "Confidential," and "Important" on the front of the envelope. Even when this is printed in a font that emulates a typewriter or a computer printer, the mere fact of this message on the outside of an envelope arouses suspicion that it is subterfuge. Truly personal mail does not usually carry such a placard. When the words are printed in bold type or red ink, the intent is even more obvious. To make matters worse yet, such words sometimes appear on an envelope that is oversize, thick, and heavy with brochures and circulars, addressed with a name-and-address label, and/or bearing an imprinted bulk mail permit, or a precanceled bulk mail stamp.

Most recipients today are either worldly enough to see through such subterfuge or become so soon after they start opening such mail, so the tricks rarely succeed. Moreover, a glance at the return name and address usually conveys a great deal to the reader.

It is probably far better either to use a plain envelope or to attempt persuasion rather than distraction to induce the addressee to open the envelope. One experienced mail-order professional commenting on this subject says that he shakes the envelope, and if he hears some hard object rattling inside, he opens it. That speaks well for the advertising novelty (e.g., an audio tape or a pen) that is small enough to enclose in an envelope. That isn't trickery because the hard object is a giveaway. Instead, it is persuasion, and although the recipient knows it cannot be of much value, the curiosity evoked by an unknown gift is almost irresistible.

Persuading the Addressee

Because of the high probability that the addressee will recognize direct-mail solicitations for what they are, many mail-order dealers decide that they might as well take advantage of all the white space available on the outside of the package and use a lot of text on the envelope. Or they use oversize envelopes to increase the amount of material that can be accommodated in the mailing. (The mail-order adage "the more you tell, the more you sell" has a great deal of truth to it, and it works on the outside the envelope, as well as on the inside!)

What appears typically as envelope copy are headline-type messages, such as these:

AN *OPPORTUNITY* TO MAKE MORE MONEY

NOW YOU CAN BE THE BELLE OF THE BALL

YOU MAY ALREADY HAVE WON $1,000,000

A BRIGHT, NEW FUTURE IS IN THIS ENVELOPE

Sometimes, especially on the oversize envelopes, there are brief textual paragraphs and even illustrations extolling the great good news to be found on the inside of the envelope.

THE FUNDAMENTAL SIN OF MARKETING

Probably *the* most basic and most commonly committed sin in marketing is forgetting that the prospective customer has not the slightest interest in what you want. The customer buys in order to get what he or she wants, not to please you or to give you what you want. Sales experts tend to refer to selling "benefits," to explain this philosophy, but this is itself an understatement; *benefit* is much too vague and weak to use here. Its definition is overly broad, and it does not really explain motivation, for the focus must be sharper than that. The sales benefit must be something the purchase will *do* for the buyer, and it must be something important to the buyer: It is not a benefit unless the buyer agrees that it is a benefit, and it is not an important benefit unless the buyer agrees that it is. Too many benefits offered are actually ho-hum as far as the prospect is concerned.

For example, a seller of computer systems and supplies sent me what he identifies as a "mini-catalog." The seller's sole inducement for me to spend time reviewing what is in the catalog is a statement that on page 3, I will find 10 and 20 percent discount specials and a free gift offer. I am not highly enthused by this lackluster, me-too, approach: Discounts, real and alleged, are readily available everywhere today, so this is really not much of an inducement unless they are truly remarkable in some way, such as discounts far greater than 10 or 20 percent. I don't care about the free gift, either; experience has taught me how trivial most of those free gifts are. I simply do not have time to look through every catalog I have received this morning, so I discard this one and go on to look at other items in my morning mail.

I find next a catalog from a seller of books. It is a catalog that promises "unique" books in its headline, with a subhead that says, "Learn how to do almost anything," and includes such lines as the following:

Save money	Publish your own book	Earn more money
Save on taxes	Win at anything	Be a real estate tycoon
Get rich	Build furniture	Improve your golf score

I am not much interested in building furniture or publishing my own book, and I don't play golf, but I am always interested in making more money and cutting my taxes. Who wouldn't be? I save that catalog to have a look through it later.

Looking further, I find that Quill® Corporation has sent me one of their special, newsprint catalog supplements, and that gets my attention: Every page is headed with a message in a banner headline that is addressed to me and my interests. Here are a few of those heads:

We've got the envelopes you need at bargain prices.

Every envelope we sell is priced to save you money.

We've got the items to make your mailings a success.

Note the difference in the approaches. The minicatalog appears to be trying to bribe me with a vague and general promise. An effort to appeal to my interest, but not a very good one because it is far too general and presumptuous: It presumes that the promise of a discount or a free gift will motivate everyone. The second example is much better: It helps the reader identify specific interests, even with a quick glance through the subheads listing the

THE
QUILL® PEN PAL

©Copyright 1989, Quill Corporation   *A friendly newsletter just for you!*   Vol. 5, No. 12, December 1989

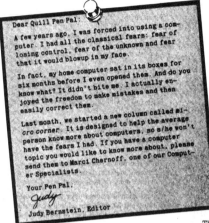

Dear Quill Pen Pal:

A few years ago, I was forced into using a computer. I had all the classical fears: fear of losing control, fear of the unknown and fear that it would blowup in my face.

In fact, my home computer sat in its boxes for six months before I even opened them. And do you know what? It didn't bite me. I actually enjoyed the freedom to make mistakes and then easily correct them.

Last month, we started a new column called *Micro corner*. It is designed to help the average person know more about computers, so s/he won't have the fears I had. If you have a computer topic you would like to know more about, please send them to Marci Chernoff, one of our Computer Specialists.

Your Pen Pal,

Judy

Judy Bernstein, Editor

QUOTE OF THE MONTH

"Before everything else, getting ready is the secret of success."

—Henry Ford

update

A TAXING ISSUE

The state of North Dakota is suing Quill Corporation to force us to collect their state's sales and use tax. Quill is challenging this suit.

"We are prepared," said Jack Miller president of Quill, "to fight this attempt by states to overturn the law on interstate taxation on behalf of ourselves and all companies, such as ours, that are involved in interstate commerce. We have absolutely no "nexus" (physical presence) of any kind in North Dakota so we intend to fight the case."

This is a case that will undoubtedly end up in the U.S. Supreme Court. Also, North Dakota is using this suit as a test case to determine the constitutionality of their recently passed state legislation designed to force out- of-state companies, such as ours, to collect their use tax.

States are trying, under their sales and use tax laws (also called "Abuse" Taxes) to collect taxes on all items purchased by their citizens—whether purchased in the state, in other states or even overseas. Furthermore, they want the out-of-state companies to be the collection agents for them. This could have quite an impact on interstate commerce.

Our founding fathers wisely reserved the exclusive right to regulate interstate commerce to the federal government. (This was reaffirmed in the 1967 U. S. Supreme Court *National Bellas Hess* case. The court said that a company must have legal presence in a state to be required to collect taxes in that state.)

Besides, collecting all the taxes would be a nightmare since every state, county and city tax differently. Potentially, there are over 7,000 different taxing units.

To keep you informed, we will periodically let you know how the case is progressing. If you have any questions, feel free to write us.

how to...

USE OPPORTUNITY $ELLING® — YOUR PATH TO SUCCESS

Selling, persuading and influencing others have changed! These "business skills" demand a high level of professionalism. Slick manipulators won't survive! Today's professional must know how to gain rapport with customers, supervisors, managers, co-workers and even family members — draw out their wants and needs, handle their concerns — and get favorable decisions.

This can be accomplished with the Opportunity $elling® sales system. It's a logical, organized and methodical approach to "selling others" on your ideas and products. It's simple, but practical and results oriented. And in order to be a successful Opportunity Seller, you must be: value driven, integrity based and non-manipulative.

1. **Open** — Your opening is your opportunity to create a positive impression. Here you must devote all your attention to your customer, client or prospect. Let them talk about their favorite subject—themselves! Value their presence and make them feel important.

2. **Probe** — The probe is your opportunity to control through questions — questions that determine the problem to be solved, need fulfilled or dream/goal to be realized. Place value in your prospect's words. Restate their wants, needs and desires to confirm their importance.

3. **Reveal** — This is your opportunity to present or "reveal" the ideas, products and services that meet your
(Continued on Page 2)

Figure 4–3. Cover page of Quill® Corporation newsletter.

subject matter of the books. And the third example is still better: It carries a specific motivator in each of a series of headlines.

SERVING THE CUSTOMER

A definition of marketing that you will not often find used is *service.* It is widely recognized by the most expert and most successful of the sales professionals that the most successful salesperson is the consultant, the salesperson who helps the customer solve problems. Neophytes in sales are thus urged to always approach prospects with the purpose of discovering the prospect's problems and offering help, relevant to what the salesperson sells. Of course, that is service.

Quill® Corporation (a highly successful cataloger of office supplies and related furnishings, fixtures, and equipment) obviously understands that. Primary among the innovations that make clear their commitment to customer service is their monthly newsletter, The *Quill® Pen Pal.* This four-page publication, now bound into Quill's monthly catalog, offers regular columns of helpful tips and other information for businesspeople. Figure 4–3 illustrates the first page of a recent issue. Other columns, found inside, include ones on writing ("Write it right!"), on computers ("Micro Corner"), on general business tips ("Clips and Quips"), information on new items ("Product News"), some editorial-style business philosophy and advice from Quill's president Jack Miller ("Entrepreneuring"), and letters from readers with the editor's answers ("Views and Questions"). A boxed notice urges readers to write with comments and questions. This "free gift" offers more than mere trickery: It offers genuine enticement by truly serving the customers' needs.

5

Marketing via Catalogs and Mail

Markets are people, so to succeed at marketing, you must understand people—what drives them, what motivates them, what they want, what they fear, and what impels them to action. That is the entire secret of marketing.

MARKETING AS THE ART OF PERSUASION

There are many activities within the function that is called "marketing," but there is only one goal: sales. A business exists only to sell something, and marketing is that set of actions that results in selling that something, whether product or service. Marketing is the set of actions that result in persuading the prospect to buy, to become a customer for the product or service. That final activity of marketing is thus sales, and sales is an act of persuasion. So it is the art of persuasion that must be mastered in order to make the sales effort (hence marketing) successful.

Whether persuasion involves selling the prospect a cummerbund or a Cadillac, or selling your spouse on going into debt for a new house or on moving to Arizona, persuasion is always based on appealing to the other party's self-interest or *perception of self-interest.* Take note of the importance of perception; it's an important qualification. It is the buyer's perception, not yours, that matters here. You may think great gas mileage—economy of operation—is important in choosing an automobile to buy, but the buyer may be more concerned with sheer horsepower or luxury features. Don't try to sell economy to the buyer who wants power or luxury features, but don't try to sell power or luxury features to the buyer who wants economy, either. Or, more

97

to the point, decide which is the most valid benefit of your product and then go out and seek the prospect—design your campaign to appeal to the prospect who wants that benefit.

APPEAL OF PRICE, BOTH LOW AND HIGH

The relative importance of selling a car's luxury, power, or economy offers a simple example, but marketing is rarely that simple. For example, while you cannot normally offer both economy and power in an automobile and in most other machines—they are usually mutually exclusive—not all benefits are mutually exclusive. It is possible that your products offer more than one benefit important enough to be the lead for a marketing appeal, but the benefits may be such that they appeal to entirely different kinds and classes of customers. People of ordinary means are not normally good prospects for high-priced luxury merchandise. Only affluent customers are likely to buy $20,000 pieces of jewelry, for example.

On the other hand, the reverse is not necessarily true: Many customers who can easily afford the best have no aversion to saving money—they are, in fact, often more conscious of the value of money than those of us in more modest circumstances. So even the wealthy often shop in bargain basements and find discounts appealing wherever they are to be found. A low price is always attractive, but it is not always decisive of itself; there are other factors in persuasion, and in some cases, they outweigh the attraction of a low price.

Oddly enough (and perhaps it is not so odd), the individual with a middle-class income often opts for the more expensive item more readily than the individual who inherited great wealth and has a greater ability to afford the more expensive item. Somehow, those for whom the more expensive item is an extravagance that wrenches their conscience a bit, the large price tag is often a proof of quality, whereas those who have always had wealth and who can more easily afford the high prices are often much less impressed with high prices. That is, it is somehow a bit troubling to many in modest circumstances to wear or own "less than the best" (as they interpret the meaning of high prices), while the wealthier customer does not necessarily see the situation in that light at all.

Money—price—thus has different meanings to different people and in different situations, and while you can and should base premises on what is generally true, you must also be aware of exceptions and of mythology. For example, you may read of some prominent person spending an astronomical sum on a party or a painting, and yet creating a scene in a posh restaurant over the price of a dinner. The two situations are not inconsistent; the individual's frame of reference is different in each case, and so is his or her sense of value. You and I are not different: We enter an automobile showroom with some sense of what automobiles cost, and so we are prepared to at least some extent for "sticker shock." On the other hand, when we have dinner at what appears to be a very ordinary restaurant, we undergo severe shock when examining the exorbitant prices on the menu.

As mentioned earlier, some catalogers list a charge for their catalogs (although it is nominal charge—$1 or $2—in most cases). For the most part, this reflects the high cost of multicolor catalogs today and the desire to avoid wasting them on the idly curious or school children who request free catalogs; the fee does not usually cover the cost of the catalog and is rarely actually collected. (More on this later.) On the other hand, it does have a psychological effect on many that supports the marketing effort because it both qualifies the requester and adds an apparent value to the catalog. That is, the payment of a dollar or two for the catalog indicates the requester's sincere interest and probable status as a good sales lead. Also, for many people, it makes the catalog far more valuable, a desirable effect.

Whether you opt to ask for a small fee for your catalog or offer it freely without charge is entirely up to you, of course, and you have ample precedents and examples of both free and priced catalogs. It is interesting to note, however, that many of the most prominent and successful catalogers offer their catalogs free of charge:

Grayarc	L. L. Bean
Fingerhut	Horchow Collection
Lands' End	Pepperidge Farm
Knott's Berry Farm	Hanover House
Scan Office Interiors	Walter Drake & Sons
Aldens	Lillian Vernon

On the other hand, Tiffany's of New York and many other upscale catalogers selling costly merchandise do charge for their catalogs, so it is impossible to generalize accurately about this aspect of cataloging. It is obviously a matter of internal policy, and as many cynics have been known to say, "it doesn't have to make sense; it's policy!" (Still, it is obvious that the majority of catalogers by far do not charge for their catalogs.) At the same time, the success of many catalogers who do charge for their catalogs, and especially the success of *Computer Shopper*, the magazine that is really a catalog, is an example: Readers pay $2.95 for single monthly issue, $29.97 for an annual subscription, so they obviously value it highly. Many catalogs do have an intrinsic value.

Figure 5–1 also illustrates this, with a nominal price of $2.00 printed on the cover of the Tiger Software catalog. Note, too, the promise of *free* Federal Express® shipping proclaimed twice, at the top and at the bottom of the cover. For many (and probably most) catalogs, prices printed on and advertised are for the record only, to discourage the idle curiosity seeker and children and to add to the average customer's perception of the value of the catalog. In fact, most will provide catalogs free to anyone who inquires, and does, of course, mail many thousands free of charge to lengthy mailing lists: The catalog business depends on doing just this. (This same practice applies to many free newsletters.)

DESIRE TO WIN

The underlying principle of persuasion is not difficult to understand: Everyone is motivated selfishly. No, that is not derogatory nor sneering; it is simple fact. We are all conscious that we live in a competitive, often predatory society, and we must be watchful over and protective of our own interests. We pursue career goals in a lengthy and sometimes never-ending campaign known as "getting ahead." We try to win the jobs that have the most prestige and that pay the largest salaries. (We compete for them.) We try to date the most attractive women or men. (We compete for them.) We try to outshine others in the way we dress and in our professional achievements. (We compete with them.) We crave recognition and strive for respect. (We compete for it.) We have a whole ethic that says that winning is the most important thing, even the *only* thing, whether it is in sports, in school, or in life generally. We judge ourselves and are judged by others on that basis: We are *winners*, or we are *losers*.

No matter what is written in those elaborate treatises and thick tomes purporting to offer sophisticated and intricate never-fail marketing approaches, the awareness and utilization of a simple winners-and-losers psychology is a key "secret" to marketing. It applies to and works equally well for all marketing, whether it is for enlisting soldiers and sailors, enrolling association members, recruiting volunteer workers, raising funds, or selling merchandise and services. (All of those activities require marketing, of course.)

The desire to *win*, therefore, whether it's called "greed," "gain," or any other term, is one of the two primary motivators. Show a prospect how to win, present convincing evidence that buying what you offer will result in winning, and you capture the prospect. Selling is much like leadership: Persuade

Figure 5–1. Cover of the Tiger Software catalog with price and express shipping promised.

prospects that it is in their best interests to follow you, to do what you recommend, and they are yours!

Some may challenge the idea that everyone is motivated selfishly. What about all those noble, selfless characters who champion self-sacrifice to help the helpless, they ask. Surely, they are not motivated by the desire for gain. Ah, but they are. Charitable people—altruists—gain a feeling of nobility, a sense of righteousness because they are so noble. Cynical as this observation may appear to be, it is still true: Self-interest is the primary motivation of all, even the noble altruists, and *even when they are not conscious of their own true motivation.* Yes, we humans can and do deceive ourselves. We can persuade ourselves to believe what we wish devoutly to believe, and we can easily reject logic that conflicts with what we prefer to believe. If you need proof of that, try using pure logic to sell liberal ideas to a conservative or conservative ideas to a liberal. The results will be enlightening. Reason cannot overcome or overpower emotion. Most of us have no difficulty persuading ourselves to believe what we have decided we prefer to believe. The marketer must understand that.

APPEAL OF BELONGING

One of our human traits is our need to belong: We share with other animals a herd instinct, and we tend to flock together. This became apparent to me when I found subscribers to my newsletters tended to say they "belonged," and it was borne out further when I found many eager to join an associates group I then formed. Note how residents associate themselves with local football and baseball teams: They become one with the Redskins, the Rams, the Dodgers, and so on, and they are devastated when "their" team loses. For many, paying for a catalog confers that special feeling of belonging to a special or elite group.

Figure 5–2 illustrates a use of this idea. It is the cover of a special holiday edition of the *Simply Tops* catalog and, as you can see, it offers a "special sale for preferred customers." (You may be sure that anyone can take advantage of this sale, however!) The regular front page of this catalog, by the way, bears the price $2.00, although the catalog arrived in the mail unsolicited and unpurchased, just as do many catalogs bearing a price on their covers.

FEAR OF LOSING

The flip side of the desire to win is the fear of losing, and this is self-interest again. This is where the insecurity that every one of us has to at least some

Figure 5–2. Cover of the Simply Tops catalog, with special appeal.

degree enters the picture. No, don't deny it: Even if you feel very confident and think that you are completely self-sufficient, capable of conquering all problems, and able to surmount all obstacles, you have at least occasional self-doubts. Society instills this in us, no matter how we fight back.

Did not the educational system teach you fear of failure?

Did not personnel managers in many companies turn you down as not good enough?

Has no insurance agent warned you of the virtually criminal neglect of leaving your family unprotected if you do not sign up for the policy that is far beyond your means?

Has no correspondence-course salesperson predicted a dismal future for you if you do not take this ultramodern training course?

Do you not lock your front door and check to be sure it is locked before you retire for the night?

Are you not at least mildly depressed when "your" team loses an important game?

Do you not worry about job security when you have been criticized by your boss, you hear rumors of layoffs, or your neighbor has suddenly lost his or her job?

Don't you feel just a bit apprehensive walking alone on a dark street at night, even in the most crime-free neighborhood?

We have cause to be cautious and fearful; everything about us inspires a sense of insecurity, and none of us is immune to it. Marketers turn it to advantage: It is a large element in marketing. Fear of losing is probably a more potent motivator than is the drive to win.

FEAR AND GREED

All motivational appeals are based on fear, greed, or both. (The terms *fear* and *greed* are used here for rhetorical purposes, not as pejoratives, and in the context of the discussion actually refer to the quite natural fear of loss and desire for gain.) Fear sells insurance, locks, alarms, fire extinguishers, and self-improvement courses. Greed (desire for gain) sells securities, tax shelters, jewelry, perfumes, and get-rich schemes.

The title of a best-selling book, *The 8-Week Cholesterol Cure* offers both, reminding us of the dangers of cholesterol while holding out the promise of a counter to it, and in a short time. That is a large part of its appeal. We are all impatient: We want it *now*. Immediate gratification is as important as convenience and effectiveness, and even more important than price. We want the gain or the means of gratification to be simple, via some easy-to-understand, easy to apply formula, a magic pill. A best-selling book of a few years ago, *How to Prosper in the Coming Bad Years*, is another example of using both fear and greed motivations in an appeal.

Not every situation lends itself to using both fear and greed in a single presentation. Most sales presentations must focus on one or the other of these motivations, rather than combining or hybridizing them. The choice of which to use is not necessarily arbitrary: There are usually certain characteristics and considerations that suggest one or the other as the more logical of the two approaches. In the case of locks and alarms, for example, the more logical approach appears to be fear motivation; for securities and business plans, the more logical approach appears to be gain motivation. The opportunity to combine both approaches effectively is not always readily apparent, nor is a combination of the two always a best choice.

Nonetheless, it is almost always possible to find both fear or greed motivations as a basis for selling anything: Each is the flip side of the other, but you must decide which is the more effective for your purposes. For example, fear motivation is not necessarily based on the possibility of some disaster; even the prospect of not getting or of not being able to get something desirable is a fear motivation.

Suppose you are selling cosmetic products of some sort, for men or women. The obvious gain motivation here is sex appeal, attracting the opposite sex and being popular. Nonetheless, it is quite easy to construct a fear motivation by simply examining the other side of the coin: What is the consequence of not being able to attract the opposite sex? It is being a wallflower, spending idle nights watching the tube instead of out on the town having fun, winding up a childless old maid or an aging bachelor, missing out on life generally. That can be a haunting fear to some people and, hence, a powerful motivator.

Of course, that argument may not be relevant to the already happily married prospect, but even married men and women want to appear attractive to the opposite sex, no matter how innocently. Thus, though fear of loneliness may be an illogical approach in some circumstances, the desire to be appealing may apply to all prospects. (No matter how much my wife assures me that I am the only man for her, she still wants other men—and women, too—to look at her admiringly.)

Figure 5-3 is a page from a recent Quill catalog offering fireproof file

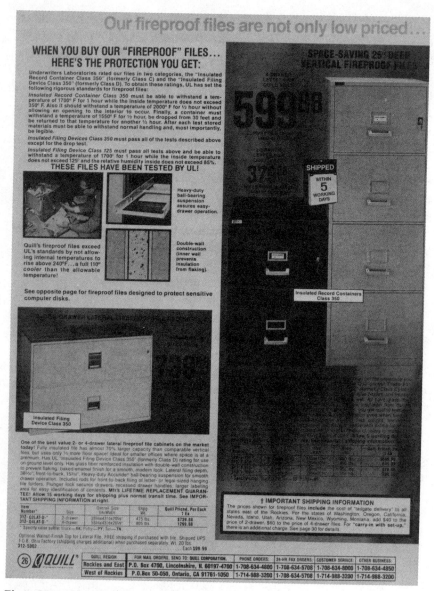

Figure 5–3. Page from the Quill catalog, using fear motivation.

cabinets for the safe storage of important records. Where Quill's principal appeal in most areas is price, supported by quality service, here the appeal is protection—fear motivation—as the caption makes plain. Figure 5–4, on the other hand, offers a gain motivation, a time-saving and labor-saving promise.

However, this is getting a bit ahead of the story, for there is much more to marketing in general and marketing via catalogs and mail especially. Discussions of actual strategies and of writing the text of the catalog (called the "copy") is covered in the next chapter, but first it's important to consider some other factors of marketing here.

At least a general understanding of niche marketing and market segmentation (closely related ideas), as well as marketing positioning is necessary before going further.

DEMOGRAPHICS

Mail-order and direct-mail specialists, especially those who advertise and mail on a large scale, find demographic studies an important element in general

Figure 5–4. Page from the Quill catalog, using gain motivation.

planning, in designing campaigns, and in developing materials. Demographic studies profile the population in various sets of terms, such as the following:

Age	Income	Buying history
Sex (M/F)	Location	Memberships
Education	Type of dwelling	Hobbies
Marital status	Political preference	Reading habits
Family status	Ethnic group	Subscriptions
Occupation	Religion	
Job title/function	Buying habits	

If you examine any list broker's catalog, you will find demographic indicators such as these identifying the choices you have available to you in renting mailing lists. You can also get such information from the U.S. Census Bureau, although their data may be as much as 10 years old (because the national census is only taken at the beginning of each decade).

Demographic Factors of Interest

Any of the factors may be of interest and important to your campaign, although rarely will you be interested in all the factors. A few of the factors are quite likely to matter.

Age.   Age is often a key factor because with certain exceptions, you do not often want to address young children, for they have no significant buying power, although they may influence their parents' buying. However, though you may not want to advertise or mail to small (e.g., grade school) children, you may want to address older children, such as high school or college age youngsters.

What's more, even among adults there are distinctions to be made. The buying habits and interests of "young marrieds" and "yuppies" are quite likely to be quite different from those of "senior citizens" and "retirees." If you are selling encyclopedias, health and hospital insurance plans, houses, or securities, for example, you will soon discover that difference.

Location.   It might be more difficult to sell air conditioning in Fairbanks, Alaska, than in Fort Worth, Texas, or Yuma, Arizona. Also, deep-sea fishing equipment, scuba gear, and surf boards probably would not sell as well in Phoenix or Albuquerque as they would in Los Angeles or Miami.

Income level. Often, income is a primary consideration. The prospects earning $25,000 per year (1990 standards) are not likely to have surplus income to invest in securities. Conversely, the $100,000 per year class is not as likely to be as much motivated by the price tag on the least expensive—"austerity model"—small appliance as the struggling single mother trying to survive on a tiny salary.

Hobbies and Memberships. If you are turning your own hobby into a catalog business—selling postage stamps, coins, or lapidary equipment, for example—you would want to know about prospects' hobbies and memberships, among other things.

Planning Based on Both Demographic Data and Acknowledgment of Emotional Appeals

These are some of the kinds of things you think about when planning and designing a campaign, deciding who are your proper prospects (and what are their demographic characteristics), what kinds of sales materials you will need, and, especially, what kinds of mailing lists you will need.

Remember always that you are dealing in emotional biases. As an officer of the Alcohol Tax Unit of the Bureau of Internal Revenue, U.S. Treasury Department a long time ago, I learned more than the average citizen knows about both beverage alcohol and industrial alcohol and the laws governing both. As a result of that experience and knowledge, without entering into detailed explanations and rationales, I have little regard for labels or for claims of superiority about alcohol products. I am convinced, for example, that paying twice as much for a heavily advertised brand as for a little-advertised brand of gin is a total waste, signifying only an underwriting of one brand's large advertising costs. I have a relative who does not agree with this, and who is embarrassed to offer his guests a bottle of gin that costs less than the most expensive (and, presumably, the most prestigious) brand. His attitude is much more prevalent than is my own, I confess: Most buyers are not at all well-informed about the products or services they seek. They tend to judge quality by price and by the impression made by the advertising. If that weren't true, no company would pay to advertise.

The power of advertising with many prospects has been called "snob appeal." It is really a matter of self-esteem: Those who insist on buying the most widely advertised and most costly brands may well be the most insecure individuals, trying to enhance their self-esteem by buying what they believe (or persuade themselves to believe) is "the best" and confusing quality with "name," when the name is entirely the result of the advertising that made the name well known. It is an emotion-based bias, for the most part, growing out of the prospect's concern with personal image. Logical argument will not shake the faith of "true believers" in some heavily advertised and supposedly superior product.

The same characteristic may have opposite effects on many prospects. For example, one individual may value shrewdness in buying and will rant and rave enthusiastically about how much he or she *saved* on some item. Another person may value the ability to afford great extravagance and may take much greater pride in buying the most expensive item and brag about how much he or she *spent* for it. Both find some comfort in thus supporting their images of themselves, according to what they believe impresses others, as well as their own egos.

This contradictory effect of appeals can extend to pride in where or from whom they buy. One individual takes great pride in buying from only the upscale or high-priced stores, whether Bloomingdale's, Nordstrom's, or Lord & Taylor. Another thinks it foolish to pay the prices charged in those stores and takes pride in being a smart shopper, which means "knowing where to shop for the best bargains."

Smart marketers take advantage of this very human need for an enhanced self-image. They invest a great deal of money to create a highly upscale catalog and work at delivering a general impression of catering to the wealthy and those of exquisite taste. Or they package the gin (perfume, vitamins, after-shave lotion, headache remedy, computer disks, breakfast muffins, or automobile service) attractively and make it appear superior to all competitors, to capture this segment of the market. However, to appeal to the "smart shoppers," smart marketers devise a different strategy. That brings up another subject: market segments.

MARKET SEGMENTS, POSITIONING, AND NICHE MARKETING

Market segmentation is a $64 way of saying "market specialization" or "niche marketing." If you specialize in some product, line of products, service, or type of customer, you *specialize* in what you offer, while you *segment* the market in which you make your offers. Market segmentation is one use of demographics: It helps both in deciding what the possible market segments are and in developing a campaign plan to pursue the segments you perceive as your best targets.

Probability statistics will work for you, usually, if the numbers are large enough to have the necessary *statistical significance* (i.e., the likelihood that the statistics didn't show a trend that really was just a chance occurrence because the sample was too small or some other variable intervened). Still, there are exceptions, which may or may not be significant for you. Not every wealthy prospect—those who can easily afford the most expensive gin or perfume—chooses to pay the price for the most heavily advertised product; wealthy customers who can easily afford the most expensive products may be quite cost conscious and be totally indifferent to the arguments of costly advertising. Nor does every prospect who supposedly cannot afford the most costly product opt for the less costly one. Even those who cannot afford "the best" may be convinced by the advertising that the heavily advertised brand is superior and merits paying more than the customer can readily afford, and many working-class people will and do manage to buy the more costly items. So there are really no truly sharp divisions or cutoffs.

You must deal in probabilities and the general rule, however, rather than the exceptions. Still, demographics notwithstanding, individuals do not always follow the paths or conform with the patterns expected according to their socioeconomic classes, at least not in American society. Americans are much more likely to react as individuals than as conforming members of a class.

The key to how prospects are most likely to react is revealed by testing, rather than by demographics or related theories, useful as demographic data may be in initial planning. That is, do use all the demographic indicators and relevant theories you can find in your early planning, but do regard these as premises that must be validated (or invalidated) by testing before you base your campaign and gamble your success on those premises. Test, evaluate the results, and implement the results as modifications to the program or the campaign. (That is, of course, the purpose of testing.)

Segmentation in Government Markets

I sold in and to a market in which I was experienced and knowledgeable— selling to the government. Still, I found it necessary to test all my premises, for they were not always valid. I found it extraordinarily easy to convince myself that certain things were true when they later proved not to be true at all. Perhaps I also overestimated how expert I was. (Or perhaps no one can be truly expert in more than one narrow segment of the vast complex of government markets.)

I grossly underestimated the segmentation of the government markets when I started marketing to federal agencies. The federal government represents a set of markets for almost every product and service known, and the governments of the more populous states are not far behind the federal government in that respect. Government markets, both federal and state or local, can thus be—*are*—segmented in more than one way: They can be segregated and classified in terms of the types of products and services purchased or the kinds of industries supplying government needs in well over 100 "supply groups" of goods and services. (These are in turn subdivided into many thousands of specific products and services, making this an almost ideal set of business-to-business markets for catalog sales. In fact, the Federal Supply Service runs supply stores and publishes its own catalogs for the use of other government agencies and for certain contractors who shop for the supplies handled by the stores of the Federal Supply Service.) What's more, these markets can also be segmented in other respects, such as types of contracts, types of suppliers, sizes of contracts, sizes of suppliers, and kinds of government agencies.

Many of the agencies have special or even unique needs. Some satisfy most of their requirements from one of the several centralized government supply organizations (in addition to the Federal Supply Service), while others contract directly with suppliers for most of their purchasing; the distinction between the two depends largely on what they buy. Some contract regularly, almost daily, while others contract only occasionally. Some buy mostly the kinds of items that are suitable for purchasing by sealed bids, while some buy items that are almost always purchased by negotiation. Some issue mostly large contracts to large organizations, while others usually make small purchases from small companies. Some are highly visible agencies, with intense competition for their contracts, while others are not well known and have short lists of bidders. Some favor one type of contract, while others favor another type. Some hold preprocurement conferences frequently, while others hold them only rarely. Some buy mostly by sealed bids, others by proposals and negotiations. Nor are these the only ways in which the government markets are segmented.

In light of this enormous diversity, I had to experiment, test, and evaluate results for a long period to determine what the significant segments were for my purposes, and then I had to design and develop a program tailored to the segments I elected to pursue. Moreover, I soon learned that government markets and their segments are no more stable or immutable than are private-sector markets, perhaps even less so: They do change, as a result of many factors, such as reorganizations, new programs, new budgets, and new legislation. So the best government markets of this year may be the poorest ones of next year or may even have ceased to exist. It is necessary to "keep up" with changes in markets in all sectors—government, business, and industrial. Old market information, even demographic data, is unreliable.

Segmentation in Private-Sector Markets

Markets in the private sector are at least as diverse as they are in government. They are even more so in terms of the diversity of customers. For one thing, both business-to-business and business-to-individuals must be considered in markets and sales to the private sector. Also, there is much wider diversity in customer budgets and ability to pay—not a small consideration.

Newcomers to business err in both directions, trying to be all things to all people and trying to be the ultimate specialists. Particularly, bear in mind the potential hazard of overspecialization and oversegmentation: Carried to an extreme, you wind up with too small a market to support your venture. You must always bear in mind at least two things when segmenting your market:

1. How large a flow of orders (i.e., how many orders) you require to survive
2. How large a market is required to provide that flow

Perhaps the second question ought to be first. It involves an estimate of how large a share of the available market you can capture. The total mail-order market has been estimated recently at $117 billion per year, but that gross figure is of no help to you. You need to get a reasonable estimate of the size of the market for the gizmos you sell or plan to sell, then guess at your share of that market. (Can you capture as much as 5 or 10 percent of it? Or is your item so necessary and so exclusive that you can hope for a much larger share? Or is the market so great that you need only a much smaller share?) It's wise to be conservative here. Specialize and segment, yes, but beware of painting yourself into a corner, too.

Positioning

Positioning is an important marketing concept that appears to confuse a great many people. It has been explained as something the marketer does to the customer's mind, influencing the customer's perception of the marketer. Put more simply, *positioning* is building an image of yourself and your product (and/or your catalog, in this case). Most major department stores publish catalogs, and the catalogs generally reflect whatever image the store has achieved. Gucci, Neiman-Marcus, I. Magnin, Lord & Taylor, and Bloomingdale's are generally regarded as upscale (expensive) stores, to the extent that some shoppers of modest means are hesitant even to look in their stores. In fact, the image rubs off on the shopper, so that there are Sears–Montgomery Ward types of shoppers and Bloomingdale's–Lord & Taylor types of shoppers, as already noted.

Position is what the customer *thinks* you are, whether the view is accurate or not, and positioning is the process of working to shape the customer's perception of you. You will acquire an image eventually, regardless of whether you make the effort to do so. In time, people will come to regard you and your catalog as representative of high-class merchandise or cheap merchandise, elegant businesspeople or schlock merchants, dependable and solid or fly-by-night, and so on. The point of positioning is to decide what image you want and then take steps to create that image.

The mistake in positioning is trying to have it both ways, to attract the kind of customers who disdain buying anything that appears too modestly priced to be of high quality, while also attracting the bargain hunters. You must decide which you want, for the two are mutually exclusive in their appeals. (The right solution, if you are intent on doing this, is to run two entirely separate and distinct catalogs, offering entirely separate and distinct lines of merchandise—in effect, two businesses.)

This is not to say that you must compete with Spiegel or with any other cataloger who publishes thick, multicolored, and obviously costly catalogs. You are somewhere near where Spiegel was 125 years ago, when their business was an infant, still a retail furniture store.

Niche Marketing

Probably the best move you can make into cataloging is as a niche marketer. (No less an authority than Maxwell Sroge, well-known writer on the subject of mail order and head of his own firm, advocates this, as do many others.) Niche marketing offers a number of advantages, such as simplified inventory and investment requirements, with at least three advantages regarding positioning and other aspects of marketing generally:

1. It greatly simplifies the positioning and segmentation problems.
2. As a specialist, you achieve visibility much more easily among your prospects.
3. It's easier to handle exclusive lines.

Perhaps you have noticed by now how much market segmentation, positioning, and niche marketing overlap and repeat each other, how often you are hearing the same arguments, couched in slightly different terms. Yes, specialization, segmentation, positioning, and niche marketing are several sides of the same question, approached from different starting positions. The merchandiser talks about "specialization." The marketer talks about "segmentation." The advertiser refers to "positioning." And the entrepreneur talks about "niche marketing." All approach similar business questions that are basic to cataloging and to any other business: What should I sell, and to whom should I sell it? Those are the basic questions of all marketing, and almost every marketing problem eventually comes down to these questions, with the addition of the *how* question: *how* shall I sell it?

INDUCEMENTS

The General Inducement: Examples of "The Offer"

All marketing and sales efforts entail inducements. The most basic and inevitable inducement is what I have called elsewhere "the offer," or what you promise to do for the customer.

Beauty by Spector, Inc., is a McKeesport, Pennsylvania, cataloger, in business since 1958 and a distributor (wholesaler) of wigs and hairpieces since 1965. The firm, headed by Myer Spector, began selling by catalog in 1984 with an initial mailing of 24,000 catalogs and accompanying literature sent out to all wig retailers. The catalog and package are simple and unpretentious, using such simple illustrations (inexpensive clip art) and offset printing as shown in Figure 5–5, a sample page from one of Myer Spector's plain-vanilla catalogs. Figure 5–6 is from another of the firm's catalogs, designed to help the retailer master the technologies of wigs and hairpieces.

Beauty by Spector, Inc. is a wholesaler selling to retailers—dealers—so the appeal is to salability and profitability of the merchandise. The catalogs, simple and inexpensive to manufacture as some of them are, offer the dealer large discounts, sales arguments to use on their customers, and guidance in understanding what they need to know about wigs and hairpieces. (Beauty by Spector, Inc., also mails catalogs furnished by the manufacturers of the products Spector distributes. Several, featuring Alan Thomas Designs, are in full color, with photographs of professional models wearing the products.)

The catalog of Specialty Merchandise Corporation (SMC), of Chatsworth, California (SMC was discussed in Chapter 1), is obviously more expensive. It is printed in full color, professionally typeset, and addressed to the aspiring

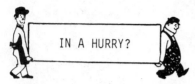

IN A HURRY?

No need to wait until your Wig catalogs arrive -- YOU CAN ORDER DIRECTLY FROM THIS PAGE! Fill in and mail the convenient Order Form on the other side of this page ..... and before you know it, you'll be wearing one of our striking Wig creations. You'll <u>look</u> and <u>feel</u> magnificent!

Available Colors

1 Jet Black
1B Off Black
2 Darkest Brown
4 Dark Brown
6 Medium Dark Brn.
8 Medium Brown
10 Light Warm Brown
12 Lt. Golden Brown
16 Dk. Golden Blonde
18 Light Ash Brown
22 Light Ash Blonde
24 Lt. Golden Blonde
27 Strawberry Blonde
30 Light Auburn
32 Dark Auburn
34 Dkst. Mixed Grey
44 Med. Mixed Grey
51 Light Mixed Grey
56 Ltst. Mixed Grey
60 Silver Platinum
101 Muted Platinum
105 Lt. Platinum Beige
4/22 Dk. Brn. Frosted
8/22 Med. Brn. Frosted
18/22 Lt. Brn. Frosted

STYLE NO.	DESCRIPTION	SUGGESTED RETAIL	YOUR PRICE
0003	2 oz. - 100% HUMAN HAIR All Purpose Wiglet	22.00	10.95
0080	3½ oz. - 100% HUMAN HAIR Cascade, Triangular Base . .	32.00	15.95
0009	3½ oz. - 100% HUMAN HAIR DeLuxe Wiglet, Adj. Wire Base .	32.00	15.95
6702	Tumble of Soft Curls from Brow to Nape. MODERN LOOK! .	65.00	32.50
0040	6-8 inch - Finest 100% HUMAN HAIR <u>All Hand-Tied</u> Wig . .	150.00	75.00
5189	<u>WIG-FALL</u> - <u>Wig</u> Cap, <u>Fall</u> Length. Lush, Exotic Beauty .	80.00	39.95
6814	Smooth Page, Sculpt Bangs. Hairstyle of Famour TV Star	70.00	35.00
7118	Skin-Tastik "Super Quality" Basic Wig, FRIZZ Resistant .	55.00	27.50
6340	NEW SILHOUETTE. Versatile, Flip-Fluff Basic Wig .	65.00	32.50
6605	Lite-Wate CLASSIC. Full Bangs, Crown, and Nape . . .	65.00	32.50
6590	Lite-Wate CLASSIC. Mid-length, Versatile <u>BLOW CUT</u> look	65.00	32.50
7350	Feminine All-over Curly, Curly, Basic Wig	50.00	25.00
6230	"Tapered Back" Neat & Trim Basic Wig - Redy t' Wear . .	65.00	32.50
6470	GYPSY PRINCESS, Feather-Wate Wig. Layered Waves & Curls	70.00	35.00
6150	Lite-Wate CLASSIC. Sophisticated Semi-Tapered Style .	65.00	32.50

RUSH <u>ORDER</u> <u>FORM</u> ON NEXT PAGE

Figure 5–5. Catalog page showing hair styles. Courtesy of Beauty by Spector, Inc.

Order Form

PLEASE SHIP THE FOLLOWING HAIRGOODS:

BEAUTY BY SPECTOR, INC.
DEPT. OR
MCKEESPORT, PA   15134-0502

HOW MANY	STYLE NO.	DESCRIPTION	COLOR	YOUR PRICE

FOR AN ACCURATE COLOR MATCH, PLEASE ENCLOSE A GENEROUS HAIR SAMPLE!

6% Pennsylvania Sales Tax Pennsylvania Residents only	
Insured Shipping Charges	3.00
TOTAL AMOUNT ENCLOSED	

PRINT YOUR NAME, ADDRESS, & ZIP CODE CLEARLY

NAME...

Address..

City .... State .... Zip ....   DATE _____

Telephone number (_____) _____

CHARGE YOUR PURCHASE

Check One   *VISA* ☐ VISA   MasterCard ☐ MASTER CARD

INTERBANK NO.   EXP DATE   MO   YEAR

X _____

Sign your name as it appears on your Credit Card

Figure 5–6. Another catalog page, including an order form. Courtesy of Beauty by Spector, Inc.

entrepreneur eager to launch his or her own business and earn some money. The theme of the catalog is that SMC all but guarantees that success by providing products and guidance, selling only to SMC dealers (called "members"). It goes on to describe several means by which the prospect can sell SMC merchandise and the array of aids and instructions offered by SMC. The catalog then offers color photographs of many of the products SMC wholesales to its "members," with three dollar-amount figures for each: Cost to member, selling price, and profit.

Computer Direct, a supplier in Barrington, Illinois, lists its offerings in an inexpensive black-and-white catalog of nearly 100 pages. It makes the usual claims of huge stocks and promises of prompt shipment (which my own experience has not disputed), but its major appeal is price. (It does offer extremely competitive prices. At least some of the items listed appear to be surplus or closeouts.)

Special Inducements

Many marketing campaigns are based on offering customers special inducements to buy. At one time, many campaigns relied on "special sales" and discounted prices as major motivators, but these have become so commonplace that it is difficult to persuade customers to conceive of them as special inducements. However, many marketing campaigns are based on offers of free gifts, bonuses, and extended guarantees.

Free Goods or Services

"Buy two and get one free" or "Five for the price of four" is a frequently used device to dangle a carrot before prospects. It's really a sale or discount, but for many people, the word *free* has special appeal, more so than the mere reduction of price. Therefore, for many customers "Buy 2 and get one FREE!" has more appeal than "3 for the price of 2" or even "⅓ off." Imaginative excuses for using the word can add a spark to any copy. Even "FREE delivery," "FREE gift," or "FREE gift wrapping" helps. (At the minimum, the word helps get the reader's attention.)

Sales

Probably second in usefulness only to the word *FREE* is the word *SALE.* Despite extensive overuse, *sale* never loses its charm: Customers never get tired of seeing it. Some successful businesses use the word perpetually, having a sale every day of the year. They or their marketing managers are geniuses at thinking up enough reasons for special sales and sale prices to keep sales as a permanent and ever-present feature. If you are ever at a loss for naming your next sale, here are just a few starter ideas you can borrow or adapt:

Fire sale	Damaged goods sale
Clearance sale	Discontinuance sale
Warehouse clearance sale	Inventory clearance sale
Spring clearance sale	Mother's Day sale
Washington's Birthday sale	Bonus days sale
Fourth of July sale	Manager's sale
Memorial Day sale	Owner's sale
Summer sale	Stockholder's sale
Weekend sale	Back-to-school sale
Winter clearance sale	June graduates' sale
Founder's Day sale	June brides' sale

Gifts

General merchandise cataloger Fingerhut has long used the free-gift device, sending surprise gifts, as well as promised gifts, and it seems to have served them well. Most people are fond of pleasant surprises, and combining *FREE* and *SURPRISE* appears to be a happy combination. In any case, Fingerhut has come a long way since the days when automobiles still used cloth-covered upholstery and a new-car buyer could expect to get a package of literature from Fingerhut offering seat covers at bargain prices.

Rebates and Bonus Certificates

Many manufacturers offer rebates on their products, and their dealers use rebate offers as an inducement, evidently in the belief that it is more appealing than other forms of discounting. (Plus the fact that probably a majority of those buying small-tag items do not go to the trouble of sending in their claims for rebates of a dollar or two, so the rebate actually costs the manufacturer much less than a true discount!)

Another device used by many catalogers is the award of credit or bonus certificates. The customer gets a kind of rebate in the form of a certificate or credit slip representing some small fraction of each purchase, possibly 1 percent of the purchase price, which the customer is to save and can use as cash for some future purchase. Sometimes this is combined with a special sale in which the credit amount is doubled. Or there may be special items offered on which extra bonus credits are awarded.

The Most Important Inducement

All of these items help stimulate sales, but none take the place of or are as effective as good service, fair prices, and generally honest treatment. Never underestimate the value of these, especially not in cataloging and mail order generally, where so many buyers tread cautiously and fearfully. For example, last year, I bought a modem from JDR Microdevices® of San Jose, California, a mail-order supplier of computers and accessories. When it arrived, it would not function. I returned it, and it was replaced promptly. The replacement worked for a time, but it too soon failed. The company advised me that they were discontinuing that line of modems and offered me a different model as a replacement. They then not only replaced it with a better modem (which is still performing faithfully), but they also sent me a partial refund because the replacement sold for less than the original model. That is integrity in a company, and they certainly won my loyalty and continued business by their courteous and prompt attention to satisfying my complaints.

On the other hand, I received what I considered to be rather shabby treatment from another mail-order supplier of computer equipment and accessories. I bought a keyboard from this company. Both the original keyboard I bought and its replacement failed electronically, and the letters on the keys rubbed off in a short time. Despite this, the company failed to respond to my letters of complaint. The president of the company wrote me snarling letters of defiance when I returned the second keyboard and asked for a refund. He denied that there was anything wrong with it, tried to silence me with an offer of a partial refund, and even threatened to sue me if I published a complaint about them. I had to write a letter of demand to get my original (defective) keyboard returned to me. (It was then in working condition, evidently repaired, but I had already bought a different model to replace it, so it now stands in a corner of my office as a testimonial to bad business practices.)

I found later that I was not this supplier's only unhappy customer. Perhaps that is why this company must advertise so heavily, seeking new customers. That seems a foolish method of doing business, however; it costs a great deal of money to get new customers. Instead, it usually makes sense to adjust complaints, even when they appear unjustified, and keep the customer.

That, too, is an important part of marketing. Keeping customers is at least as important as making them.

GETTING RELIABLE ANSWERS

Premises Versus Measurements

Premises, theories, and conventional wisdom have certain usefulness when properly employed, but the only reliable indicators are actual measurements. Chapter 4 showed how misleading percentages can be in determining profitability. A response of 0.5 percent on a $200 item can produce profits, while a response of 10 percent on a $5 item will probably bring substantial losses. Only return on investment (ROI) is a significant measure, and testing is the only way to minimize risk and maximize success. You may be interested in rates of response for statistical or other purposes, but they are almost meaningless unless qualified by average order size, gross profit per order, and other cost-of-sales figures.

Testing must be carried out according to a properly designed plan, and you must know how to conduct a test properly. In one unfortunate case, Gwenda Schanzle and her daughter Pamela ventured into catalog sales with a new item, Australian style moleskin jeans; they "tested" the two dozen odd lists of 5,000 names each by mailing to *every* name on each list, rather than to some fractional percentage of each list. Only later did they learn that this was not the way to test the lists. The tragedy was that this left them without money to spend on additional lists so that they could apply what they had learned ("Never Give a Sucker an Even Break," Dee Henry, *Catalog Business*, August 1, 1989). Nor was this their only mistake. They suffered many defeats and disappointments before they finally identified their proper market and got their venture to begin returning a profit. They learned everything the hard way, but they were fortunate to be tough enough and determined enough to stick it out and eventually find success.

What Good Are Response Rates?

Despite the fact that response rates have little real significance in terms of testing and evaluating the viability of a given campaign, they do have some utility. The chief usefulness of response rates is for estimating future promotions, judging the size of the gamble. That is, if you have some historical figures on response rates, they can be useful in designing test runs by providing a basis for estimating selling prices and other costs. Of course, the response rates must be tested before making a major commitment to them, but they give you a better starting place for designing your test program than the off-the-cuff guesses you would otherwise be forced to use.

The next chapter looks at the practical matter of implementing these marketing ideas when creating your *catalog copy* (i.e., the text you write for your catalog).

6

Writing Catalog Copy
That Sells

People do not buy (despite a few exceptions); they have to be sold. With catalog shoppers, the selling is accomplished by catalog copy—words and illustrations.

COMMUNICATION AND PERSUASIVENESS

The Word Is Not the Thing

The general semanticists will advise you that "The word is not the thing." That catch-phrase points out that words are only symbols for objects, concepts, and images. They are useful only to the extent that they mean the same thing to both or all parties concerned with the intended communications. Therefore, if it is true that "people usually do not buy; they must be sold," all businesses must be concerned with what form of communication sells merchandise to people. In the case of cataloging, the communication is via a print medium—words and pictures.

Communication as a Prerequisite to Persuasiveness

Communication is not a one-way street. It hasn't happened simply because one party has uttered, verbally or by other means, a stream of words in a language understood generally by the recipients. Unfortunately, the receiver often does not get the message intended by the sender. When this happens and communication does *not* take place, senders tend to react defensively. Senders are sure that they were clear enough, and that the receiver is to blame if the communication did not take place. Of course, the receiver has the opposite view. The study of semantics addresses the problem of what words do and do not mean to all parties involved in a communication.

In addressing the problems of communication and persuasiveness, not only is communication essential to persuasiveness, but also the same elements, functions, and malfunctions apply both to communication and to persuasiveness.

The Art of Persuasion

If selling is the art of persuasion, as I alleged it to be in earlier chapters, writing effective sales copy must be the art of persuasive writing. It is. Effective selling means persuading prospects to become customers—to buy. Experience dictates that certain words and certain expressions are more persuasive than others.

There are, however, two sides to this coin: Some words and expressions are highly persuasive in a positive regard, while others have the opposite effect: They alienate, polarize thinking, and create hostility. For example, most of us like to believe that we are determined, steady, conscientious, or persevering; we would object, however, to being characterized as bull-headed, obstinate, or even stubborn. The second set of words are generally regarded as negative traits, whereas the earlier set of terms are positive and even laudatory. Is this true for everybody? No, indeed; some individuals are delighted to be regarded as bull-headed, obstructionist, even totally intransigent. They are the exceptions, however; do not permit yourself to be misled by a few exceptions.

The differences among synonyms and their various effects on emotions relate to a semantic quality called "connotation." Many words that have the same *denotation*—literal meanings, which make them synonyms of each other—have conflicting nuances or shades of meaning. This is largely because many words have an *emotional* content that suggests or implies certain meanings beyond their literal meanings or dictionary definitions.

Connotative meanings are not static because language is not static. Language that is living—in daily use, actively spoken and/or written by a society—grows and changes. In the process, many words take on new connotations. Less than a century ago, the word *rascal* was synonymous in both denotation and connotation with the word *scoundrel*. Today, the word *scoundrels* still describes unscrupulous, untrustworthy, and evil people, but *rascals* can refer to mischievous children, and that term is used more in fondness than in condemnation. Rarely will you find the word used today to describe someone regarded as a true scoundrel.

Even more dramatic change takes place with some words. The word *gay*, for example, certainly has taken on a new connotation in recent years. Many who are now known as "gay" have "come out of the closet" and do not object to being identified by that adjective in its current meaning. However, many men and women who are "straight" (another word with a new and different connotation), especially men, would be indignant (and some even horrified) to be referred to as being "gay" now. So it is not only necessary to understand the classical connotations of words but also to keep up with changes as they come into existence.

The context in which a term is used often identifies the intended connotation, especially when the word is used as an obvious metaphor, rather than in its literal meaning. Thus, prices may be "chopped," "demolished," "smashed," or even "assassinated," and the reader or listener has no difficulty in grasping the intended meaning, which is *reduced*; the advertiser is simply dramatizing the reduction in cost.

There are also regional problems with words: Words still do not mean the same thing everywhere even today, despite the leveling influence of modern travel and communications. Most waiters and waitresses in Philadelphia, for example, would not know what a "sweet roll" and "Bismark" were any more than waiters and waitresses in Chicago would be likely to know what you referred to if you requested a "coffee cake" or "jelly doughnut," their terms for these things.

There are even international problems involving language. After the Second World War, the Western allies referred to Allied Military Governments of Occupied Territories as "AMGOT," until they learned that the word was a not-so-nice word in Turkish and offensive to Turkish nationals. The term was then shortened to AMG. Many Americans probably now know that "bloody" is a not-too-nice term in England, but few know that "knocked up" used to mean being awakened in hotels by a knock on the door, when a wake-up call was requested. (Telephones were not then standard fixtures in hotel rooms there as they were and are here, and morning calls were achieved by a bellman knocking on doors at requested hours each morning.)

Words also take on meaning from the ways in which they are expressed, from the *implications* of the construction. "It's a nice product, but it is quite expensive" clearly does not have the same implied meaning as "It is quite expensive, but it is a nice product," despite the fact that the words are identical; only the order—that is, the construction—has been changed. The first expression clearly suggests disapproval and evades recommendation. The second expression clearly implies a recommendation.

Finally, there is the matter of individual biases that cause readers and listeners to attach their own meaning to words. Persistence is regarded as an admirable trait when indoctrinating individuals in the benefits of refusing to quit too easily in the face of obstacles. The word may take on a quite different meaning, however, for the individual who has been unreasonably harassed by a salesman who is described by that word.

These facts of language affect advertising and selling. The significance is not just academic; it has practical applications and consequences.

The Additional Constraints of Written Presentations

Up to this point, the discussion has concerned language, communication, and persuasiveness in general. The real concern here, however, is with *written* persuasiveness—catalog copy—which imposes greater constraints than those of verbal presentations in face-to-face, radio, or TV presentations. Catalog copy cannot rely on mood-setting music, suggestive intonations, sound effects, facial expressions, gestures, or other nonverbal modifiers and influences. Only words and illustrations are available to do the job of appealing to the emotions and to the intellect.

THE ELEMENTS OF WRITTEN SALES COPY

According to commonly accepted ideas about advertising, the necessary elements or functions for successful copy are four: (1) Get attention; (2) arouse interest; (3) generate desire; and (4) ask for action. Exactly how these objectives are to be realized is not even suggested by their statement, unfortunately. What may be inferred from these descriptors, also unfortunately, is that these are all separate objectives—that is, that getting attention is not necessarily related directly to arousing interest and that generating desire is still another and separate function or objective, also not necessarily related to the others. The inference one may draw that these are separate elements and objectives leads to some highly ineffective copy.

The "Hook" in Sales Copy

If you watch TV for only a short while, you learn to recognize what fiction writers have often referred to as the "narrative hook" or, more simply, "the hook." That is the curiosity-piquing or dramatic event with which the program opens, especially if it is a TV drama or movie. It may or may not be a scene from the beginning of the story, and often is not. The purpose is to "hook" the viewers—capture their attention—so that they sit, albeit impatiently, through the stream of opening commercials, announcements, and, in the case of movies and lengthy TV dramas, the almost endless roll of credits, which might otherwise cause a great deal of channel switching to take place quite rapidly. (Do we really care who manages and dispenses the props? No, but you would if you or someone you know did it.) The hook is a sample of what the producer of the show believes to be the most exciting, dramatic, or curiosity-arousing moments of the show, which not only captures attention but also does so with enough intensity to hold the viewer long enough to get back to the meat of the program.

The counterpart to the narrative "hook" in written sales copy and advertising is either the headline or the caption and/or the illustration, when illustrations are used. However, when headlines and illustrations have little to do with the overall goal of the copy, they do little to sell the merchandise. If the "hook" is force-fitted solely to capture the reader's attention, no matter how momentarily and how irrelevantly, it actually detracts from the persuasiveness of the copy. For example, a seller of computer printers advertises, "Our prices aren't just lower. They're authorized." That headline is meaningless to Mr. and Ms. Average. Even when it's explained later that the advertiser is an authorized dealer in the printers advertised and the claim is then made that being an authorized dealer means something to the buyer if or when something goes wrong with the printer purchased, it's a weak and even nebulous argument with little in it to motivate the reader. In fact, that copy suggests that something is likely to go wrong with the printer and is therefore negative advertising that is more likely to alarm the reader and discourage the sale than to encourage it.

The seller of a variety of computer disks runs an advertisement in that magazine cum catalog, *Computer Shopper*, and headlines his copy **DISKOVER US!** You may find that headline clever and attention getting, but it is not good advertising. Despite its vague relevance because the advertiser does sell disks, the headline suggests no reason whatever for patronizing that advertiser rather than any of the many other sellers of disks. It is, in fact, a good example of another common fault in copy writing: the use of pointless and irrelevant humor (and often quite bad and unfunny humor) in advertising copy.

Another bad example of inept humor based on the pun is the headline that describes a computer company as "tops," making a bad joke of it because it refers to two subheads, *Desktops* and *Laptops.* This makes it one of the many banal attempts to impress a reader with the cleverness of a bad play on words, rather than on a benefit—a reason to buy what is being advertised. The result of what is to me "klever kopy," usually copy based on puns, is almost always totally unmotivating, reeking of amateurishness. It has a negative effect on many readers, especially those who are weary of sophomoric cleverness. Many readers even feel indignation at such a clumsy attempt to demand their attention because it merely wastes their time.

Better, although not by a great deal, is copy that says "Now you can afford to be in a powerful position," which is followed by a pictorial listing of six computers with scant descriptions of each. Perhaps some readers will link the headline with the body copy, perhaps not; the linkage is not obvious. Only highly experienced computer users might read in some relevant meaning to the word *powerful* as a reference to some computers being more "powerful" than others and the more expert computer users being referred to often as "power users." Those less expert are likely to be mystified by the cryptic message and to sigh resignedly as they go on to other pages, wondering why the advertiser thought they would know what was being discussed.

The preceding examples reveals one of the worst sins of advertising: using a headline that the advertiser thinks will attract attention, but having no message that directly and meaningfully relates to the rest of the copy for the average reader. (Is the real sin that the advertiser does not understand who the average reader is? Or is it that the advertiser makes totally unwarranted assumptions about the reader?)

In the preceding examples, the headlines did not even effectively grab the reader's attention. But what would have happened if it did succeed in grabbing attention? Is the rest of the copy linked to it? Does it arouse interest? Generate desire to buy? Not in these cases. The answer to all these questions is "no." The rest of the copy is about as dull as copy can get. Each computer illustration is followed by three lines listing basic characteristics of the system, followed by an "only" price quotation.

There are many other examples of ineffective copy writing. The fact is that there are many approaches to copy writing. Several are good approaches, and many are misconceived and indicate complete amateurishness—utter lack of talent or, at least, of knowledge and training in the art of writing sales copy. (Unfortunately, writing advertising copy is one of the several special fields in which most people who can read without moving their lips believe that they are as capable as anyone in writing effective copy.) Here are some examples of the various "schools" of copy writing:

Figures 6–1 and 6–2. Pure price appeal—probably the most common approach to copy writing. You certainly will have no problem finding examples of this.

Figure 6–1. Price appeal copy.

Figure 6–3. We've got it all. Come see us.

Figure 6–4. We are the greatest. No one does it better.

Figures 6–5 and 6–6. Secondary benefit.

Figure 6–7. Fear motivation: We can save you.

Figure 6–8. Special feature(s).

There are many miscellaneous ideas, as illustrated in Figures 6–9, 6–10, and 6–11. These hardly merit being called advertisements, for they do not make very energetic efforts to sell; they are hardly more than announcements. Even if they win enough sales to earn their way, that is not evidence that they are

Figure 6–2. Another example of price appeal copy.

well-conceived advertisements or that they could not and would not produce far greater results with a few judicious changes.

The point is that getting attention, arousing interest, and generating desire (not to buy, really, but to gain the promised benefits) are not truly separate elements or functions of the copy; they are all part of the same function, and they must be addressed directly in the headline and in the copy that follows immediately. There must be *linkage* between the hook and the desire to buy, and perhaps that requires some explanation of its own.

Linkage: Converting Attention into Interest and then Desire

Distinctions among getting attention, arousing interest, and generating desire to buy are not truly separate elements; they are really only different aspects of the same process. Everyone acts out of self-interest. That does not necessarily mean material gain, of course; people strive for other kinds of gains too: gains in self-esteem, gains in feelings of greater security, gains in perceptions of happiness, and gains in many other nonmaterial matters. Dramatic and curiosity-arousing gimmicks may capture a reader's attention momentarily, but an effective appeal to self-interest does a great deal more: It captures attention and *holds* it. That is far more important.

Some of the approaches illustrated in the figures are meritorious; others are poor ideas, as far as their sales and persuasiveness characteristics are concerned. Figures 6–1 and 6–2 offer headlines promising low prices and little more than that to commend patronage. Figures 6–3 and 6–4 base their appeal on headlines that claim superiority of some sort or other—just what kind is not clear—as sources for laptop computers. The headlines of Figures 6–5 and 6–6 offer spin-off or secondary benefits, which is not a bad approach. Figure 6–7 employs a fear approach, although the hazard is only implied and not expressed in the headline. Figure 6–8 uses the hardy, never-fail perennial FREE!, along with a direct benefit—a calculator built directly into the keyboard—which is an innovation. The illustrations of Figure 6-9 are simply announcements and hardly merit being called advertising.

Rarely does a reader decide immediately (or within seconds of reading the copy) to make the purchase. More often, the buying decision comes on gradually, as the initial attraction does combat with reason, discretion, and caution. That is, arousing interest is not enough; the interest is a spark, and it must be fanned into a flame, which is the irresistible desire to buy and enjoy the benefit promised.

A weight-loss product advertisement offers a good example. The head-

PC's TO GO
THE LAPTOP SPECIALIST

"For All of Your Laptop Needs"

ZENITH

* Z184-1, Z184-2
* Z286/20
* Z286/40
* TurboSport 386
  $CALL

Spark by Datavue
* 640K memory
* Two 3 1/2" 720K drives
* EL backlit screen
* 20Mb hard drive optional
* 4.77/9.54 MHz
* One year warranty
  $CALL

TOSHIBA

* T1000
* T1200F/FB, H/HB
* T3100e, T3200
* T5100, T5200
  $CALL

Accessories

Carry Case/Spark	$ 49	5.25" Ext. Drives	$225
Carry Case/Toshiba, Zenith	60	JT Fax Portable	325
1.7 Battery/Spark	69	Diskette Case	10
1200 Baud Int. Modem	211	Fast Lynx	69
2400 Baud Int. Modem	275	Battery Watch	25
WorldPort 1200 Pocket Modem	189	Numeric Keypad	129
WorldPort 2400 Pocket Modem	275	Box of 10/3.5" disks	18

Specials

*Datavue Spark with 20 MB Hard Drive	*$1995*
*Mitsubishi mp286L with 20 MB Hard Drive	*2299*
*JT Fax Portable with Laptop Purchase	*299*
*Discovery 2400 Baud Pocket Modem	*199*

* Limited Time Offer

800-992-3236

PC's TO GO
THE LAPTOP SPECIALIST

15-day money-back guarantee. Shipping charges non-refundable.
All non-defective returns subject to 15% restocking fee. Returns
must be in original factory condition. Prices subject to change
without notice.

Figure 6-3. "We've got it all."

Figure 6–4. "We're the best. See us first, last, and always."

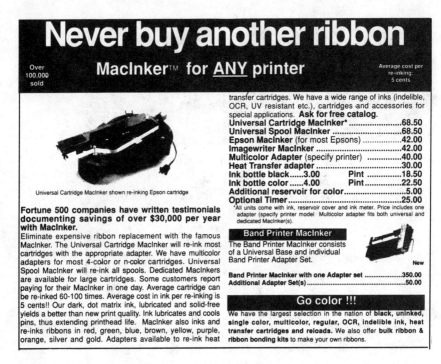

Figure 6–5. Secondary benefit.

line says, "LOSE WEIGHT FAST, EASILY, WITHOUT STARVING." "Before and after" photographs of men and women show how much weight each lost. The blurb beneath the headline said something about a dramatic new breakthrough, a major scientific advance in the science of nourishment that meant everyone could now lose weight while eating three hearty meals every day.

The reader is thinking, "Wow! That sounds marvelous! But wait; isn't that what they all say? I would like to believe it, but I have heard that one before. But wait—there's more; I'll read on."

At this point, the advertiser has gotten attention and aroused interest, despite the fact that the copy is not exactly original or especially imaginative. It offers something better: It appeals to something a great many of us *wish to believe*, and it does so in apparently reasonable terms. What overweight person, possibly a perpetual dieter in perpetual quest of the perfect figure, could avoid being interested, at least initially?

Going from interest to desire to buy is another matter, however. The reader may be expected to be somewhat skeptical, for a wide variety of reasons, such as previous disappointments and reading or viewing on TV many

The Smart Business Person's Way to Save on FAX Machines

Most FAX Buyers Will Wish They Had Read This Before They Had Purchased Their Fax Machine.

This is the way to cut your cost to the bone and you don't have to even move to do it.

You can save hundreds of dollars without ever leaving your chair and without giving up top name brand quality or full service.

Your savings can exceed thousands of dollars for purchasing one or more units from us.

But dollar savings are not the only factor to consider. Getting the service you need easily and inexpensive-ly is very important and you can count on us to help take care of your FAX Machine easily, quickly, and with a minumum amount of down time.

Because so many of you will purchase from us, we are able give you huge savings. We will only make a "small" profit on each unit but we sell a large number of units. We don't try to get rich on one sale as some other dealers do.

Since 1984, FAX of America has been "making it our business" to help you save even more on fax machines, the smart business person's way. You too can join the tens-of-thousands of satisfied FAX of America customers by picking up the phone and dialing 1-800-342-FAXX.

We don't just save you time, we don't just offer good service, we just don't want you to pay too much for a fax machine. We do want you to save money and be happy. If all this sounds too good to be true, it isn't Call us today.

CALL 1-800-342-FAXX NOW
We'll Beat Any Price From Anyone Who Offers All The Service We Do.
CALL FOR CURRENT PRICE QUOTE

SHARP*
FO220 . . . .$728.00
FO300 . . . .$799.00
FO330 . . . . $1029.00
FO510 . . . . $1199.00
FO230 . . . . .CALL

MURATA*
M900 . . . .$610.00
M1400 . . . . .CALL
M1800 . . . . .CALL
Call for other models not listed.

RICOH*
RF850 . . . .$699.00
RF920 . . . .$1188.00
Call for other models not listed.

PANAFAX*
UF250 . . . .$1280.00
UF260 . . . .$1499.00

XEROX*
Plain Paper Fax Machines
7021 . . . .$2995.00
7021 Faxmaster $3425.00
Computer controlled Fax. Unlim-ited memory and page storage.

Eliminate dedicated phone lines, hook up a phone, answering machine, and modem on one phone line. Automatic switching to each device.
TF500 . . . . .CALL

COPIERS by Sharp
SF-6000 . . . . .CALL
SF-7300 . . . . .CALL
SF-7350 . . . . .CALL
SF-7750 . . . . .CALL
All Sharp copier supplies at discount.

LAPTOPS by Toshiba
T1000 . . . .$ 652.00
T1200 Hard Disk/Reflective . .$1828.00
T1200 Dual Floppy/Reflective . $1370.00
T1200FB Dual Floppy/
Reflective $1436.00
T1200HB Hard Disk/Backlit . .$1958.91
T1600 . . . .$3299.00
T3100E $2799.00
T3200 286 . . . .$3499.00
T3200 286 with 1.44 MBFD . .$3499.00
T5200 386 40 MB $5029.00
T5200 386 100 MB $5421.00
T5100 386 . . . .$4245.00

FAX PAPER Sale Prices
Price per roll/6 Rolls per case

	98'	164'	328'
	roll	roll	roll
8 cases	3.49	5.99	8.99
6 cases	3.99	6.49	9.49
4 cases	4.99	6.99	9.99
2 cases	5.99	7.99	10.99
Regular Prices	7.99	9.99	13.99

PRINTERS
by Panasonic
KX-P1180 . . . . . .$ 179.00
KX-P1191 . . . . . .$ 215.00
KX-P1124 . . . . . .$ 316.00
KX-P1524 . . . . . .$ 540.00
KX-P1595 . . . . . .$ 434.00
KX-P4450 . . . . . .$1460.00

*Prices shown do not reflect FAXCare Kit which must be purchased with every machine.

Panamax Telemax 1 . . . .$89.00

No surcharge for COD certified check. Personal checks allow 21 days to clear. Indiana residents add 5% sales tax. All sales final. Refused shipments subject to 15% charge. Prices subject to availability and change without notice.

MODEMS
by Pratical Peripherals
External
M1200 BPS EX . . . .CALL
M2400 BPS EX . . . .CALL
Internal
1200 BPS IN . . . . . .CALL
2400 BPS IN . . . . . .CALL

COMPLETE PCs
Complete FAX Board 4800
Complete FAX Board 9600
Complete Answering
  Machine
Complete Hand
  Scanner/400
Complete Half
  Page Scanner
Complete Full Page Scanner

Faxcessory Cleaning Kit . $29.95

FAX OF AMERICA
CALL TOLL FREE 1-800-342-FAXX (3299)
P.O. BOX 1032 • SOUTH BEND, IN 46624

Figure 6–6. Another example of secondary benefit promised.

Figure 6–7. Fear motivation at work.

widely publicized exposes of advertising excesses and marketing hoaxes. Still, hope springs eternal, so the reader almost surely *hopes* to be convinced by the rest of the copy. He or she may be saying unconsciously, "Please prove that this is true. Please . . . ."

The fact is that the first two elements are almost the same: Make the headline and/or illustration appeal directly and immediately to the reader's self-interest (especially to an intensely felt self-interest), and you have the first two requirements satisfied almost simultaneously. What follows to arouse that desire to buy is something slightly different, but it should be so closely linked to the attention-grabber and the interest-arouser that it is difficult to find the dividing line. Desire to buy results when the reader is convinced that the

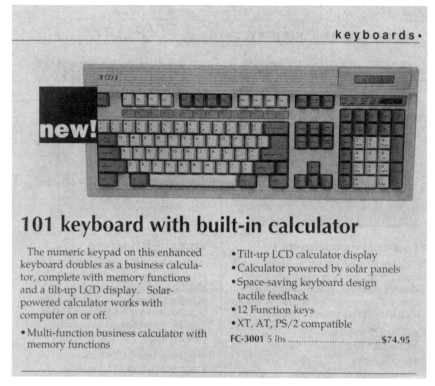

keyboards•

101 keyboard with built-in calculator

The numeric keypad on this enhanced keyboard doubles as a business calculator, complete with memory functions and a tilt-up LCD display. Solar-powered calculator works with computer on or off.

• Multi-function business calculator with memory functions

• Tilt-up LCD calculator display
• Calculator powered by solar panels
• Space-saving keyboard design tactile feedback
• 12 Function keys
• XT, AT, PS/2 compatible

FC-3001 5 lbs $74.95

Figure 6–8. Special features (and implied benefits).

advertiser can and will deliver—that the purchase will produce—the promised benefit.

I call the portion of an advertisement that generated desire to buy, "proof," although it might be more accurate to call it "evidence," because proof, like beauty, is often in the eye of the beholder. That is, in the case of advertising, proof or evidence is never absolute. It is whatever the customer perceives and will accept as proof. Of course, the prospect's earnest desire to believe the promise will help a great deal; it's much easier to convince prospects to believe even the unbelievable if they want enough to believe it. At the same time, prospects are not entirely naive: the more extravagant the promise, the more proof is required. It is one thing to promise a $50 ring for $19.95 and make the explanation behind the marvelous offer sound plausible. It is quite another thing to promise a $500 ring for $19.95 and make that plausible; it won't be easy to persuade viewers or readers to accept rationalizations of that.

Figure 6–9. Miscellaneous approaches.

Figure 6–10. Some examples of "asking for action."

In my view, there are three, not four elements in the process of selling. Though I agree that the final element is "asking for action," I call the first two elements, "the promise," and "the offer" (mentioned in previous chapters). What's more, I do not rate all three elements as being equally necessary or equally important. In terms of priority or order of importance, I rate promise first or highest, then proof, and then asking for action. Both the promise and the proof have been discussed, but the request for action has yet to be discussed.

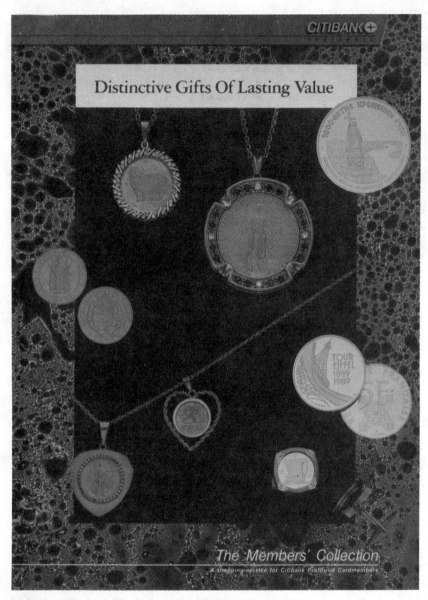

Figure 6–11. Cover of Citibank card special catalog.

Request for Action

One thing you will perceive in mail order is that many prospects are indecisive. Many are simply procrastinators. They want to act, but it's too much trouble to do it now, or they still have a lingering doubt and they need time to allow the notion to mature and take hold. Some will get around to ordering eventually. (You will get orders resulting from offers you made two or three years earlier and had long forgotten, a well-known phenomenon that the late Joe Karbo referred to as the "drag.") Many others will never get around to it. Some simply cannot make decisions unless they are led, goaded, or ordered to make them. Others are almost totally without initiative: They are simply unable to act without specific directions. If you have been in mail order for a time you already know this. If you have not, you may have some trouble believing this, but experience will educate you!

Because of the indecision and procrastination of prospects, it is necessary to "ask for action"—that is, to instruct the customer in the steps you want him or her to take in giving you the order—in effect, asking for the order. Examples you will probably recognize or can easily find by reading print advertisements (see Figure 6-10) are along the following lines:

> Simply fill out the order below, recording your credit-card number or enclosing your check or money order, and mail it TODAY in the enclosed postage-paid envelope.

> Call the toll free number below, and order your FREE SAMPLE issue TODAY. This offer is for a LIMITED TIME ONLY, so act immediately.

> Send the enclosed *special bonus certificate* in today, with your order, and qualify for your FREE GIFT and special drawing for the big prize, a trip to Hawaii for two.

Note that each of these is an *imperative*, issuing direct instructions to the customer. Copy that fails to do this pays for the omission in many missed orders. An amazingly large number of people will not act unless literally *ordered* to do so and instructed step-by-step. (Surprisingly, this is as true with well-educated "upscale" prospects as it is with others.) Other important factors must be considered when asking for action:

- Urgency
- Ease
- Clarity

Urgency.   Try to impart a sense of urgency, a need to act immediately. More people than you might imagine tend to procrastinate. They intend to order, but it is not convenient to do so at the moment, which means that it may never happen. It helps to combat this unfortunate tendency to postpone action if you furnish a special reason for acting promptly. That is why you see so many ACT NOW, LIMITED OFFER, and THIS WEEK ONLY exhortations in advertising and sales copy.

Ease.   Make it as easy as possible for the customer to do what you ask. Furnish clear, easy-to-fill-out forms and an addressed, postage-paid card or envelope. Arrange to accept as many credit cards as possible, and encourage their use. Make all forms as simple as you can, using check-off items, rather than write-in items, and otherwise making the ordering process as painless as possible for the customer.

Clarity.   Be highly specific in your instructions. Subtlety has no place here. Tell the customer *exactly*, not approximately, what to do. Provide very clear instructions.

All of these steps help urge the customer into action, but to reach this point, you must have effectively provided the main elements, proof and promise.

PROOF AND PROMISE: THE HEART OF PERSUASIVE COPY

Reduced to its essence (the need to ask for action notwithstanding), the two most critical steps in the selling process are these:

1. Make the ***promise***, which will then get attention, arouse interest, and generate desire to believe the promise. (Ideally, summarize it in the headline, but at least introduce it there and then complete the thought in a subhead or blurb following immediately.

2. Provide the ***proof***, or evidence that will enable the reader to believe the promise and thus justify the decision to buy.

Actually, if the promise was appealing enough, or the customer wanted to believe it earnestly enough, the decision to buy may have been made even before the proof is offered. However, the customer almost surely would still not have bought because most people have a degree of caution. It may be simply a need on the part of the customer to rationalize a buying decision, but you must furnish help in making that rationalization.

WHAT CONSTITUTES PROOF, AND WHAT CREATES CREDIBILITY?

The point was made earlier that proof is whatever the customer will accept as proof; it is the customer and only the customer who must be convinced. The word *proof* is therefore rather a loose and flexible term as used here. And the proof may not always be direct; it can be indirect, as in the case of arguments and material used to build credibility.

Credibility is an important characteristic. The customer must have faith in your integrity, in your honesty. Major firms, such as Sears, Montgomery Ward, and Spiegel, are well known and have little problem with credibility; most customers accept them as responsible and honest firms, simply because they are so well known and have been in existence for so long a time. Little-known firms have a different problem: They must provide evidence of their reliability and honesty so that their claims have a degree of credibility with the average customer. This is, in a sense, a subset of what is referred to here as proof, but it must be borne in mind as a necessary ingredient of an image that supports marketing success.

Some kinds of organizations, such as banks, have a certain inherent credibility: Most people tend to think of the bank as the epitome of propriety and integrity. So the bank need not do much more than provide the symbols that convey and reinforce that impression. Citibank, certainly a well-known and major player in banking, issues gold credit cards they identify as *Citibank Preferred,* and in a recent mailing to holders of those cards, they offered a catalog listing "The Members Collection" to their "members," noting that it offers "A shopping service to Citibank Preferred Cardmembers." (See Figure 6-11.) The collection is of American Eagle 22 karat gold coins and gold accessories of various kinds. The brochure is quiet and in good taste, of course, as befits a prestigious banking institution, and it is in full color.

Other catalogers, ordinary merchants, are less fortunate, and their integrity is not automatically accepted. They must work at achieving credibility in their various sales presentations, using such devices as the following to generate an image of credibility and furnish proofs to customers:

- Photographs

- Samples of the product
- Logical argument
- Testimonials
- Guarantees
- Claims of widespread acceptance
- Repeated mailings
- Wise choice of trade name

Photographs

Photographs can be used to support promises and claims in a number of ways. "Before" and "after" photos showing actual weight reduction achieved by users are effective in diet and weight-loss programs. Photos of physical facilities— exterior views of plants, interior views of laboratories and platoons of workers, views of special equipment, and other such photographs—convey the impression of qualifications and of well-established bases of operations. Hence, such photographs generate credibility generally, as well as support the validity of specific promises.

Samples of the Products

It is possible to provide samples of many products. I received a catalog of greeting cards this morning (The Windsor Collection, Sunshine Art Studios of Springfield, Massachusetts), with both photographs and actual samples bound into the catalog. Other printed products (e.g., labels, forms, cards, and stationery) are easy to furnish as samples. (I get many samples of such items from Quill® Corporation and others.) Perfume scents are added to printing inks to create "scratch and sniff" pages. Computer disks may be enclosed, as may inexpensive phonograph records. (They are still used, despite the audiotape and compact disk trend.)

Logical Argument

Logical argument is used widely and is effective in many cases, even if the logic is less than flawless. Sometimes, simply explaining the process that produces the product is itself a logical or, at least, a logical-sounding argument. Sometimes, the argument is that the product (or the company) has been in existence for some large number of years, which presumably is a testimonial to excellence. The guarantees offered, the large quantity already sold, and other such items may also be used as logical support for the promise.

Testimonials

There are three basic types of testimonials or endorsements: (1) Those of ordinary customers who are satisfied users willing to recommend the product to others, (2) those of well-known public figures, and (3) those of authorities or apparent authorities. For example, selling a health product may be enhanced by using the photograph and statement of a working physician, biochemist, or other professional with suitable credentials. (The credentials must be stated.) Some advertisers, however, use an actor who is dressed as and appears to be a physician or other professional authority (e.g., in a white jacket or smock, perhaps in a laboratory or other supporting environment). For some products, a testimonial or endorsement by a well-known sports or entertainment figure may be useful to establish your credibility and to reassure your customers. Give some thought to the type of testimonial or endorsement most likely to persuade those to whom you address your offers.

Guarantees

Many customers find boldly stated guarantees reassuring and will accept these as proof, on the assumption that you would not make the guarantee if you had doubts about your ability to deliver what you promise. That is a kind of logical argument in itself, and having made the guarantee you may wish to point that out, as many advertisers do. Modern statutes affecting mail order, policed by the Federal Trade Commission, provide automatic guarantees to the customer anyway (especially to those using credit cards), so you have little to lose by trumpeting the terms of a guarantee that you are required by law to make, whether you advertise it or not!

Claims of Widespread Acceptance

Use the track record of your sales to advantage. There are various ways to do so. Find the most favorable or most impressive set of numbers—number of years in business, number of customers, volume of sales, low incidence of returns, or other. If you are too new in business to have such numbers, use the numbers of those whose products you sell. (In fact, many manufacturers will gladly furnish you advertising materials and information.) Numbers are always good evidence; readers tend to accept them as proofs.

Repeated Mailings

Simply being in business for a while helps to build credibility. That is why many firms proclaim the many years since they were founded. In fact, one reason the major catalog houses have little problems with credibility is that they have been in business for a long time and are consequently very well known. Many people believe firmly that it is much smarter to buy a "name brand" than any competing product, regardless of price or other considerations. Familiarity offers reassurance and builds credibility.

The assurance that comes from familiarity is one reason that mailing repeatedly to the same list tends to produce better results with each mailing until it peaks, probably about the fourth or fifth time, on the average. On the first mailing, you are an unknown quantity, and it is quite easy to discard your literature summarily. The second time the recipient gets your literature—provided you have not permitted too much time to elapse since the first mailing (probably not more than a week or two)—it is slightly familiar, enough to reinforce the slight impact of the first mailing. By the third, fourth, or other repeat mailing, the reader is not sure that you are new and unknown. A surprisingly large number of recipients come to believe by this time that you are an old and familiar firm, and they begin to study your offers much more seriously!

One cataloger I knew made it a practice to mail to each new list once a week for four weeks, then once a month until he felt that response had peaked.

Wise Choice of Trade Name

The name you assign to your firm is not unimportant. It is probably a mistake to use your personal name, unless yours is already a well-known name that will help. Otherwise, it is simply an exercise in vanity and a wasted opportunity. Of course, Spiegel, Sears, and Montgomery Ward, among others, tend to disprove this, but they were pioneers, creating a new industry, whereas you are a fledgling trying to break into the highly competitive field that they dominate. Why add handicaps to your task? Or, conversely, why not take advantage of every angle you can employ?

It is also a mistake to select a lengthy and grandiose name. To some knowledgeable cynics, that is a giveaway that yours is a tiny venture trying to impress people. The great ones can afford to be modest, and it may pay you to emulate them.

It is still another mistake to select a cryptic or humorous name. One new cataloger named his firm PDN, which stands for "Pretty Darn Nice," he says. The initials are meaningless to customers, and if you reveal the jest and tell customers what the initials mean, you are confessing newness and implying frivolity, rather than serious business.

It is best if your business name makes a statement. "GE" stands for General Electric, and that, in its day, was a statement. "RCA" was the set of initials for the Radio Corporation of America, which also said something. "IBM" is for International Business Machines, a statement that has been heard around the world. And "GM" is General Motors, of course, the largest of American automobile manufacturers.

Something interesting happens when you choose a logical, conservative name that makes a statement, no matter how simple and straightforward. It does something for your image. In my own case, when I set up the first of my corporations, I named it Government Marketing News, Inc., with the acronym GMNI. That was a simple name that made a statement. A strange thing happened: An incredibly large number of people who received my literature were sure that they had "heard of" Government Marketing News and *knew the name well*! The name simply had that quality: It was as unpretentious as are the names of some of the largest corporations in the country, and it was a *logical* name, so logical that people hearing of it could not believe that it had not long existed. So they persuaded themselves to believe that it was a long-established name they knew quite well. From the beginning, credibility was never a problem for Government Marketing News, Inc.

Of course, that kind of reception and reaction can be a great aid to you, helping you create the right image and saving you both time and money in building credibility and a customer list. You would therefore probably do well to avoid using an overblown business name. Seek an unassuming and reasonably conservative business name that somehow summarizes or at least suggests what your business is all about in a quiet, simple, and straightforward manner. (Simplicity exudes confidence, whereas brash names suggest feverish need for attention.)

HOW MUCH PROOF IS NEEDED?

Aside from the question of what is proof, there is the equally important matter of how much proof is necessary to sway customers and persuade them to place their orders. It's a true concern, for it varies along with or in response to at least two main parameters: the price tag and the promise.

Price Tag as a Factor

The average customer is not going to ponder long or agonize over a decision to buy a $5 or $10 item. Many people will spend that much merely to satisfy curiosity or to enjoy a transient amusement, such as a witty bumper sticker or a greeting card. Therefore, you do not need to make a very elaborate promise or drag in a ton of proof to close that sale. However, a sale that involves thousands, or even hundreds of dollars is another matter: The average customer does not spend that amount of money frivolously. Without question, the size of the purchase is one determinant of how much proof is needed: the larger the price tag, the greater or more convincing the proof must be.

Credibility of the Promise as a Factor

Another factor is equally critical: the nature of the promise—how credible/ incredible the promise is. If I promise you that I can guide you to sound investments that will reward you with 10 percent of your investment in dividends each year without great risk, you probably will not have a great deal of difficulty in accepting this, as long as you can find the backup data reasonable. However, if I promise you investment guidance that is risk-free and will return 25 percent each year, you probably grow immediately skeptical. You assume at once that (a) I am deliberately stretching the facts to the breaking point in my anxiety to win your investment, b) I am a fool who doesn't know how risky an investment of that sort must be, or c) I am a charlatan trying to take you in with an obvious fraud. In short, you require a great deal of proof before you can even take my offer seriously, much less believe my promise.

One thing that aids me is your natural wish to believe in a risk-free investment that pays 25 percent. You may even wish so much to believe in it that your judgment is clouded. If I help you enough, you may try to believe in it. You may even rationalize as much as you can to try to put your doubts aside and persuade yourself to let your fondest hopes overcome your good sense.

The preceding example is a bit extreme, of course; I certainly do not intend to commit a fraud. Nonetheless, it does illustrate that the more elaborate or extreme the promise, the harder it is to accept it and, therefore, the more persuasive the proof must be.

Thus, there is an inevitable trade-off between promise and proof, as there is between price and proof. You have only limited control over price, but you do have control over the promise. You may find it possible to make quite a startling promise and still be telling the truth, but that may not be good business, for it makes it more difficult to present satisfactory proof. In fact, if the promise is extreme enough, customers may not "buy it," no matter how true it is. It may be better in the end to tone down the promise, therefore.

A FEW FACTS AND MYTHS ABOUT COPY

There are many widespread myths about copy writing that ought to be debunked immediately. (In fact, some of the myths contradict other ones!) Here are some of the common myths:

Myth: People will not read solid text. They want to see lots of white space, short sentences, short paragraphs, and frequent paragraphing.

Fact: People will read whatever they find interesting, especially when they see it as affecting their direct interests. Many full-page, solid-text advertisements have been wildly successful. The late Joe Karbo ran his full-page advertisement, "The Lazy Man's Way to Riches," and pulled over $6 million in orders; it earned millions and is still earning in a slightly modified form. (It set a new standard for such advertising, widely imitated today.)

Karbo's was only one of many such advertisements that succeeded, and it succeeded for a simple reason: Everyone would like to be rich, and readers could not help but read all of the copy, despite their common sense cautioning them that there is no easy way to succeed. Moral: Capture the reader's interest, and you won't need a hatful of tricks and gimmicks; you won't be able to stop the prospect from reading every word.

Myth: People will not read long copy. Their attention spans are too short.

Fact: A mail-order platitude (and a truism) opposes this myth: "The more you tell, the more you sell." Short copy may do the job for inexpensive items; it won't do the job for the more costly items. In any case, tests have shown rather clearly that longer copy invariably improves results. People will read whatever appears to be in their own interests to read—whatever "strikes a nerve"—whether it is long or short, as pointed out in regard go the previous myth. If they find the subject truly of great importance to them, they will actually want long copy because they want to know more about the subject. For example, when one of my early mailings produced disappointing results, I did not change what I was using, but I added to it. I was using a letter and simple brochure. I added a second brochure, offering more information and additional sales arguments, and the response almost doubled.

Myth: It is essential today to offer elaborate guarantees and display the guarantee boldly to be sure the customer is fully conscious of it.

Fact: There is no evidence that this is so. Making the guarantee too prominent a feature in the mailing may be a negative factor, suggesting an inferior or unreliable product. Offer the guarantee, but don't make a major production of it—don't let the guarantee dominate the copy. You are selling a product, not a guarantee.

Myth: You must have a "response device"—an order form and return envelope.

Fact: Not always. These are probably definite assets in business-to-consumer cataloging but of far less importance in business-to-business cataloging, where the customer has full office facilities at hand.

WHAT ARE YOU REALLY SELLING?

Benefits

In presenting seminars, I often start by asking a number of attendees what business they are in. The answers are always enlightening. Here are some typical ones:

> "I am a computer consultant."
> "We sell high-tech equipment."
> "We provide custom training services."
> "I am a security specialist"
> "We are in electronics R&D and manufacturing."
> "We sell management services."
> "We do surveys and polls."

The emphasis and orientation is almost always on "I," "us," or "we"— what "I" or "we" do, offer to do, sell, or offer to sell. It is almost never on what the customer wants or gets—what "I" or "we" *do* for the customer. That orientation is at the heart of what is wrong.

Sometimes, I follow up by asking a pertinent question; "What do you *do* for your customers?" or "What does your customer get out of it?" I am, of course, trying to provoke listeners into viewing the situation from the customer's viewpoint because what anyone really sells is the benefit to the customer. The customer does not buy aspirin or antacid tablets; he or she buys relief from physical discomfort or pain. Consider the thrust of Alka Seltzer TV commercials for an excellent example of selling the benefit: The advertising is invariably based on what the product does to relieve suffering. Alka Seltzer is only one of many examples, for all effective advertising and selling does that. The alleged benefit of drinking the advertiser's beer is good fellowship and fun, as the typical beer commercial shows. The benefit of a cosmetic is the enhancement or even the acquisition of sex appeal. The benefit of a dishwasher detergent is the enjoyment of others' approbation and envy.

Even selling against direct competition, you sell your service or product as a *better way* of achieving the benefit—more of the benefit, more effective delivery of the benefit, more dependable delivery of the benefit, or other such improvement vis-à-vis the promised benefit. Talk of better quality is usually either an afterthought or supporting copy, for rarely is the pursuit of greater quality the primary motivator, much as we try (as customers) to rationalize our motivations in buying. (We humans, all of us, hate to admit even to ourselves that we are less than totally rational.)

Something More Than Benefits: The Promise

However, even the benefit is not what sellers really sell. In the final analysis, businesses do not sell the benefit either; businesses sell the *promise* of the benefit! All advertising is based on the promises it makes, even at the point of sale where the customer can see, touch, feel, and smell the product, for only by owning it can the customer hope to enjoy the benefit promised. Until then, the customer is buying the promise. In fact, when a salesperson presents an excuse or an argument to a customer and privately comments colloquially, "I think he bought it," or the reverse, "I don't think he bought it," the colloquialism is particularly appropriate!

7

The Important and Necessary Elements in the Mailing

Catalog sales is primarily a mail-order business, although cataloging is a rather special area of mail order. It therefore is wise to review the verities of the mail-order business for basic how-to guidance.

DIRECT MAIL: BASIC EXAMPLES

Five sheets of 20-pound paper in a standard-sized business envelope (a number 10 envelope) weighs about one ounce, and may be mailed in a first-class envelope for the same cost as mailing a single sheet of paper in that envelope. With the high cost of postage today, it is usually wasteful to mail less than the maximum allowed. The same philosophy applies, of course, to other classes of mail because all are based on weight. Another factor encouraging the enclosure of the maximum amount of sales material is the mail-order platitude, "The more you tell, the more you sell."

In any case, it is generally considered that a direct-mail package must include at least four basic items: a sales letter, a brochure, an order form, and a return envelope. That is theory. In practice, the content of a direct-mail package varies a great deal. The typical package often includes far more than those four items. It often includes more than one brochure, a circular or two, and even special sales devices, such as contest or prize offers, plastic cards, advertising novelties, and one of those little folded notes that says something along the lines of "Do not read this unless you have decided not to order." As noted in a previous chapter, copy on the outside of the envelope is also often included as an element of the sales effort. A quick look at a few typical direct-mail packages offers a sampling of the variety being distributed.

A direct-mail package from Worldwide Bargain Hunters, of Holland, Michigan, furnishes a good example. (This firm sells information on surplus, imports, closeouts, and other sources of goods at what are purported to be bargain prices.) The package includes a two-page sales letter, three circulars, an order form, and a return envelope. The sales letter is a bit different from most such sales letters. Where most are printed in what appears to have been a typed original, with many handwritten underlines, exclamation marks, and marginal comments, this is definitely typeset in a rather small type (not larger than 8 points—the size used for footnotes in textbooks) and printed in black and red ink on an inexpensive white offset lightweight paper. In fact, it is really only a one-page letter because the first side is a letter, addressed "Dear Friend," with a signature, but the second side is more sales argument, technically not part of the letter itself.

The other circulars are printed in black ink on lightweight colored papers, one yellow, one blue, and one green. Each side of two of the circulars makes a different offer, with an order form imprinted on each side. There are, in fact, six order forms included in the mailing, only one of which is a separate element. The separate order form can be used for buying the whole package—all the items offered in all of the circulars.

In all, this is a package that is quite inexpensive to prepare: Both sides of ordinary lightweight letter-sized sheets of offset paper are used for the simplest kind of printing, with no binding expense, and a colored ink is used on only the sales letter. In fact, this package violates some of the "rules" others insist must be followed. Yet this firm has been doing this for many years (at least 15 to 20 years that I can personally recall), so it is obviously successful. (The right rules are whatever works for you.)

From well-known Rand McNally & Company of Skokie, Illinois comes a direct-mail package of quite another stamp: It is in an oversize (6" x 9") window envelope with ample envelope copy: "Finally Revealed: The True Picture of 5-Digit Zip Codes Throughout America!" In the envelope are four pieces: a two-page sales letter, a slick multicolor brochure, an order form ("$25.00 Introductory Savings Certificate"), and a postage-paid return envelope.

The sales letter is addressed "Dear Executive," appears to have been typed rather than typeset, and is printed in black ink with blue ink underlines of certain words and phrases. It is not nearly as "noisy" as many I have seen, but is relatively quiet and dignified. It is printed on both sides of a single sheet of heavy offset paper, and it is signed by a vice president of the company.

The brochure is expensive. It is printed on glossy—calendered or enameled—paper, in several colors, and it includes an acetate transparency to use as an overlay on an illustration, which demonstrates the product offered. The transparency, too, is an expensive item to include.

A package from Anka Company, jewelry wholesalers of Warwick, Rhode Island, is still another matter. It arrived in a 6" x 9" manila envelope with some envelope copy, but without a letter. Instead, it has a four-page set of instructions for customers (who are prospective dealers in the Anka line), a four-page price list and order form, and two full-color catalogs. (Color is essential, in this case, due to the nature of the products.) The envelope says "Information You Requested Is Enclosed," a common enough statement on the outside of envelopes that are sent in response to inquiries generated by advertising in the media. The envelope reveals that it was mailed via bulk mail, which accounts for the delay that often occurs before you get information you have requested after reading an advertisement: The sellers must have a certain minimum amount of mail before they can use bulk mail and reduce their postage costs, and so they wait until enough inquiries have been accumulated before they respond to them.

The newest mailing from SMC (Specialty Merchandise Corporation of Chatsworth, California) is hard-hitting. This is the fourth or fifth package of literature I have received from them over the past few months. Each package has been different, and it is quite obvious that SMC believes in perseverance and understands the benefit of repeat mailings in a regular series. This newest package includes the classic elements, but on a somewhat exaggerated scale, and so it is different in that respect: Few mail-order packages I have seen are quite that busy, "loud," and aggressive.

This one is in a 9" x 12" window envelope, covered with copy on the front and back, with lots of red and black ink, several typefaces, all large and bold, and a generous number of exclamation marks. In fact, there is little white space to be seen on this unusual envelope, which was probably designed especially for SMC.

The back of the envelope is of special interest here because it suggests a number of ways and orientations by which one may use the SMC catalogs and merchandise to earn profits. It includes in the listing, for example, mail order, wagon jobbing, fund raising, party plans, flea markets, swap meets, retail store sales, advertising specialties, incentives, premiums, rack merchandising, and subwholesaling, which is presumably a kind of multilevel marketing.

An unusual element in this package is a 12-page tabloid titled *The Specialty Wholesaler*, with many arguments and reports supporting the SMC concept, an order form, a separate "certificate" offering full credit for the membership initiation fee when a certain sales volume is reached, and the usual postage-paid return envelope.

The sales letter in this package is based on the customary direct-mail model, with many handwritten notes, comments, and punctuation marks in blue ink. It also has the almost obligatory (for this kind of approach) postscript, once again urging action. The envelope and the letter are almost hysterical in the "noise" they make. Altogether, this is quite a package, quite expensive, I would judge, and probably highly successful.

THE SALES LETTER

The centerpiece or main element of the typical direct-mail package is the sales letter. Sales arguments are presented in other pieces—brochures, circulars, envelope copy, and elsewhere—but the main forum for selling, and the focal point of the entire presentation is typically the sales letter. It is here that the seller speaks directly to the prospective customer, addressing him or her as "Dear friend," or by some other personal term. Here is where so many adopt an apparently sincere tone (e.g., "If I had a brother, I would give him this same advice," or "You owe this to your family, but you owe it to yourself too"). Others are more objective or matter of fact: "This is a $111 billion market. You don't need to capture more than a a tiny fraction of 1 percent of this market to begin making a great deal of money." Or "Don't take my word for it. Just read the letters enclosed of those who are grateful that they discovered this in time and are writing to thank us."

I know of no good evidence that one approach works better than the other. The evidence is that there are many approaches that work. (There are usually many ways to achieve any end.) That means to me that you start by selecting the approach that is most comfortable for you and that appears to best suit your product and your prospective customers. Use and test that approach, but use and test others also. Test them, and see which works best for you. In the end, I think, you must make your own rules, based on your own experience.

An example or two of such sales letters may help you. Figure 7–1 is one example. Its basic appeal is to the urgent desire of so many to be successful freelance writers. (This assumes that the mailing went out to a list of individuals

HRH COMMUNICATIONS, INC.
P.O. Box 1731   Wheaton, MD 20902
Fax: (301) 649-5745   Voice: (301) 649-2499

BECOME THE WRITER YOU DREAMED OF BEING
WITH THE NEW AJAX WORD PROCESSOR

<u>It's an investment in your future!</u>

The new Ajax word processor was designed especially for professional writers. It's a platitude but still true that good writing is rewriting. Even the masters produced their best work by revisions. The Ajax word processor was therefore designed to make revision easier than it has ever been before, easier than with any other word processor on the market today. That is why the Ajax word processor is more than a convenience to today's serious writers; <u>it is an absolute necessity.</u>

It's simple: With the Ajax word processor, it is so easy to rewrite that rewriting becomes almost a pleasure. (In fact, it *is* a pleasure for writers who caress words lovingly, as William James did.) The difference will show up in the results—<u>in responses from delighted editors</u>.

There is also the matter of simple efficiency. You can turn out <u>much more work every day</u> when you are using this superfast new system.

Writers are only as good as their tools. You know you cannot send in a handwritten manuscript and expect it to be read or taken seriously. Only neatly typed manuscripts can hope to vie for an editor's attention. But "neatly typed" today does not mean something typed on a battered old portable. That will not fare much better today than one written with a quill pen. Image counts, and the image of success today is the word processor.

Best of all, the new Ajax word processor can be yours for only $69.50 per month, and it will earn far more than that for you every month, as you turn out your articles, short stories, fillers, and whatever else you want to write.

We are so eager to have you try this fantastic new system, with its fabulous price breakthrough, that we offer all the following <u>if you order within 10 days:</u>

FREE INSTALLATION AND TRAINING: Our representative will come out with your new Ajax to install it and train you.

FREE TRIAL: Use for 30 days <u>at our cost</u> and return it <u>at our cost</u> if you are not delighted.

FREE GIFT, just for <u>trying</u> the Ajax: Desk set—handsome mahogany and onyx stand with pen and pencil set and digital clock. Yours to keep <u>even if you return the Ajax!</u> Value: $45.

Figure 7-1. First page of typical sales letter.

who had expressed such an interest, perhaps the subscription list of a writer's magazine.)

Note that there is no salutation, such as "Dear friend," here. The omission is deliberate. My own experience suggests to me that the salutation contributes nothing to the letter, and so I prefer to omit it in most cases.

This is another case of conventional wisdom being accepted without question. I could perceive no difference in response between sales letters bearing a salutation and those without it, and I have occasionally run across articles in which others have expressed the same conviction. On the other hand, I do believe in using a headline, with or without a subhead or blurb and with or without a direct salutation.

As an example of the "sincere" approach, consider the sales letter offered as Figure 7–2. Here, for comparison, a salutation is used. Note how that sincere tone is achieved in this case by the "in group" or familial appeal of such terms as *fellow writer* both in the salutation and in the body of the letter. Everyone, apparently, wants to belong, and this is reassuring to those aspiring writers who are struggling for a foothold in the writing profession or trying to improve the foothold they have already gained. The author of this letter knows exactly to whom he or she is speaking, and has fashioned the appeal accordingly.

The specificity of the letter in Figure 7–2 points up something: Don't make the beginner's typical mistake of trying to be all things to all people. It simply doesn't work. Confine your appeal to that special interest that is important to your reader. The argument or appeal in this letter would probably fall flat if presented to well-established, successful writers, whose concerns are probably earning more money with less effort. You need a different approach and a different sales argument for them, possibly one that promises a great improvement in productivity with the product. That headline might be along this line:

HOW TO BOOST YOUR INCOME OVER 30 PERCENT!

Try the new Ajax word processor for 10 days.
Return it if it does not increase your productivity by at least that much.

Frankly, I am unconvinced that all those interlined and handwritten interjections, frantic punctuation, and other excited demands for attention make a positive difference in the final result. In fact, I am not at all sure that even if they do make some difference that the differences are beneficial ones: Copy marked up in this manner is the mail-order version of high-pressure selling, and

HRH COMMUNICATIONS, INC.
P.O. Box 1731   Wheaton, MD 20902
Fax: (301) 649-5745   Voice: (301) 649-2499

IT'S HERE AT LAST! THE OPEN SESAME TO WRITING SUCCESS!

The ultimate writer's tool is now yours.

Dear fellow writer::

I want to share the good news with all other professional writers: It is my absolute delight to tell you that the Ajax word processor is finally here!

We writers have waited a long time for this superb writing tool. Believe me when I tell you that no one has been more impatient in waiting for this day or is more excited than I to make this important announcement. I can tell you that I personally oversaw every test and tryout, insisted on every improvement and refinement in this word processor that was designed especially for the professional, creative writer. It is as different from all other word processors as a Picasso is different from a political cartoon. This is the word processor for the true professional.

It's a platitude but still true that good writing is rewriting. Even the masters produced their best work by revisions. That's why I insisted that the Ajax be designed to make revision easier than ever before. That is why the Ajax is more than a convenience; it is an absolute necessity. The difference will show up in the results—in responses from delighted editors.

There is also the matter of simple efficiency. You can turn out much more work every day when you are using this superfast new system.

The new Ajax word processor can be yours for only $69.50 per month, and it will earn far more than that for you every month, as you turn out your articles, short stories, fillers, and whatever else you want to write.

We are so eager to have you try this fantastic new system, with its fabulous price breakthrough, that we offer all the following if you order within 10 days:

FREE INSTALLATION AND TRAINING: Our representative will come out with your new Ajax to install it and train you.

FREE TRIAL: Use for 30 days at our cost and return it at our cost if you are not delighted.

FREE GIFT, just for trying the Ajax: Desk set—handsome mahogany and onyx stand with pen and pencil set and digital clock. Yours to keep even if you return the Ajax! Value: $45.

Figure 7-2. A "sincere" sales letter.

that kind of selling turns some prospects off completely, killing any chance of a sale. I cannot help but feel that such devices reveal only the lack of a good sales argument, the failure of the marketer to use some imagination and, even more important, to be introspective and insightful enough to reason out the reader's true concerns, desires, and worries. Hence, the eager effort substitutes blue smoke and mirrors for a proper sales presentation. When you examine sales letters that engage in that sort of agitated arm-waving, you often find that the sales arguments are too weak to stand on their own. They simply are not strong appeals to the readers' interests.

In the two cases represented here by the two figures, the arguments are probably powerful enough to stand on their own, to do without the gimmicks. Look at the two of them in Figures 7–3 and 7–4, with the gimmicks eliminated and the handwritten comments simply incorporated into the copy. Read them and try to visualize their impact on the readers to whom the copy is addressed—aspiring and hopeful writers.

Because word processors and their printers are in such common use today, with all their versatility, it is no longer necessary to use underlines exclusively to simulate typewriter copy. You can now also use oversize type, italics (which used to be represented by underlining), boldface, and other devices to emphasize key points without losing the impression of spontaneity, as represented in the two figures. It is time, I believe, to take full advantage of what the new technology has brought us and to modernize old ways.

Not every sincere letter is of the tearful "if I had a brother" type, with superlatives and other assorted hype. Some are of what we might call the "quietly sincere" variety. One letter that comes in a package from Jack Hurshman Advertising of San Francisco exemplifies that type. His quiet letter begins with a simple headline: *Let Us Show You How to Get **Better Results** From Your Advertising.* The rest of the letter is in the same tone, pointing to 30 years of successful experience and service to clients, with a simple, dignified exhortation to investigate what the agency can do for the reader.

There are just three other elements in the package: A one-sheet flyer with an order form offering advertising in *The New York Times*, another flyer with its own order form offering a special deal on inquiry advertising, and a 3" x 9" brochure explaining the advertising services offered.

Some catalogers bind their sales letter into the catalog itself, as in Figure 7–5. This is the inside of the cover of a catalog titled *Books to Help Your Business.* Listed in the catalog thus introduced are page after page of books for businesspeople. The back cover sums up the message by saying "This Catalog Will Help You Attain SUCCESS . . . MONEY . . . KNOWLEDGE."

BECOME THE WRITER *YOU DREAMED OF BEING*
WITH THE NEW AJAX WORD PROCESSOR

It's an investment in your future! Make it all come true now!

The new Ajax word processor was designed especially for professional writers. It's a platitude but still true that good writing is rewriting. Even the masters produced their best work by revisions. The Ajax word processor was therefore designed to make revision easier than it has ever been before, easier than with any other word processor on the market today. That is why the Ajax word processor is more than a convenience to today's serious writers; **it is an absolute necessity.**

It's simple: With the Ajax word processor, it is so easy to rewrite that rewriting becomes almost a pleasure. (In fact, it <u>is</u> a pleasure for writers who caress words lovingly, as William James did.) The difference will show up in the results—<u>in responses from delighted editors.</u>

There is also the matter of simple efficiency. You can turn out <u>much more work every day</u> when you are using this superfast new system.

Writers are only as good as their tools. You know you cannot send in a handwritten manuscript and expect it to be read or taken seriously. Only neatly typed manuscripts can hope to vie for an editor's attention. But "neatly typed" today does not mean something typed on a battered old portable. That will not fare much better today than one written with a quill pen. Image counts, and the image of success today is the word processor.

Best of all, the new Ajax word processor can be yours for only $69.50 per month, and it will earn far more than that for you every month, as you turn out your articles, short stories, fillers, and whatever else you want to write.

THIS IS A GOLDEN OPPORTUNITY. DON'T MISS IT!

We are so eager to have you try this fantastic new system, with its fabulous price breakthrough, that we offer all the following **if you order within 10 days**:

FREE INSTALLATION AND TRAINING: Our representative will come out with your new Ajax to install it and train you.

FREE TRIAL: Use for 30 days <u>at our cost</u> and return it <u>at our cost</u> if you are not delighted.

FREE GIFT, just for <u>trying</u> the Ajax: Desk set—handsome mahogany and onyx stand with pen and pencil set and digital clock. Yours to keep <u>even if you return the Ajax!</u> Value: $45.

Figure 7-3. First page of "straight" sales letter.

HRH COMMUNICATIONS, INC.
P.O. Box 1731   Wheaton, MD 20902
Fax: (301) 649-5745   Voice: (301) 649-2499

IT'S HERE AT LAST! THE OPEN SESAME TO WRITING SUCCESS!

The ultimate writer's tool is now yours.
Now you can make it all happen!

Dear fellow writer::

I want to share the good news with all other professional writers: It is my absolute delight to tell you that *the Ajax word processor is finally here!*

We writers have waited a long time for this superb writing tool. Believe me when I tell you that no one has been more impatient in waiting for this day or is more excited than I to make this important announcement. I can tell you that I personally oversaw every test and tryout, insisted on every improvement and refinement in this word processor that was **designed especially for the professional, creative writer. It is as different from all other word processors as a Picasso is different from a political cartoon.** This is the word processor for the true professional.

It's a platitude but still true that good writing is rewriting. Even the masters produced their best work by revisions. That's why I insisted that the Ajax be designed to make revision easier than ever before. That is why the Ajax is more than a convenience; **it is an absolute necessity. The difference will show up in the results—in responses from delighted editors.**

There is also the matter of simple efficiency. You can turn out *much more work every day* when you are using this superfast new system.

The new Ajax word processor can be yours for only $69.50 per month, and it will earn far more than that for you every month, as you turn out your articles, short stories, fillers, and whatever else you want to write.

YOU MUST ACT NOW.

We are so eager to have you try this fantastic new system, with its fabulous price breakthrough, that we offer all the following *if you order within 10 days*:

FREE INSTALLATION AND TRAINING: Our representative will come out with your new Ajax to install it and train you.

FREE TRIAL: Use for 30 days *at our cost* and return it *at our cost if you are not delighted.*

FREE GIFT, just for *trying* the Ajax: Desk set—handsome mahogany and onyx stand with pen and pencil set and digital clock. Yours to keep *even if you return the Ajax!* Value: $45.

Figure 7-4. Another "sincere" letter.

Forum Publishing Company

383 East Main Street • Centerport, New York 11721
Tel: 516/754-5000 • Fax: 516/754-0630 • Telex: 804294

Success comes to those who learn! Knowledge is power and information is the vital fuel to success. Attaining the valuable resource of information is the single most important challenge to an entrepreneur.

No longer does a fledgling businessperson have to enroll in the school of hard knocks to educate himself. Today, literature is available which makes costly mistakes and indecision obsolete. A novice has the rare opportunity to peek into the brain of business giants and grasp concepts that took lifetimes to accrue.

With all the business and finance books on the market, it is difficult and sometimes confusing to find the information your particular business requires. FORUM PUBLISHING, a leader in the field of business literature, has done the work for you. We chose for our catalog only the most valuable, up-to-date and reputable publications from the hundreds our staff reads yearly.

Whether you are embarking on a new career in the business field or are an old hand at business and finance looking for fresh ideas, FORUM has what you need. Our selections are comprehensive and include a vast array of business directories, legal and tax help, as well as books for just starting out. Our motto: "With books . . . pennies can make you millions". Quite frankly, no one is too successful to pass up that kind of bargain.

Invest in your business library--- it will mold your perspective and your future. When choosing books, periodicals and directories, we hope that you will consider FORUM your key to knowledge.

Private Business Consultation

FORUM PUBLISHING has established a small business consulting service designed to help clients start or expand their businesses. FORUM founder, Martin Stevens, heads this group which provides members with individualized assistance at reasonable fees.
-- *Please call or write for our complimentary prospectus.* --

---

Figure 7–5. Inside cover of a catalog used as a sales letter.

STRATEGIES OF THE DIRECT-MAIL PRESENTATION

Remember always that the sales letter has selling as its main objective; it, like all the other elements in the mailing, is a sales presentation. In the present discussion, the presentation may have any of three immediate purposes, depending on the individual circumstances. The cost of producing catalogs is quite high today, running to several dollars per copy, in many cases, so many catalog sales organizations no longer send them out on an unsolicited, mass basis, where a large portion of them are consigned to the trash heap unopened and so are entirely wasted at great expense to the sender. Many organizations today make a small charge for their catalogs, although many—perhaps most— offer to refund the money by crediting it on the first purchase made. The purpose is not to make money on the catalog, of course, but simply to distinguish between requests from idle curiosity seekers and requests from those who are seriously interested. Even those who do not charge for their catalogs use various means to make that distinction and avoid wasting money on futile mailings of an expensive item. There are several ways to do this, other than charging a dollar or two for the catalog, so that the immediate purpose may be one of these:

1. Inducing respondents to formally request the catalog
2. Inducing respondents to order from the catalog (when the sales letter accompanies the catalog)
3. Inducing the respondent to buy something offered and thereby qualify to get the catalog

Media advertising is often used to stimulate a respondent to make a qualifying purchase. Well-known cataloger Walter Drake, for example, runs many media advertisements offering name-and-address labels at a break-even price as a loss leader to attract new customers. They get the Walter Drake catalog and accompanying sales literature with their labels. Each buyer of labels thus becomes a new lead or prospect to become a Walter Drake catalog customer.

Every sales presentation must have a strategy, some rationale for inducing the reader to do what you ask. The argument must always be presented in terms of what doing so will do for the reader. As some sales trainers observe, good salespeople never sell; they solve problems. Never forget, however, that the reader may not be aware of the problem, so you must usually describe it or explain the problem that you are solving for the reader.

This is entirely aside from such other considerations as price and convenience. Those are secondary arguments. That is, they are arguments for buying from you, rather than from some competitor. Before those arguments are useful, however, the readers must be shown why they should be interested in the purchase to begin with.

The sales letters presented in Figures 7–1 through 7–5 are examples. They promise to help the reader solve the problem of wanting to become a successful writer. They do so by offering to facilitate rewriting, a must for all writers. The strategy is simple: First, the appeal is to the cherished dream of many individuals, to become successful as writers. This copy does *not* make the mistake of sounding like so many other advertisements to help the reader become a success in writing through training and guidance in the mechanics of grammar, rhetoric, and composition; this copy presents an indisputable rationale regarding the need for rewriting, of rewriting as an important key to writing success. Moreover, it promises to eliminate most of the drudgery of rewriting, which is a chore that many writers dread. So the promise is an effective one, and the rationale is one that readers are likely to accept as validation of the promise. Installment terms are offered, and gifts are offered as a bonus for merely trying the product.

Regardless of the brilliant sellership of a sales letter, you cannot sell an expensive product, such as even the smallest and simplest computer, on the strength of a single letter, even one of several pages. In practice, the advertiser would probably devote three or four pages to the letter, presenting many details of the product and more extensive sales arguments for it. Even given a very long sales letter, more—much more—is usually required to sell even moderately priced items, let alone something as expensive as a computer (which is what the lay person is really referring to by the term *word processor,* whether consciously or not). So a brochure is a virtual requirement in direct-mail selling.

BROCHURES

Some people consider the writing of brochures or *brochuremanship,* as some refer to it, a special art. While the lay person refers to almost any literature printed in panels and folded accordingly, others make distinctions among them. Noted and expert copywriter Robert W. Bly, for example, writing in *Create the Perfect Sales Piece* (John Wiley & Sons, 1985) distinguishes carefully between booklets and brochures, pointing out that the *booklet* is merely informative, whereas the *brochure* is a sales piece. More significantly, however, he points out that a brochure is generally written to help sell a single product or product line, but a catalog offers a much wider array of an offeror's products. One might even say that a catalog is an extension of the brochure idea, or the brochure on a grand scale.

If the sales letter is normally the centerpiece or main element in the typical direct-mail promotion, the catalog is the centerpiece or main element in the catalog sales promotion. The sales letter is a great aid in urging the prospect to send for the catalog and in introducing the catalog when it is sent, as well as in encouraging its use, but the orders result from the catalog itself and, in some cases, from the special enclosures and flyers that accompany it.

CATALOG PACKAGING

The catalog of Forum Publishing Co. does not change often and has a simple cover. That stability and simplicity reflects the nature of that venture. At the other end of the spectrum is the Quill catalog, with a major, slick-paper edition published every six months, a monthly catalog, and other special catalog editions. Figure 7–6 presents the cover of one of Quill's regular monthly editions, and it speaks for itself. The nature of the highly competitive office and industrial supplies business is reflected by the copy shown. Note the guidance to an index provided in a small box in the lower right corner of the cover.

Each month, Quill's catalog carries a column called *Quill Business Tips*, offering the reader useful suggestions to use in business, and the business is supported also by a monthly newsletter that goes out under separate cover with a large number of full-color brochures. Quill is obviously mail-order oriented and is dedicated to heavy use of direct mail.

For many businesses, and especially for many catalogers, the perpetual sale is a way of life. The special sale items illustrated on the front page of Quill's catalog of Figure 7–6 is only a sampling: Every one of the 64 pages of this heavily illustrated catalog offers sales and bargains. At the least, all items are shown priced "as low as," with a reduced price based on ordering some quantity required to qualify for the lowest price, as shown in Figure 7–7.

This is a bit different than selling special items, such as computers, furniture, and fax machines. (Quill sells some of these kinds of items, too.) Most office supplies are consumables and are standardized items that are readily available from many sources, so the focus must be on reasons to buy these items from Quill and not some other supplier. The reasons are price, convenience, and service, and all must be emphasized. The importance of service must not be overlooked, for service and convenience (which are not unrelated to

Figure 7–6. Front cover of a monthly catalog.

Figure 7–7. Typical catalog page.

each other!) are two opportunities to offer something unique, unlike sale prices, which are offered by your competitors and may be even lower than your own in many cases.

One approach is to make your catalog easy to use by telling the reader on the front page where to find the index and the order form and otherwise making it easy to find things. Another is to design your order form to make it easy to order. Still another is to design the order form in a way that minimizes the probability of mistakes in understanding what the customer wants. One way to do this is to ask the customer to fill in not only the item number and name, but also the page number and color of the item, where appropriate.

You can provide a separate order form, but most catalogs bind an easily removable order form into the catalog. (See Figure 7–8 for an example.) Some catalogs also attach an envelope, to make ordering even easier. (Nowadays, many catalogers are adding fax machines and providing fax numbers, as well as toll-free lines, to facilitate convenient and swift ordering.)

INDIVIDUAL BUSINESSES AND INDIVIDUALIZED CATALOG COPY

The nature of catalog copy varies with the nature of the business. You must not lose sight of the fact that catalog sales is not a business in itself, but is a way of doing business, a medium for the exchange between seller and buyer that actually is the *business*. Herschell Gordon Lewis, in his book, *Direct Mail Copy that Sells* (Prentice Hall, 1984), makes an indirect (and perhaps unintended) allusion to this in a chapter titled "Catalog Copy—How Long and How Strong?" He points to the incongruity of some catalog copywriters imitating others' catalog copy even when the other catalogs are for totally different kinds of products. He remarks on the passing of the old days, the days when all catalog copy tended to be inspired by and to emulate the classic Sears catalog.

The aforementioned Quill and Forum catalogs are of two totally different kinds of businesses. Both businesses are highly competitive, but the similarity ends there. Quill sells items that are consumable and items that most customers buy routinely as necessities—from paper clips to trash bags, but including also computers and furniture. Forum Publishing Company sells one-purchase items (i.e., books that are purchased only once by each customer). Quill's copy must, by its nature, emphasize price, and price is always featured so prominently (refer to Figures 7–6 and 7–7) that it tends to dominate the copy, perhaps dominating even the illustration. Forum's copy (see Figure 7–9) uses an illustration of the book as the dominant element, with the price in small print.

ORDER FORM   89

FORUM PUBLISHING CO.
383 East Main Street
Centerport, New York 11721

1. Sold To PLEASE FURNISH STREET ADDRESS

Name _____

Street Address _____

City/State/Zip _____

Phone Number ( ) _____

Credit Card Orders: **800/635-7654**
Fax Orders: **516/754-0630**
Customer Service: **516/754-5000**

VISA   MasterCard

For Faster Service on Credit Card Orders Only

2. Form of Payment

❏ Check or Money Order Payable to Forum Publishing Co.

Charge to: ❏ **Visa** ❏ **Mastercard**

Call 800-635-7654
Mon. - Fri., 9:30am - 5:30pm (EST)

Account No.

Month   Year   Authorized Signature

FAX Your Credit Card Order To Us 24 HOURS A DAY!
516/754-0630

3. Items Ordered MINIMUM ORDER $15.00

QUAN.	BOOK NUMBER & TITLE	PRICE

Delivery Information: Please allow 2-4 weeks delivery of books and 6-8 weeks for magazine subscriptions.	ADD POSTAGE CHARGE *(Includes Insurance)*		Merchandise Total	
	Orders up to $50.00 add **15%**	Orders over $50.00 add **10%**	N.Y. Residents must add local sales tax.	
			Postage & Insurance	
			TOTAL	

Thank you for your order

Figure 7–8. Typical catalog order form.

20   MANAGERS BOOKSHELF

How to Develop a Personnel Policy Manual

This 508-page manual is the definitive guide for establishing personnel policies for the purpose of maintaining fair and equal employment opportunities through effective personnel administration. Even small firms can benefit from this manual from learning how to keep their employee relations stable. Covers wages, absenteeism, promotions, benefits, discipline, grievances. Have the knowledge of a labor leader at your fingertips.

Order #27 *Originally $79.95* - **$29.95**

Personnel Administration Handbook

This worthwhile 1,088 page hardcover book features the tools and methods you need to achieve your company's goals for profit and growth. This book fully details your role with your employees. Originally published at $69.95.

Order #28 - *Special* - **$24.95**

The Complete Portfolio of Tests for Hiring Office Personnel

Avoid Hiring the Wrong Employee

It's a complete collection of 12 different scientifically designed tests. And each test is actually a combination of tests that will help you determine whether a person has the necessary skills for the job including: clerical, secretarial, bookkeeping positions and more. These tests were created to help you:

❖ Predict success or failure on the job
❖ Differentiate among candidates with similar backgrounds
❖ Identify a person's strengths and weaknesses
❖ Make more objective hiring decisions

Order #HQD-682 *234 Pgs., Ring Binder* - **$69.95**

The Complete Portfolio of Time Management Forms

Take Advantage of these Reusable Forms to Organize Yourself and Your Employees

180 of the most practical, unique and well thought-out time management planners- to instantly organize your time, set schedules, and establish priorities. This extensive, professionally designed collection consists of worksheets, fiscal planners, yearly and multiyear forecasting sheets, general and academic schedules and timetables. Plus scores of forms for projects, assignments, priorities, delegation, goal setting and more.

Order #HQD-676 *184 Pgs., Ring Binder* - **$49.95**

TOLL FREE: 800-635-7654   VISA & MASTERCARD

Figure 7–9. Page from a catalog selling books.

Other differences between the businesses also affect the copy. Quill is a generalist in selling office and industrial business necessities. The company therefore inventories and sells an enormous array of products and must present many items on each page if the catalog is to do the sales effort justice and yet be of manageable size. (Exception: The Quill catalog does devote more space, usually a full page at least, to the more costly items, such as office copiers or computers.)

Forum Publishing, with a more specialized and therefore smaller inventory, can devote more space to its items. A few pages present as many as eight or more books, but many pages present only two books, and probably the average is three to four items per page. In most cases, the headline of each item description is a repeat of the book title, for most of the book titles are descriptive enough and fill the other requirements of a headline: They present or at least clearly imply the direct benefit, which presumably should induce the reader to become interested. In many cases, however, the copywriter has added a blurb or subtitle to increase motivation. The subtitle to the copy for *The Complete Portfolio of Tests for Hiring Office Personnel* bears the subtitle "Avoid Hiring the Wrong Employee," and another bit of copy for a book titled *Direct Mail and Mail Order Handbook* is subtitled "To help you carve a bigger slice of the 60 billion dollar mail order market."

In still another example, a catalog of jewelry, such as the Anka catalog referred to in Chapter 6, depends primarily on color illustrations, for perfectly understandable reasons, and it devotes space to each item in some proportion to its cost, again for understandable reasons.

INFORMATION REQUIRED IN CATALOG COPY

The information required in the copy varies, but it should include at least information to satisfy the following four basic needs:
1. What the product is
2. What it does and what it is useful for
3. What options are available to the buyer
4. How to order it

What the Product Is

Even with an illustration, some verbal description is necessary, and readers expect it. For a three-ring binder, Quill's catalog says, "D-ring holds 25% more sheets than round rings," following the illustration and the "SAVE UP TO 49%" headline. Forum also provides amplifying information about each book listed. The lead-in, "For Flea Marketers . . . " introduces the book title (and headline), *The Directory to U.S. Flea Markets.* A text expansion follows and includes the "Alphabetized Listings," "Detailed Information for Each Market," and "Booth Rate Facts for Dealers," with text expansions of each of these items.

What It Does and What It Is Useful For

What a given product does and what it is useful for is often implicit in the description, or the item is so common that no such information is needed. No one needs to know what copier paper or ball-point pens do and are useful for doing. In other cases, such information is highly crucial. It is not necessary to explain the use of an envelope, but the customer is probably interested in the strength of a manila envelope and is perhaps not at all familiar with Tyvek envelopes and how they are different and perhaps superior. New products are constantly appearing, and prospective customers need to learn about them. Try always to remember that what is obvious to you is often anything but obvious to a customer.

What the product does or what it can be used for is often synonymous or nearly so with the benefit the product offers. You can usually kill two birds with one stone by structuring capability and physical descriptions so that they also furnish a description of benefits.

What Options Are Available

Many products offer various options to the buyer, including the following:

Size
Color
Model/features
Quantities/prices
Maintenance and repair service

The customer should be aware of all available options. Even the option of color may be highly important, and certainly some of the other options will affect the customer's decision.

How to Order

Never underestimate the customer's need for guidance in ordering. It is axiomatic in marketing that the easier it is for a prospect to order, the more likely he or she will do so. Here are some things you can and should try to do to make it easy for the customer to order:

1. Assign each product offered a unique ordering code of some kind. It may be a simple number or letter and number, but the more complex the ordering code, the more difficult it becomes for the customer (and the more mistakes you will have to correct later, when you are filling orders).
2. Make charging easy, either by setting up open accounts or by arranging to accept credit card charges.
3. Provide check-offs to the maximum extent possible in order forms.
4. Supply a toll-free (800) number, and accept orders thereby.
5. Install a fax (facsimile machine), and accept orders by fax.
6. Supply a postage-paid return envelope or an order form that folds into a postage-paid envelope.

These techniques are not as difficult or as expensive as they may appear to be.

For example, regarding Item 1, try to keep your order codes simple, but try also to make them as *mnemonic* (memory assisting) as possible. For example, all paper items might be coded with "PAP" and a number following, all computer items coded "CMP" and a number, and so on. That helps both you and the customer, and it makes errors less likely. It also does not give your computer any problems in handling ordering, invoicing, inventory accounting, or any other related task you might ask of your computer.

Regarding Item 2, it is not difficult to set up an account that enables you to handle VISA and MasterCard charges. Ask your banker about this.

If you are unable to design your own check-off forms (Item 3), there are many specialty printers and vendors of such items. A few inquiries will bring you many sample order forms that you can examine to select one that best suits your needs and desires.

To implement Item 4, you do not have to install a toll-free telephone in your own establishment. There are support services who will accept 800 calls for you and charge you only for each call.

Given that fax machines (Item 5) are getting cheaper every day, there is no good reason not to have one when it can add so much business. Simple machines—those that don't have the paper cutters, automatic dialing, and other bells and whistles—are selling today as cheaply as $450.

Talk to your local postmaster about implementing Item 6—postage-paid return envelopes. He or she will explain how simple it is to set this up.

GETTING HELP

Perhaps all of this seems like a tall order, especially the task of writing those catalog pages. Take heart; a great deal of help is available. Many consultants, copywriters, and other support specialists can help you do all the work and solve all the problems. You can find their advertisements in publications (see Appendix B at the end of this book). You can also get a lot of free help from the manufacturers of the products you handle if you are selling commercial merchandise. Almost all manufacturers whose goods you sell can and will (gladly) furnish you with photographs, drawings, text, and other aids on request. This material may even be composed into catalog pages and ready for the printer, after combining them with whatever else you have. Some manufacturers will probably even be able to furnish still more help than that in the form of circulars, flyers, brochures, and other printed matter in quantity so that they can actually be bound into your catalog, or they may even be able to furnish catalogs, in some cases. When you buy merchandise, be sure to inquire about such help.

8

Mailing Lists: A Critical Necessity

The list business, which is at the core of direct mail and catalog sales, has its own share of mythology, misrepresentation, and deadly misunderstanding.

HOW CRUCIAL IS THE MAILING LIST?

It is understandable that those who vend (i.e., rent out) mailing lists to marketers insist that the mailing list is all, *the* single most important factor, in whether direct-mail campaigns succeed or fail. Vendors of mailing lists certainly have a direct interest in maximizing the importance of the mailing lists that produce their incomes. Still, although there are other factors that must not be overlooked in planning and evaluating the results of a direct-mail campaign, the mailing list *is* important. For that reason, it's important to understand the nature and importance of the mailing list by looking closer at just what the mailing-list industry is, who does what in it, and how it functions generally.

THE LIST VENDORS

Basics Regarding the Use of Mailing Lists

DM News, Target Marketing, and *Catalog Business* are prominent journals of mail order generally and of direct-mail marketing especially. Every issue of these periodicals carries advertising by a variety of individuals and organizations who support mail-order and direct-mail marketers with related services and products. The advertising in these periodicals tends to be dominated, however, by the copy of organizations whose business is vending mailing lists—more specifically, renting them to direct-mail marketers.

As mentioned previously, mailing lists are normally rented, not sold, and the user is expected to rerent the list—pay the rental fee for another use—each time he or she wishes to use it, except for those who respond to the mailing with an inquiry or an order. Those names and addresses become the property of the renter. These are the basic ground rules of list rental, although there are some exceptions to this rental methodology: Some advertisers of lists for rent will offer rates for multiple use of their lists, and some will even rent lists on an annual, unlimited use basis. However, they definitely do not sell the lists; the lists remain the property of whomever is the owner of record. (As mentioned previously, the owner is not usually the vendor who rents the list to others.)

In most cases, vendors of lists rent mailing lists as their sole income-producing activity, or at least as their primary profit center. Direct-mail marketing is a major industry, in which many billions of dollars are at stake every year. Mailing-list rental is a major component of the industry. In fact, almost all direct-mail professionals (not just the renters of lists) regard the mailing list itself as the critical element in the success of a direct-mail campaign (i.e., success is considered to be tied directly to the quality of the mailing lists).

The key to succeeding, then, is to have a high-quality mailing list. But what does "quality" mean here? It is anything but a precise term, no matter where applied, and a useful definition is as difficult to establish for direct-mail and mailing lists as it is for other industries. Nonetheless, its importance to success makes its definition—with respect to rented mailing lists—essential.

Before defining "quality," however, several other mailing-list terms must be understood. The terms by which these suppliers of mailing lists identify themselves and describe what they do can be highly confusing to those not familiar with the field. Most of those suppliers have several basic functions in what is a fairly complex business, and each perceives the major functions in his or her own terms. Many of the list vendors (e.g., Direct Media of Greenwich, Connecticut, and the Kleid Company, Inc., of New York City) label themselves "list managers," which does describe one facet of their businesses. Some claim "database management" as their primary service, also a valid term for what they do. And some describe what they do as "list maintenance," "list enhancement," or even simply "list services." Most also identify themselves as list brokers where that is a more appropriate description. That is what most truly are, for most of the mailing lists that are marketed by the vendors are indeed lists that they broker and do not own: Most of the mailing lists that they market are the property of others, and the broker earns a commission for marketing the lists he or she manages (or "maintains," "enhances," or "services").

Dual Roles: List Broker/Manager

The difference in description and definition of the broker/manager roles occurs because there are actually two roles being served: (1) The broker must first "sell" his or her management services to the owner of the list—to persuade the owner to permit the broker to handle the list as the list manager and broker; (2) The broker must rent the list to prospective customers. In some cases, the broker/manager must even enter the list into computer files, which is an expensive "keyboarding" task. This task is decreasingly necessary today, however, in this era of inexpensive and abundant desktop computers: Most owners of lists have their own computers and have already "computerized" the lists, simplifying the process. Even so, the broker must understand the market and must code the lists in a way that maximizes the utility and marketability of the lists. (As mentioned previously, the current trend is to use computerized databases, rather than actual printed mailing lists.) In any case, managing lists means establishing and coding the lists so as to enable the broker to assemble or select a wide variety of lists from a single database, a collection of lists that are not homogeneous but have widely different characteristics.

Once coded and incorporated into a main database, the list manager is also marketing the list. Finding customers to rent the list is also part of the management task. That means that the broker/managers must understand their markets, of course. Hence, these list broker/manager firms are list managers to the lists' owners and list brokers to those who wish to rent the lists for use in their own direct-mail campaigns.

Thus, the typical vendors of mailing lists play a dual role, in which they are both list managers and list brokers. *List maintenance* and other terms describe some functions, secondary functions, that they must perform as necessary elements in list management and vending. That duality of roles is what makes for confusion when confronting this field for the first time.

Examples of Mailing Lists

The average list broker may have some in-house lists, lists that he or she owns, but usually most of the lists are the property of someone else, who has entrusted the list to the vendor to organize and market. For example, here are just a few of the lists offered by one firm, AZ Marketing Services of Cos Cob, Connecticut:

American Airlines In-Flight Catalog Buyers
Bloomingdale's by Mail
Bloomingdale's Charge Cards
National Gardening Magazine
Oreck Mail Order Buyers

Meredith List Marketing of Des Moines, Iowa offers many lists of subscribers to periodicals, among other lists, including the following as examples:

Better Homes and Gardens Books
Ladies Home Journal
In-Fisherman
Successful Farming
Craftways

Roman Managed Lists, of New York City, recently sent me descriptions of two new databases they now manage. One is the list of active subscribers to a trade journal named *Appliance Manufacturer*. The other is a list of subscribers to the government publication of NASA, titled *NASA Tech Briefs*. These are offered here as Figures 8–1 and 8–2, and by scanning these, you can easily see some of the demographic data available.

Another well-known figure in the industry is Ed Burnett of Ed Burnett Consultants in Englewood, New Jersey. Figure 8–3 is a single page of his alphabetical listings. His catalog also provides listings according to other parameters, such as number of employees, sales volume, industry (using the Standard Industrial Code numbers). He also can provide lists of families by age, by income, by length of residence, by type of automobile, and by other such labels and descriptors.

Others offer such diverse lists as subscribers to *Sesame Street Magazine* and respondents to the Physicians' Mutual Database, a list of Physicians' Mutual insurance customers.

What Is List Management?

You may wonder why anyone's mailing list needs "management." Why don't Physicians' Mutual or *Time* magazine just rent out their lists themselves and

ROMAN MANAGED LISTS, INC.

20 Squadron Boulevard, Suite 650, New City, NY 10956

NASA TECH BRIEFS
Active Subscriber Mailing List

Subscribers by name	161,264	$85/M
Competitive offers		$95/M
Fund raisers		$75/M

For List Clearance call:

Lee Roman
Jeannette Hyman
Brian Ingber
Call Toll-free
800-FAB-LIST
(800-322-5478)
In New York State
Call (914) 638-2530
Fax: (914) 638-2631

Description:

NASA Tech Briefs active subscriber mailing list is comprised of over 161,000 engineers and executives whose business is keeping abreast of technological developments within the Aerospace, Electronics, Defense and Communications industries.

These professionals have qualified themselves to receive the official magazine on innovation and technical data from the NATIONAL AERONAUTICS AND SPACE ADMINISTRATION (NASA).

This highly regarded, well respected publication is known as NASA Tech Briefs.

NASA Tech Briefs is one of the most consistently strongest pulling lists on the market. Nearly 80% of the mailers testing this list return for continuation. These test & continuations reflect on the list's appeal for a wide range of offers — from scientific/technical to business to consumer.

NASA TECH BRIEFS ACTIVE SUBSCRIBERS CLASSIFIED BY JOB FUNCTION:

Company Management	21,588
Engineering Management	38,891
Engineering	71,234
Research	17,276
Design & Development Engineering	80,276

NASA TECH BRIEFS ACTIVE SUBSCRIBERS CLASSIFIED BY TYPE OF BUSINESS (INDUSTRY):

Aerospace	25,144
BioMedical	6,214
Communications	9,795
Computers	12,173
Consultants	6,743
Chemicals	4,212
Defense	10,129
Electronics	22,300
Government	8,885
Industrial Equipment	12,271
Library	373
Materials	5,635
Nuclear	1,616
Power and Energy	4,927
Research Laboratory	8,512
Transportation	4,732
Education	5,303
Others allied to the field	9,180

(See Additional Selections on Reverse Side)

STATE COUNTS			
MA	6,865	WI	3,304
RI	626	MN	3,488
NH	1,151	SD	164
ME	334	ND	129
VT	297	MT	164
CT	3,773	IL	7,807
NJ	6,622	MO	2,299
NY	10,987	KS	1,192
PA	8,239	NE	631
DE	534	LA	1,081
DC	882	AR	505
MD	4,818	OK	1,209
VA	4,529	TX	9,127
WV	385	CO	3,392
NC	2,507	WY	94
SC	1,254	ID	436
GA	2,293	UT	1,392
FL	6,055	AZ	2,714
AL	2,336	NM	1,362
TN	1,744	NV	433
MS	605	CA	29,531
KY	906	HI	269
OH	8,325	OR	1,434
IN	3,410	WA	2,894
MI	5,384	AK	116
IA	1,077	US Terr.	150
TOTAL			161,264

SELECTIONS

Title Selections	$5/M
Demographic Selection	$5/M
Industry Selections	$5/M
State Selection	$5/M
SCF Selection	$5/M
Zip Code Selection	$5/M
A/B Splits	$5/M
Key Coding	$1/M
Pressure Sensitive Labels	$7.50/M
Minimum Order	5,000
Magnetic Tape	$25

Delivery Schedule:	Restrictions:	Commission:
10 working days after receipt of order	All rentals for one-time usage. Sample mailing piece required for every order. List Rental Agreement Required.	20% to recognized brokers, 15% to agencies.

Lists are updated continuously and guaranteed to be at least 95% deliverable.

NASA TECH BRIEFS is managed exclusively by Roman Managed Lists, Inc.

We believe the information concerning this list to be accurate, but we cannot guarantee its accuracy or the outcome of the mailing. Prices are subject to change without notice.

Figure 8–1. A list of subscribers to an industrial trade journal.

ROMAN MANAGED LISTS, INC.

20 Squadron Boulevard, Suite 650, New City, NY 10956

APPLIANCE
MANUFACTURER

Active Subscriber Mailing List

Total Active Subscribers .... 35,644 .... $85/M

For List Clearance call:
Lee Roman
Jeannette Hyman
Barbara DiMarsico
Call Toll-free
800-FAB-LIST
(800-322-5478)
In New York State
Call (914) 638-2530
Fax: (914) 638-2631

Description:
APPLIANCE MANUFACTURER devotes itself to the solutions of problems and the interests of the Design for Manufacturing team — in the Consumer, Commercial and Business Appliance Industry. This is accomplished with an editorial mix of product technology and manufacturing applications, and is addressed to those engineers and managers who are responsible for managing product design and manufacturing in high-volume manufacturing plants.

Every issue contains editorial on: Design for Manufacturing, Manufacturing Systems and Design Trends and Technology, plus product information covering Materials, Components and Equipment.

APPLIANCE MANUFACTURER ACTIVE SUBSCRIBERS CLASSIFIED BY JOB FUNCTION:	
Product Mgt. &/or Prod. Engineering	14,431
Product Engineering &/or Design	16,900
Administrative &/or Financial Mgt.	4,915
Quality Control/Quality Assurance	7,583
Materials Handling/Storage/Retrieval	4,897
Research & Development (including Mgt.)	12,653
Purchasing/Procurement	6,658
Mktng./Sales/Advtg. or Srvcs. (inc. Mgt.)	4,708
Other	1,703

APPLIANCE MANUFACTURER ACTIVE SUBSCRIBERS CLASSIFIED BY TYPE OF BUSINESS:	
Home Appliances	10,311
Consumer Electronics	4,410
Commercial Appliances/Coin Op. Equipment	2,837
Business & Office Equipment and Systems	9,607
Appliance Components & Subsystems	3,608
Other Manufacturers	3,936
Appliance Mchdsr./Consultants/Designers	73
Industry Association	70
Other Services	62

APPLIANCE MANUFACTURER ACTIVE SUBSCRIBERS CLASSIFIED BY EMPLOYEE SIZE:	
1–19	3,333
20–49	2,364
50–99	2,759
100–249	5,823
250–499	5,457
500–999	4,861
OVER 1000	9,698

STATE COUNTS

AL	285	MT	7
AR	270	NC	653
AZ	349	ND	1
CA	4,103	NE	80
CO	318	NH	244
CT	917	NJ	1,761
DC	20	NM	48
DE	74	NV	78
FL	757	NY	2,890
GA	480	OH	2,395
HI	11	OK	162
IA	643	OR	210
ID	69	PA	1,666
IL	3,695	RI	137
IN	1,369	SC	310
KS	175	SD	58
KY	994	TN	991
LA	104	TX	1,307
MA	1,728	UT	139
MD	519	VA	429
ME	66	VT	65
MI	1,216	WA	237
MN	1,217	WI	1,474
MO	648	WV	41
MS	150	WY	19
		TOTAL	**35,644**

SELECTIONS

Title Selections	$5/M
Demographic Selection	$5/M
Industry Selections	$5/M
State Selection	$5/M
SCF Selection	$5/M
Zip Code Selection	$5/M
A/B Splits	$5/M
Key Coding	$1/M
Pressure Sensitive Labels	$7.50/M
Minimum Order	5,000
Magnetic Tape	$25

Delivery Schedule:	Restrictions:	Commission:
10 working days after receipt of order	All rentals for one-time usage. Sample mailing piece required for every order. List Rental Agreement Required.	20% to recognized brokers, 15% to agencies.

Lists are updated continuously and guaranteed to be at least 95% deliverable.

APPLIANCE MANUFACTURER is managed exclusively by Roman Managed Lists, Inc.

We believe the information concerning this list to be accurate, but we cannot guarantee its accuracy or the outcome of the mailing.

Prices are subject to change without notice.

Figure 8–2. A list of a different type of subscriber.

Alpha Listing

Electronic/Fallout

	NATIONAL QUANTITY	SIC CODE
Electronic Research & Devel.	2,510	7391E
Electronic Resistor Mfrs.	150	3676
Electronic Testing Equipment	940	3825A
Electronics Consultants	390	7390G
Electrotypers & Stereotypers	30	2794
Elevator & Escalator Mfrs.	1,000	3534
Elevator Installation Contractors	2,020	1796A
Elevators Supplies & Parts Mfrs.	420	3534A
Embalmers	1,800	7261B
Emblems (Wholesale & Manuf)	940	2399C
Embossing Equipment & Supplies	70	2799B
Embossing (Service)	480	2799A
Embroidery (Service)	2,080	7400X
Embroidery Supplies	210	5949H
Emergency Medical Service	890	8081S
Employment Agencies	13,970	7361A
Employment Agencies, (Exc. Temporary)	32,780	7361
Employment Consultants	180	7361E
Enameling Japanning & Lacquer	420	3479A
Encyclopedias, Retail	580	5963E
Endocrinology	1,350	8011E
Endodontics	1,870	8021B
Energy Conservation Engineers	4,030	8911X
Energy Conservation Equip - Solar - Whl	290	5074F
Energy Conservation Products (Retail)	1,900	5211Y
Engine Electrical Equipment Mfrs.	1,440	3694
Engineering Equipt Supplies	1,220	5086R
Engineering & Scientific Instruments	1,930	3811
Engineering Services, N.E.C.	4,300	8911Z
Engineering, Surveying & Architecture Firms - All	85,590	8911
A.C. Heating & Ventilation	800	8911K
Acoustical	150	8911U
Architectural Services	25,800	8911A
Building Construction	5,490	8911G
Civil	8,570	8911E
Consulting	20,560	8911D
Electrical	3,050	8911J
Energy Conservation	4,040	8911X
Environmental	570	8911M
Fire Protection	570	7400C
Industrial Designers	2,370	8911C
Marine	560	8911T
Mechanical	2,450	8911L
Mining	350	8911N
Professional Engineers	7,200	8911H
Sanitary	1,280	8911Q
Surveyors	13,030	8911F
Engineering Services, N.E.C.	4,300	8911Z
Engineering Systems	310	7362J
Engineers - Designers - Industrial	2,370	8911C
Engineers Acoustical	140	8911U
Engineers Agricultural	70	8911O
Engineers Geotechnical	410	8911P
Engineers Marine	560	8911T
Engineers Metallurgical	140	8911S
Engineers Petroleum	630	8911V
Engineers Solar	10	8911Y
Engines - Gasoline Or Diesel, Whls (Tm)	6,710	5084L
Engines-Gas (Tm)	14,430	5261D
Engines Industrial	10	3621B
Engines Rebuilding (Various)	7,240	7599A
Engines Supplies Equip & Parts	2,840	5063C
Engravers - N.E.C.	2,360	2753D
Engravers - Plastic,wood,etc.	2,550	7390X
Engravers-Mechanical	510	2753B
Engravers & Plate Printers	4,610	2753
Engravers-Stationery	630	2753A
Entertainers	4,660	7929B
Entertainment Bureaus	2,600	7922J
Entertainment, N.E.C.	10,370	7929
Envelope Mfrs.	1,240	2642
Envelopes Retail	350	5943D
Environmental Conservation	3,030	8641C
Environmental Controls Mfrs.	580	3822
Environmental Engineers	570	8911M
Episcopal Churches	6,480	8663P
Equipment Rental & Leasing Services (See..	57,010	7394
Erosion Control	190	0762G
Escort Services	620	7299K
Escrow Services	3,810	6059B
Estates	790	8811
Etched Products-Metal, Glass, Etc.	260	3993G
Eviction Services	140	7390E
Excavating Equipment Whl.	1,300	5082J
Excavating & Grading	30,800	1794A
Excavation & Foundation Work	37,410	1794
Excercise Equipment Stores	3,250	5941R
Executive Offices	760	9111
Executive Recruiters	4,730	7361D
Executives	1,200,000	
Expansion Joints (Mfg.)	330	3441A
Experimental Work	360	7391C
Explosives Mfrs.	130	2892
Explosives, Wholesale	650	5161O
Exporters	8,310	5099G
Exposition Trade Shows & Fairs	700	7319D
Express Service	1,930	4213E
Exterminating & Fumigating Equip	140	5087H
Exxon Stations	8,440	5541J

Middle Management Executives

The best and the brightest. Sales and Marketing
Managers on the move — and the direction they're
headed is straight to the top of the corporate ladder.
As managers who oversee the activities of other
executives, they're prime prospects for seminars,
business and self-improvement tapes, books,
magazines and travel — for themselves, or for their
staffs.

Select them by company size and by industry.

F

	NATIONAL QUANTITY	SIC CODE
Fabric - Coated, Not Rubberized	340	2295
Fabric Mills - Nonwoven	100	2297
Fabric Mills - Smallware	490	2241
Fabric Shops	11,610	5949B
Fabricated Metal - Structural	4,410	3441
Fabricated Textiles, N.E.C.	6,250	2399
Facsimile Communication Equipt	1,310	3662A
Facsimile Transmission Svce	430	4821A
Factors	220	6153A
Factory Outlets	1,770	5999G
Fairgrounds	360	7929F
Fallout Shelter Contractors	10	1521N

16   **SAVE TIME** — SEND IT BY FAX! **CALL (201) 871-3649**

Figure 8–3. A page from the Ed Burnett Consultants list catalog.

earn all the income from them? The answer is probably obvious: Renting mailing lists is a business—an industry, in fact—in itself. Most owners of lists are not interested in nor equipped for getting into that business. Yet, their lists of customers, subscribers, or members are valuable assets, worth money, and ought to be put to work to produce additional income. Hence, list managers developed organizations that (1) gather the lists of names, addresses, and other information; (2) use the lists to create new databases designed to support and enhance the value and income-producing potential of the names; and (3) market the lists sorted from the databases.

A few list owners do their own list marketing, although they tend to set up separate organizations for the purpose. Dun & Bradstreet, for example, market their own extensive lists through Dun's Marketing Services, one of the corporation's companies. Book publisher Doubleday operates Doubleday List Marketing, featuring lists of book club subscribers. And *Boardroom Reports*, New York publisher of newsletters, offers their own lists through their own Boardroom Lists organization in New York City.

THE KEY FUNCTIONS OF MAILING-LIST MANAGEMENT

Classifying and Categorizing Each List

The list broker's most important function from the list owner's viewpoint is managing the marketing of the lists to produce maximum income for the list owner (and for themselves too, of course, since they earn a commission). However, from the user's viewpoint, the list broker's most important function is classifying and categorizing the lists accurately (and truthfully) so that the user can target markets with great precision. Price is a consideration, of course—the owner wants it maximized, and the user wants it minimized, naturally—as are a few other factors, but those are secondary considerations, relatively unimportant if the primary goals are achieved. The list manager therefore classifies each name on each list as precisely as possible in terms that have usefulness for the user of the list.

For example, Chilcutt Direct Marketing of Edmond, Oklahoma advertises some of the subcategories by which it has classified the 1,700,000 names of the Physicians' Mutual database. The categories include these:

132,000 preteenage kids
59,000 boating enthusiasts
59,000 fishermen

19,000 collectors

50,000 gourmet cooks

58,000 do-it-themselfers

178,000 donors

50,000 exercise/fitness enthusiasts

76,000 gardeners

91,000 sewing and needlepoint enthusiasts

833,000 home decorators

84,000 pet owners

86,000 VCR owners

Being able to order a list of gardeners or gourmet cooks obviously offers you a marketing advantage. In addition, lists may be and are classified by many other categories than just hobbies or personal interests, such as by the following:

Age

Occupations

Types of employers

Income levels

Types of residence

Home owners versus renters

Urban, suburban, rural

Zip codes

Employment status (e.g., worker versus retiree)

Previous purchases by mail

Memberships

Ethnic group, religion

Political affiliation

Educational level

Qualified Lists Corp. of Armonk, New York, for example, advertised its list management of names associated with the periodical *Cars & Parts* in the *DM News* issue of March 1, 1989. The advertising described the periodical as part magazine and part catalog, offered "78,000 active subscribers" and "80,000 book buyers," referring to the lists as "98% direct mail buyers." The copy went on to provide a reader profile of "$59,000 average income, 46% college graduates, 77% married, average age 47, 98% men." That amount of detail about a list indicates the value of using the right lists.

Merging and Sorting Specific Lists

Anyone on one list may also appear on many other lists: A name on a list of insurance salesmen may appear also on several other lists, such as those of home owners, suburban dwellers, computer owners, fishermen, book buyers, middle-income citizens, college graduates, and countless others. Obviously, if the broker were to keep separate lists, a roster of 1,000,000 names would soon swell to one of 50 million names through massive duplication, hardly an efficient way to manage the lists. With computers, however, that is no problem: Each name needs be in a master file only once because it can be encoded with a number of keys so that the computer can be ordered to print out all names of fishermen, insurance salespeople, home owners, or whatever else is wanted. In fact, it is easily possible to have the computer print out only the names of insurance salespeople who are also home owners and fishermen!

Databases

The master list of names from which selected names can be withdrawn and assembled has its own name: *database*. That word has already been used to identify the Physicians' Mutual mailing lists as a database. Technically, a database is any set or collection of data that has a common relationship of any kind and/or that the user wishes to group together as a database for whatever reason. So the size and nature of databases can vary enormously. The list broker could logically identify all the names and addresses in his or her care as a single database. However, because the list broker must credit rental fees accurately to the list owners, combining the various owners' lists would probably become a problem, although with a sophisticated enough computer program, it would be possible to do so. Without a sufficiently sophisticated computer program, however, the logical thing to do is to designate the entire list or set of lists of a given list owner as a database. Thus, if you order 25,000 names of civil engineers and the broker must go to the lists of several different list owners to collect that many names for you, the broker can identify the money owed to each database owner.

ASSESSING THE QUALITY OF LISTS

Deliverability

In mailing lists, one measure of quality is "deliverability." Any piece of mail that is undeliverable for any reason is a *nixie*. The tendency of all list brokers is to guarantee their lists in terms of deliverability, promising some minimum percentage of nixies, such as not more than 1 percent, and sometimes offering to replace each nixie with two additional names.

Nixies are, of course, inevitable because people move, die, get divorced, get married and leave home, and otherwise change status, among other events, thereby invalidating some names and addresses. Removing nixies from mailing lists or correcting them when the problem is an incorrect entry is known as "cleaning" or "purging" the list, and it is a part of the broader function of maintenance of the list.

Customized Suitability

Deliverability is not the only characteristic that determines the quality of a mailing list. Other maintenance activities include various manipulations of the lists, usually via computer these days, such as updating the list by adding new names and codes, using "merge-purge" to eliminate duplicates, and correcting any errors discovered. Also, inevitably, regardless of whether this is pointed out to you or whether the word *quality* is even used, *quality* also should refer to the demographic or other data that characterizes the list, and that should include both the amount of detail known and the accuracy of the coding. In fact, the more highly stratified with demographic data, the more valuable is the list.

Further, a list of known *buyers* is superior to a list of *inquirers*. If you sell books by mail, a list of known mail-order book buyers is more valuable—of higher quality, that is—than a list of known mail-order buyers whose specific interests are not known. Further, if you specialize in mystery stories, a list of known mail-order buyers of mystery stories is of even higher quality. The more closely you can match a list to the precise characteristics you have decided describe your best prospective buyers, the more useful and valuable that list is to you.

In fact, quality also includes or should include the accuracy with which the list conforms with those characteristics you have asked for and which have been promised you. The problem is that there is no practical way to determine how well the list conforms with what it is claimed to be. In fact, there is no way to be sure about the number of nixies when the mailing is at other than first class rates unless return postage is guaranteed. So in the end, quality is, for the most part, something that one accepts from any list broker who appears to be dependable and ethical. Most are, and most work hard at tagging their lists in ways that enable them to tailor their mailing lists to your order.

KINDS OF LISTS

Known Buyers

The lists discussed up to this point have been primarily lists of buyers of one sort or another—subscribers to periodicals, owners of credit cards, purchasers of merchandise by mail, home owners, hobbyists, and others who have been customers. These kinds of lists, it is generally agreed, are the best kind because they are lists of *known buyers*—individuals who buy from catalogs, use charge cards, and/or are or have been mail-order customers of one kind or another. They are also valuable because there is usually some demographic data about them available, such items as age brackets, income levels, occupations, education, and other information highly useful in evaluating them as prospective customers. They are, in a large sense, "qualified," and that is itself an important element of quality.

Qualifying a prospect is a simple enough idea: It means establishing that the prospect is a true prospect—that is, someone who is (a) sincerely interested in the product or product line, and (b) capable of making the purchase, in that he or she has the money, the credit, and/or the authority to make the purchase. If the prospect lacks such qualification and is not really interested in the line or could not make the purchase in any event, the sales effort is obviously a total waste of time and money. Hence, professional salespeople learn to qualify prospects—determine whether it is worthwhile to make the effort—before investing a major amount of time and effort. Known buyers are already qualified by virtue of their history as buyers, credit-card owners, or whatever is evidence of their general interests, ability to buy, and willingness to buy. That qualification is itself a valuable asset, and the lack of it can easily become the fatal flaw in the campaign.

The lists of known buyers of one type or another are the cream of the crop. But there are at least two other broad kinds of lists, each generally deemed to be considerably less valuable because they are, presumably, lists of people whose potentials as buyers is less clear—that is, they are not as well qualified as those on the lists of known buyers. One of these other kinds of lists is that of "inquirers," and the other is the compiled list.

Compiled Lists

Generally speaking, compiled lists are considered to be of the least value when compared with lists of known buyers or lists of known inquirers. That is primarily because they are generally almost totally unqualified lists. If they are compiled from a telephone directory, for example, little or no information, other than that they have a telephone and live in some given area is known about them. Of course, the names may be compiled from other sources that do provide a bit of additional information. For example, if the names are drawn from the membership roster of an association of psychologists, they are known to be practicing professionals. Here are some of the kinds of sources from which lists may be compiled (as you may recall from brief mention in Chapter 1):

Membership directories, all kinds
Voting registration lists
Automobile owners
Home owners
Boat owners
Computer owners
Hobbyists
Advertisers
Convention goers

None of this is to say that compiled lists are totally without worth. Quite the contrary, there are situations where there is no other way to get the names and addresses desired or even where a compiled list is the most suitable one. For example, if you wanted a list of all the antique auto enthusiasts in the world you might or might not find such a list offered by the regular list brokers. You would therefore have to compile the list yourself or turn to one of the companies that does such compilations. (There are a few who specialize in this.) Or you might run inquiry advertising and/or public relations (PR) campaigns to solicit inquiries from antique auto enthusiasts as a source of inputs from which to compile a list.

Inquiry Lists

Inquiry lists provide names of prospects more likely to be qualified than those found on compiled lists. For example, when you respond to an advertised invitation to send in a card or letter requesting more information about the subject advertised (e.g., an insurance or drug company advertisement about the dangers of hypertension and offer of more information upon request), your name generally speeds its way onto a list of inquirers. You are now a prospect, and your name is now a sales lead to be followed up with a mailing, sending you what you asked for, plus a complete direct-mail sales package.

If you respond to that with an order, and if the advertiser is keeping his or her lists up to date, your name gets transferred to the customer list, the most valuable list of all. If you do not buy, your name remains on that inquiry list, and you continue to get sales literature, in a continuing attempt to win your order. Even if the advertiser eventually decides that you will never become his or her customer and gives up on you, your name is still worth something as a prospect who has shown an interest in hypertension (or in whatever the original advertisement was about). Thus, you are still more valuable as a prospect than is a list compiled from a source unrelated to hypertension (or any other subject of inquiry).

A list of inquirers will not rent for the top rates, but it still can be rented. Probably, someone else with another service or product can sell to you. To that limited extent, at least, inquirers are qualified or partially qualified. (In some cases, the advertiser requires more extensive qualification by requiring the inquirer to make inquiry on an official business letterhead or accompany the inquiry with a business card.)

You can rent lists of inquirers, although you should pay less for renting lists of inquirers than you pay for lists of known buyers. In spite of the fact that lists of inquirers are of less value than lists of known buyers, they are not without value and they are certainly not totally unqualified. The fact that they are names of individuals who have shown some specific interest itself is at least a partial qualification, so the list is not a totally cold one.

BUILDING YOUR OWN LIST OF INQUIRERS

As mentioned in Chapter 1, you can develop your own lists of inquirers, by using that same inquiry advertising that gets your name on so many mailing lists. In principle, it is quite simple: It consists of running advertisements calculated to elicit responses—generically "inquiries," although not always literally *inquiries.*

There is more than one way to go about this. The simplest and most direct way is to insert small advertisements—they may be classified advertisements or small display advertisements. Here are a few actual classified notices (with names omitted), selected from a recent issue of an "opportunity seeker" magazine:

THOUSANDS OF THINGS TO SELL. Free info! Sell business firms. We'll put you wise to sensationally profitable business. Confidential, no obligation.

HERBS—YOHIMBINE, PAU D'Arco and others. Catalog $1.00 (refundable).

ATTRACT LOVE, MONEY, HEALTH. Send stamp.

Small display advertisements attract more attention and provide a bit more space for the message, but the approach is the same:

SEND FOR OUR NEW CLOSEOUT CATALOG
New designer jeans & clothing • Cosmetics • Army/Navy
Accessories Line of recycled clothes • Videos
$1 for giant catalog.

MAIL ORDER PROFITS
Sell books, manuals, directories
Up to 1,000% profit. The secret to big profits.
Buy $10 books for $1. Free report, profit making facts

Of course, the advertisements are worded and inserted in the types of publications that will appeal to the kinds of individuals you wish to attract. The idea is to offer something that will encourage the readers to respond. If you are going to offer them a catalog, be sure to word your offer so as to provide a good reason for wanting your catalog.

Another way to attract names for your lists, perhaps a much better way, in fact, is to run small advertisements in the right publications, selling a small item at an unusually attractive price. One cataloger does this with name-and-address labels. Moreover, he does not do it occasionally, but always, as a standard marketing method. Everyone who orders labels gets a catalog returned with the labels and suitable direct-mail sales literature. Of course, there are many items you can find that you can sell for a dollar or two, perhaps even as loss leaders. One advantage of doing this is that the appeal is probably much greater.

Reader's Digest ran a test many years ago, offering an item free in one advertisement and asking for 10 cents in another otherwise identical advertisement. The copy asking for 10 cents outpulled the other advertisement by a wide margin. Why? Perhaps the readers assumed that anything free could not be worth much, while something costing 10 cents (which would be at least a dollar today) had to be something of value. Others have found at times that advertising asking for $2 produced better results than advertising asking for $1, probably because most of us do not believe that $1 will buy anything worth having, other than a cup of coffee or a candy bar.

Another, and possibly more important advantage of winning inquiries through selling some kind of leader, is that you are getting names of *customers*, rather than of inquirers, when you sell a leader to attract new names. No matter how small the sale represented by the leader, it is a sale and it is a new customer. The names indicate people whom you know will order by mail and who now have had a buying experience that should encourage them to buy again, overcoming their resistance to buying by mail, if it existed before. That is quite an advantage to gain.

You do have to find out what works best: What is the best kind of item to offer? What is the best price range in which to work for a first sale? What are the best places to advertise? What is the best copy to use? And so on.

Of course, the best way to find out what works best is to take the guesswork out of it by testing your ideas. Run the advertisements and tally the results. (Forms and methods for testing appear in Chapter 12.) You may eventually decide that you want to run ads as a permanent feature of your marketing, if it works well. Nonetheless, continued testing is a necessity to make it work well, for only with tests can you be sure that you know what you are doing.

You can use PR techniques to get free publicity that will also bring inquiries. Chapter 12 discusses PR, publicity, and the tools and methods used for these activities. Among the useful tools are the publicity ("press") release and the product release. They can be used for general advertising and promotion, but they can also be put to work to produce inquiries. In brief—see Chapter 12 for more details—you can build releases around the most novel or most interesting items you handle, and if you cannot find an item that you believe is novel enough or interesting enough, you can invent an excuse for the publicity by making an "introductory offer," in which you offer some attractive item as a loss leader. Or you can choose somewhat more expensive items—a few of them—and conduct a contest, giving those items as prizes. With a little imagination, you can get a great deal of what amounts to free advertising.

DATABASE MARKETING

Whether a list includes known buyers, inquirers, or members of a compiled list, it can be manipulated and utilized more effectively if keyed as a computerized database. The term *database marketing* is now used frequently in connection with direct mail and cataloging. It has, in fact, been the subject of many articles and discussions at meetings of direct-mail professionals. The terms *database* and *database management,* often referred to by computer specialists and computer users as *db* and *dbm,* respectively, are probably regarded as unintelligible *computerese* or computer jargon by the lay person.

Even many direct-mail professionals are not comfortable with the term, nor do they fully understand it: Despite the fact that they use the term casually and frequently, they understand only that the term is used to refer to the mailing lists, but they often do not truly comprehend the nuances that distinguish database marketing from list marketing. That is understandable: The considerations that distinguish database marketing from list marketing are rather subtle to those not fully at home with computer technology.

Sometimes, it seems as though many people who profess expertise are actually dealing in jargon they have learned rather than in the concepts that they ought to have learned. It does require a fair amount of explanation to achieve a full understanding and appreciation of the difference, and it is no disgrace to profess ignorance as a necessary first step in learning about it. Recognize in advance, however, that the term refers both to the lists used in direct mail and to the data associated with and part of those lists, for they are the heart of direct-mail marketing. Thus, database marketing is unavoidably an alternative to and perhaps may even be considered to be an extension of list marketing because it refers also to marketing via the mailing lists that are the heart of direct mail.

What Is a Database?

The profusion of terms may have you temporarily overloaded and confused. A somewhat simplified preliminary statement of the difference may set the scene and help bring understanding about: A *mailing list* is merely a list of names and addresses. A *database* (as used in this connection) is a list of names and addresses with a great deal of information about those whose names and addresses are on the list.

The essence of the distinction is that database marketing really refers not to what names and addresses are on the list but to how the list is handled, manipulated, and maintained, to what information about the list is available and may be extracted from manipulations, and how such information is put to use in behalf of more profitable and more successful operation. *Database* may thus be equated to *mailing list*, but the more significant term in designating a difference is the addition of *management*, as in *database management*. That is, database marketing is distinguished from list marketing due to the manner and means by which the list is managed. For example, database marketing, properly used, enables you, the cataloger, to gather volumes of pricelessly valuable information about your list of prospects, from creditworthiness to preferences in toothpaste and reading matter. It begins to permit direct mail to implement scientific methodology, at least to some extent.

Depending on how nitpickingly technical you wish to be, defining the general term *database* is easy: Any set of data that you group together for whatever reason (some commonality that is significant for your purposes) may be designated a database. In the direct-mail business, the set of data is a mailing list. (In other applications or other industries, a database can be and usually is a set of data having completely other significance—perhaps a list of slow payers, a list of research scientists, a list of prospective clients, or a collection of documents.) Therefore, in the strictest sense, a simple mailing list may be considered a database, and many databases are just that—a simple list of names that have some common factor, such as all being subscribers to the same periodical or all owning homes in the same zip code area.

For the purposes of direct mail, however, such a broad definition only adds to the confusion. For direct mail, the definition must be simpler and thus clearer: Although anyone can designate any collection of information a database, for practical purposes, a simple list of names about which nothing is known except their addresses is not a direct-mail database. A list of names about which more than their addresses is known (e.g., whether they own or rent the houses in which they live) is a *database* because it can already be subdivided by that data into owners and renters. There is no definite dividing line that dictates how much more than an address one needs before a mailing list becomes a database, and so for our purposes the dividing line is whatever enables the first subdivision of the names into two or more classes.

Database Management Programs

In computer applications generally, a simple list may be handled by any of many basic computer programs, including simple editors and word processors. "Handled" means stored, added to, erased from, sorted, or otherwise manipulated in several basic patterns. That is the practical extent of such programs, however. To manipulate data in more complex and sophisticated patterns requires more sophisticated software programs, and there are database management (dbm) programs available for the purpose. With such programs, many other functions become easily possible. Before analyzing different kinds of dbm programs, an excursion into some related matters may help make a related consideration clear.

Methods of Storage

Most lists today are stored "in computers." Technically, the data is not actually in the computer but is stored in some computer *medium* from which it may be transferred to the computer's memory area (for temporary residence there) when necessary to do something with it. With the large, mainframe computers, that storage may be and often is on magnetic tape, those large spinning reels that you may have seen in TV representations of computer rooms. There is some advantage in overall efficiency, but there is at least one disadvantage: The list of names is sequential in every sense of the word. To get to any name anywhere on the reel, the computer must read ("pass") every name that precedes the one wanted. That makes it a rather awkward system, one that is time-consuming, which means that it is expensive.

Floppy disks and other random-access storage media have helped simplify the problem because data can be accessed at random instead of sequentially. Storage on disks, as an alternative to tape and as a method that is almost universal with desktop computers, offers the advantage that names in the middle of a list can be accessed almost directly (which means almost immediately). This rapid access is an important factor in database management, which requires frequent, swift, and generally ready access to any file and to any record in a file.

WHAT IS A DATABASE MANAGER?

Database management software was conceived to handle stores of data used for operations, for research and development (R&D), and for almost any other purpose in which the ability to store, organize, sort, and otherwise manipulate the items is advantageous. One key advantage of the diverse capabilities of database management programs is the way in which such capabilities facilitate testing, which has been emphasized in several earlier chapters. Such testing is an essential of the direct-mail industry because the industry operates primarily on statistical probability (i.e., the probability that some percentage of prospective customers addressed will respond with orders and/or become repeat customers). When success and failure hinge on a percentage point or two, such research and the information it provides becomes a decisive factor in mere survival. When the study of results achieved produces information that makes future efforts more successful, that study clearly becomes valuable.

Before the advent of the computer, such research was manual, depending on file cabinets full of paper records, such as mountains of index cards. The computer changed that, making paper files and index cards obsolete. The desktop computer was revolutionary in providing widespread access to these automated processes.

Database management programs are appropriate for many kinds of data—mailing lists, customer records, inventory, and others. With dbm, you can code every entry in many ways to enable you to select names and to compile lists of almost any kind, as already described. In addition, you can carry out valuable research of many kinds, such as determining what kinds of offers produce best results, what kinds of customers buy what kinds of products or services, what the seasonal patterns are, what campaigns have produced the greatest returns on investment, and many other such data. However, there are several kinds of dbm programs, each of which offers different capabilities for sorting and merging mailing lists according to different criteria.

Mailing-List Managers

There are many computer programs designed especially to manage mailing lists. They are, in fact, dbm programs designed especially for mailing-list management, and they are easy to run because the design decisions have been made for you. However, they are also relatively inflexible because the designer of the program has decided for you how many lines you need and what information you need. In one such program that I used in the early days of my computer experience, for example, I could not use the 9-digit zip code; the program allowed me only five digits for the zip code. I found it rather awkward to record a Canadian address because the program did not easily lend itself to the Canadian postal codes, and it was even more difficult to record addresses in other foreign places, such as Singapore and Maylasia. I was also limited in the number of ways in which I could code entries for later retrieval and analyses.

I concluded, finally, that mailing-list managers are probably ineffective for large lists (which mine wasn't) and for small lists requiring flexible manipulation. Because I wanted something with greater flexibility, I turned to a regular dbm program. It proved to be an education in itself. Aside from that special variety of database manager I have referred to as a mailing-list manager, there are two main kinds of database managers: *flat-file* dbm programs and *relational* dbm programs.

The Flat-File Database Manager

The flat-file dbm, which is simpler than the relational one, is what I use because my needs are quite modest. I use my own dbm for more than one mailing list and for other purposes than mailing-list management. In fact, I keep seven separate files in my dbm: (1) a generalized mailing list of customers for my own modest catalog operation, (2) subscribers to my monthly syndicated column, (3) a list of reviewers of my books, and (4—7) other generalized purposes, such as a computer version of a rolodex-type of file in which I keep all those other, miscellaneous numbers of friends, associates, suppliers, editors, and all those classes not numerous enough to justify enjoying their own individual files or databases.

The beauty of the full-scale (unqualified) dbm (either flat-file or relational, as opposed to mailing-list managers) is that its flexibility permits you, the human manager, to design your files pretty much as you wish. Some of my files have eight lines (*fields*, in computer jargon) for each entry (*record*, in computer jargon), while others have either fewer or more fields for each record, as I saw the need. I designed the file formats, and when I gained more experience and perceived the shortcomings of my original design, I redesigned the files without having to rekey (re-enter) any of my mailing lists.

I can code and sort files by any of the fields I have designated for them, and I can thus retrieve and print them on labels or in any report format by any code. These are very simple records because my lists are short, and my needs rather simple. Others might have much larger files, with many more records, and two or three times as many fields. The form should follow the function (i.e., the design should be dictated by your needs).

My rather basic dbm system permits me to design my labels and to print out individual names and addresses, entire files, or lists of names and addresses selected by codes I have designated according to how I perceive my own needs and desires. It also permits me to design my own reports and to either view these reports on the screen or print them out. (I can do the same with the mailing lists.) Further, I can transfer any of this data to other programs, such as word processors by creating a report and copying the report to the disk, to be available to another program. Although those comprehensive abilities suit my needs, they exhaust the possibilities of the flat-file dbm. I am happy with it despite its limitations, but you may need more.

The Relational Database Manager

The relational database manager can do all that the flat-file dbm can do, plus a few other things, chief of which is that it can handle information from more than one group of files at a time (i.e., it can summon up other files and/or data from other files while it is already within a given file). It can *relate* data directly from one file to another, justifying its designation as "relational." It is thus considerably more sophisticated in its capabilities than the flat-file dbm and is thus preferred for the larger and more complex applications. However, whether you use a flat-file or a relational dbm, the use of any dbm for handling lists greatly expands what you can do with your lists.

This great expansion of your ability includes searches, analyses, trial fits, and many other manipulations for on-screen study; you need not print anything out until you have gotten some answers and decided what you want. With today's technology, you can handle almost any list on a modern desktop computer: Reliance on large, mainframe computers is dwindling to a large extent, as desktop computers are expanding in their capacity and even now come equipped to handle files running to many millions of names. Too, in many cases, desktop computers are used as links to mainframe computers, serving as remote terminals or work stations.

DATABASES VERSUS MAILING LISTS

Today, if you read the periodicals devoted to mail order generally and to direct mail especially, including the advertising addressed to those who are prospects for mailing lists, you will see more and more reference made to databases offered. The essential difference between renting mailing lists and renting databases is primarily a matter of the difference in the information you will get about the names on the list. Jocularly, you might say that a database is a mailing list with a college education and not be far from the truth!

A *database*, as the term is used by advertisers, is a mailing list or a set of mailing lists with a great deal more information about the people on the lists than people were able to compile in the days before modern computers. That makes the difference between mailing lists and databases a matter of degree (of information) more than a matter of kind. However, the distinction also reflects a vast difference in value and usefulness: You can *do* a great deal more with a database than you can with a simple mailing list or set of mailing lists, making the database almost incomprehensibly more versatile and valuable.

Judging by the amount of literature devoted to explaining this, the subject is perhaps a bit complicated. However, it is probably easiest to appreciate this fully by the example of how you would handle your own in-house lists. On the most basic level, in-house lists are of two kinds: customers and prospective customers. On a slightly more sophisticated level, customer lists may be subdivided into recency and size of purchases, and prospect lists may be subdivided into inquirers and other prospects.

Over time, a great deal more information about customers may be developed, and the more information you have, the more valuable is the list. (Now you know why you are often asked to fill out questionnaires and supply what appears to be irrelevant information about yourself!) You might, for example, start coding customer lists—and, where possible, prospect lists also—with such additional information as the following:

Zip codes
Age
Education
Residences
    Home owners
    Condominium owners
    Apartment dwellers/renters
Length of residency
Credit ratings
Size of families
Frequency of purchases
Types of purchases or other patterns of buying
Average size of purchases

Obviously, such information makes it much easier to market effectively to customers and to prospects. When you have a special item to offer or want to run a special sale of some kind, you can go into your database files and develop a profile of the ideal prospects among both your customer and your prospect lists. For example, apartment renters would not usually be good prospects for aluminum siding or for major appliances; you would want to reach home owners and possibly condominium owners with such appeals. You also would not appeal to retired people with school supplies or children's clothing ordinarily; instead, you would want to search out names of young couples with small children. Whether you sell shoes, insurance, automobiles, or furniture polish, the more you know about customers and prospects, the more you will be able to sell.

Computers and dbm software makes the compilation and retrieval of such vast amounts and kinds of data possible. A relational database manager begins to shine above the flat-file database manager because with it, you can combine names from different lists to meet any given need.

The value of such data as part of your in-house lists for your own marketing is rather obvious. However, it has another great advantage: When the time comes that you wish to begin renting out your lists, whether directly or through a list manager/broker, as most list owners do, that store of data about the people whose names are in your database makes your lists a great deal more valuable. Your list manager can command prices for rental of your lists in some proportion to the amount and kind of data available about the names on the list. It thus has a double value for you as the list owner: It rents more easily and for higher prices than do simple mailing lists.

On the other hand, when you are the renter, you seek the most effective lists you can find. If you rent an ordinary mailing list, it comes to you with only a parameter or two qualifying and describing it. When you rent a database, however, you get a volume of information that enables you to use the list more effectively than if it were a simple mailing list. Whether it is your own list or a brokered list, you can specify what you want—the list that most closely approaches the ideal prospective buyer for what you offer. Undoubtedly, as time goes on, databases will increasingly dominate the list rental industry.

9

Costing, Pricing, and Accounting

The more you know about accounting, the more control you will have over your business.

COSTING AND PRICING

Setting prices for what you sell is never easy. There are several influences, but they fall into two categories: (1) Marketing—that is, determining prices that aid and support marketing (i.e., encourage sales), and (2) costs of doing business and of individual products, which determine the prices you must charge to turn enough profit for survival. At least one of the benefits of effective accounting is to help you with this and even to help you exercise a degree of control over costs. First, consider the influence of marketing when determining prices.

Why People Shop by Mail and Catalog

Most people who shop by mail do so either for convenience or for economy. That is, they use mail order because they do not have the time or the inclination to go out shopping personally, or they believe that they can usually save money by using mail order for their shopping.

I confess to both motivations for my own shopping for certain items, especially those items I use in my everyday work—office supplies and computer supplies. I have never been able to find local sources of supply for a great many items at prices that even approach those of many mail-order houses. For example, I bought my fax machine, a Murata 1200, for $600 by mail order. It has since been offered by other mail-order dealers for even less than that low price (as low as $459 at the moment) but at the time I am writing this, I have yet to find it offered in the local, across-the-counter stores for less than $629, and I have seen it in department stores at its list price of $900. The same thing is true for a great many other items.

Every Monday, the *Washington Post* publishes its business section as a rather thick tabloid insert, and the display advertising therein is inevitably dominated by computer sellers: The tabloid is almost as much a computer catalog as it is a newspaper business section. It is preponderantly advertising for local computer sellers, usually offering discounted prices, or what are claimed to be discounted prices. But even they are rarely price competitive with the mail-order computer sellers who advertise regularly in *Computer Shopper* and other nationally distributed computer periodicals.

I read the newspaper's computer advertisements every Monday with great interest, but I turn to mail-order dealers for most computer items that I buy for my serious business use. The exceptions are usually major equipment or those few cases where I cannot afford to wait a week or two for delivery and am not spending enough to justify overnight delivery service. (Many mail-order suppliers offer this overnight service at extra cost on small purchases, and some at no extra cost on large purchases.)

Must You Discount Your Prices?

Am I typical in my buying habits? Are all mail-order buyers seeking bargains, low prices? I can't answer that with certainty, but obviously many mail-order sellers believe they do. A substantial part of the market is dominated by sellers appealing primarily on the basis of price. The low prices also largely result from the heavy competition in the computer field, which "trains" or conditions the public to expect discounted prices in their other mail-order purchases. That expectation drives down prices in all mail-order fields. Because many catalogs feature or at least allege low prices, it seems to be clear that discount pricing is expected by a large part of the catalog-shopping buyers. Although the marketing strategy of many catalog businesses is based either on offering items not found elsewhere or on appealing to the convenience motivator, it is even more often based on discount pricing and its appeal.

Low prices, or apparent low prices, particularly characterize catalogs that are business-to-business (BTB) sales oriented. I do not find it strange that BTB cataloging should be price-based; business executives certainly find keeping costs to a minimum very much in their own interests and are likely to do so without much conscious deliberation. In addition, many other kinds of merchandise are commonly sold by catalog on a discount or bargain-prices basis. Vitamins and related drug items are quite commonly sold at discounts, probably because the normal markups for such items are quite high and thus allow ample margins for price cutting. Also, price-cutting and discounting are quite common in catalog sales of many other items, such as photographic equipment and supplies, books, gadgets and novelties, magazine subscriptions, and just about any kind of item that is readily available elsewhere and easy to compare for prices—that is, for all highly competitive lines, even those that do not offer high margins for markup.

The Influence of Comparison Shopping

It is not difficult to "shop around" for many items, especially if brand names are unimportant to you. However, there are also many kinds of merchandise where comparison shopping is so difficult as to be impractical. Furniture and clothing are good examples. It is very difficult to go off and find another dealer offering the identical sofa or jacket you just looked at in another store or another catalog. Hence, catalogers of such merchandise may use such words as *sale, discount,* and *low, low prices,* but the drive to sell price rather than quality does not usually have the same impact as it does in selling merchandise for which the prospect can verify the truth of your price claims. You must try to persuade the reader that your prices are, indeed, low, but it is not easy to prove your case. In fact, it often helps to tell the reader why you are able to offer such a ridiculously low price. That is why sales of such merchandise are often introduced with an explanation of how the seller has just bought out the entire inventory of some warehouse, the bargain is made possible by a sudden model change, the cataloger's merchandise buyer made a stupid error and bought too many of the item, the cataloger fortuitously discovered a large inventory that had been resting forgotten in a remote corner of the warehouse, or other such story.

Making Customers Versus Making Sales

Still another factor affecting prices and markups is the possibility or probability of repeat sales and the frequency of such repeat sales (i.e., of how frequently the customers are likely to buy from you), which is sometimes a question of whether the items (or at least most of the items) in the line are consumables.

Supermarkets sell their food at relatively slender markups, as little as 10 percent and even less in some cases. The great volume of sales and, especially, the regular frequency of repeat sales permits dealers to engage in this kind of pricing. Supermarket business is based heavily on selling to the same customers week after week, and perhaps even more frequently than that. There certainly are other factors. For example, the great buying power of such stores results in the advantages of leveraged buying, and the great competition compels highly competitive pricing.

Nonetheless, probably more important than any other factors is the fact that most of what a supermarket sells is consumable and is consumed daily, forcing the store's customers to replenish stocks frequently and regularly. Frequency of purchases (especially of consumable items) is a consideration in cataloging, too. If you sell a line of consumables, the potential for continuing sales to the customers you make must affect your thinking and decisions about pricing and cost strategies.

It Is a Numbers Game

To pursue a sensible and useful discussion of costs and pricing, you must have at least a limited understanding of accounting. No, you should not leave that entirely up to your hired accountant, no matter how expert he or she is. It is as important to understand basic principles of accounting as it is to understand basic principles of the catalog business (which your accountant need not understand). Ignorance of accounting is hazardous to your (business) health.

ACCOUNTING FOR THE LAY PERSON

First, a frank admission: I am not an accountant, and I profess to no real expertise in it. I have never had formal training in the subject. What little I know or think I know about the subject is simply what I have picked up over many years in managing my own and others' businesses, which has made me responsible for the bottom line and for all the lines above it.

My ignorance may actually be more an advantage than a handicap here because I can't dazzle and bewilder you with the special professional argot of accountants. I am compelled to use lay language and present simplified and perhaps even oversimplified explanations. Nonetheless, there are some terms that have specific meanings for accounting. When I am forced to use an accounting phrase that means something quite different than it appears to mean to the lay person, such as *cash basis* or *cost of sales*, I will explain what I think it means to an accountant and, at least, what *I* mean by it.

For example, I once thought that "cost of sales" referred to the cost of winning the order or of making the sale. I have since discovered that *cost of sales* includes the total cost connected with making the sale and with *fulfillment* (i.e., filling the order represented by the sale). I also thought that keeping my system on a "cash basis" meant literally selling strictly for cash. Instead, a *cash-based* accounting system means that the bookkeeper posts items in the ledgers only when they were actually received or paid. The other system—*accrual-based* accounting—posts items when they are billed and posts expenses when they are charged, whether paid or not. So have no fears; I won't confuse you or leave you behind because I can't. If I know more about accounting than you do, it is not much more, and it may very well be less.

Why You Need Accounting: The True Purpose

Ask lay people why it is necessary to have accounting systems, and you may be surprised at how often you are told that it is because the IRS requires it. (That is a response I often get from seminar attendees when I ask the question.) However, that belief is a half-truth and is misleading. The IRS does require you to keep records, but not necessarily as a formal or full-blown accounting system. Technically, you could probably satisfy the legal requirement for records by keeping boxes of bills, receipts, and canceled checks and check stubs, along with a school kid's copy book in which you have logged transactions or each day's business in chronological order with dates, as many small business owners did in the past. (*That* ought to discourage future IRS audits!)

The problem with this kind of recordkeeping is that it is of little use to you for anything except responding to an IRS complaint or proving that you did pay a bill that is in dispute. It doesn't help you much if you are trying to determine (a) whether your costs—either in general or for any specific item—have gone up or down, (b) whether you are making or losing money on any given item, (c) whether you are getting a fair return on your investment (ROI), (d) whether you have reached your desired net worth, or (e) whether you are even turning a profit in general.

"Shoebox recordkeeping" leads to a failure to be able to discover such facts about your business, which can lead to far more serious failure in today's world. In fact, it has led many businesses to the edge of bankruptcy and sometimes over the edge. It is not unheard of for companies to lose money steadily for a long time and be unaware of it—unaware until, that is, it is too late to save the venture from liquidation or from the auction block. It is even more common for companies to have unprofitable areas that drain the profits earned elsewhere, preventing the company from achieving its full profit potential. For example, you might be earning substantial profits on your line of perfumes, while your line of lipsticks is a consistent loser. Yet if you weren't monitoring your accounts, you might not know it. The lipstick disaster could even destroy you or, at least, prevent you from achieving the full potential of your business.

It is also true that some individuals get caught up in mistaken views of the importance of vindicating their own judgment. They champion the selling of a favorite item that does not sell well, and they fiercely resist all signs that the item is a drag on the business and ought to be dropped, believing that their own prestige is at stake. Accounting ought to reveal clearly the truth about the item by providing the numbers. It is easy to assure yourself that something "ought to" do well, but it is quite another matter to look at the numbers on a page; they tend to have a coldly sobering effect on misplaced wild enthusiasm.

In short, the purpose of an accounting system is to provide information for intelligent management. You need to *know* how well your perfume is doing and how poorly your lipsticks are doing, and you need to know it before you are too deeply in trouble to salvage the situation by raising lipstick prices, changing the line, dropping the line, mounting a special lipstick-marketing program, or doing whatever you think is a proper remedy. Your chosen remedy may or may not prove to be the right one, but at least you can be aware of the problem. In that way, you can do something about it while there is still time, using the unemotional, hardheaded numbers from the accounting system as a guide. Your business can tolerate or even survive mistakes, and undoubtedly you will make a few, but your business cannot tolerate and survive ignorance of the truth. The major role of accounting is to provide you with the truth on a regular, continuing basis.

Size and Nature of Accounting Systems

Large and complex corporations have large and complex accounting systems. They need such systems to manage their businesses. Unfortunately, sometimes small and simple corporations choose to have large and complex accounting systems. (Or they permit their accountants to talk them into large and complex accounting systems.) That is often a mistake and a misfortune because such systems tend to be too ponderous for the small organization. The reports take too long to be developed so that they can be studied carefully. Perhaps the multibillion-dollar supercorporation can survive a year or two of undetected losses or other problems, but the small business usually cannot do so. (Large and complex accounting systems tend to be far slower in reporting than small and simple systems are, and they may even fail to report one year's business results or even its current condition in any detail until the following year.) The small company usually cannot afford to wait until December to learn how it was doing the previous summer, for example.

The accounting system ought to be proportional to the size and complexity of the company. I am very small, as a corporation, so I have a very simple accounting system, a proprietary one (Dome®), available in most office-supplies emporiums, that tells me early each month how I did the previous month. In fact, if I wish to take the time to examine the records, I can determine quite easily and quickly how I did as recently as last week!

Being Profitable

In one sense, there are only two kinds of dollars in business, as in life generally: those that come in and those that go out. The trick is to keep the two at least in balance, to see to it that outgo does not exceed income. That is, outgo may exceed income momentarily—this week or this month—but they must at least balance over the long haul. That's the minimum, that is. The real goal, of course, is have an imbalance in which the income is considerably more than the outgo. Having said that, it must be recognized that there is a great deal more to be said on the subject, for nothing is really quite that simple.

Profit. A true understanding of the simple proposition of income versus outgo requires that the dollars be subdivided. In business, the basic excess of income over outgo is known as "profit." For accounting purposes, however, that must be subdivided as *gross profit, net profit,* and *pretax profit.*

Net profit and *pretax profit* are not precise terms. *Gross profit,* however, is relatively easily defined. *Gross profit* is the difference between what an item costs you to buy or manufacture and what you receive when you sell it. If you pay $5 for the item and charge customers $8.95, the gross profit is then $3.95 on the item. This can also be translated into total gross profit for the year. For example, if you paid out $100,000 to buy or manufacture whatever you sold, and you sold it for $175,000, you had a gross profit of $75,000.

Net profit takes into account the additional costs of selling the item— overhead, advertising, packaging, fulfillment, and other such costs. It is not easy to assess these on each individual item or individual sale, so it is usually determined for the entire year's operation. Using the figures of the first example (for gross profit), if it also cost you $20,000 to advertise, sell, and ship the products, you would have had a net profit of $55,000.

Pretax profit refers to federal—IRS—taxes on company or corporate income, and it is usually the same as *net profit*. However, *pretax profit* differs from net profit when applied to fairly complex corporate structures that have special costs (e.g., G&A [general and accounting] costs, write-offs, or other such special costs). In such complex cases, the special costs are deducted before taxes are assessed, to identify the pretax profits of the corporation—that is, the profits before the IRS exacts its toll. Finally, the term *net net profit* refers to a final profit after all deductions, including taxes, are made.

Assets.   Even the three terms for *profit* oversimplify the income or profit you receive. Income or profits are not always represented by cash on hand. After processing by the accountants, profits may emerge as *assets* of various kinds. Assets can include cash on hand, negotiable securities, fixtures, equipment, supplies, inventory, billed and unbilled receivables, mailing lists, and, for some kinds of ventures, labor inventory (custom work not yet fully complete and thus not yet billable), and even R&D in inventory.

The Cost of Doing Business

Aside from all this, the important thing is to understand costs, but even that is not uncomplicated, for costs must be sorted out and classified if they are to be controlled. On the most basic level, all costs are either *direct* or *indirect*, and an understanding of that is a first step in controlling them.

Direct Costs.   A *direct cost* is a cost that is incurred for a given sale and can be identified as being confined to that sale. If you sell a wrist watch that costs you $11, you have a direct cost of $11. You also have the costs of getting that sale and of packaging and shipping it. If you can positively identify all those costs for each given sale, you can count them as direct costs. Of course, you may not be able to do that as a practical matter. If you use a contractor to do your fulfillment and get billed a unit price for each order filled, you will probably be able to assign fulfillment expenses as direct costs. Otherwise, it is quite difficult to pin down these costs, which means that you must count those as indirect costs.

Indirect Costs. Those "other" costs that cannot be isolated and as-signed to each sale are real enough, despite the inability to connect them specifically with each sale. They include labor, printing, postage, materials, and shipping expense (assuming here that you do your own fulfillment). That's not all: Rent, heat, light, telephone, insurance, taxes, licenses, salaries, and possibly even other items have to be deducted from income. They are indirect costs because there is no way to know just what portion of those costs should be applied to each sale. Still, the business must bring in at least as much as it pays out if it is to survive, let alone show a net profit, after all the bills are paid.

There is yet another kind of indirect cost. When you started the business, you invested start-up capital for furniture and equipment. You must recover that too, for the furniture and equipment ("capital items," in accounting parlance) wear out and lose their value as time goes on. They depreciate, as your automobile does, and the loss represented by that depreciation of value also must be recovered by the business.

Another name for all those indirect costs is *overhead.* In fact, indirect costs are often broken down into various categories, but that does not affect the principle that all those costs are necessary to keep your business going, even when things are slow. Some of those costs are *variable* and decline when business is slow. But many of those costs are *fixed*—rent, for example—and are as high when you are doing zero business as they are when you are swamped with orders.

Profit. Most businesses count profit as a rate, a percentage of all costs. Here is a simple illustration of that:

Direct cost:	$10.00
Overhead (@ 60%):	6.00
Subtotal:	16.00
Profit (@ 25%):	4.00
Total (selling) price:	$20.00

The rates charged vary widely with the nature of the business and with the merchandise or services sold. The figures furnished by your accounting system are important in many ways. For example, suppose that a competitor sells an item for $15, while you find it impossible to sell that identical item for less than $16 without losing money. Suppose also that you can buy the item at the same price your competitor does. How is it that she or he can sell it for less?

The answer may be that your competitor (a) has a lower overhead rate, (b) is selling the item as a loss leader, (c) has grossly overestimated the market for the item, or perhaps (d) is losing money on it and does not know it. (That does happen and is responsible for some bankruptcies.) That illustrates the absolute need to know what "the numbers" are.

How Much Is True Profit?

The earlier example may help in understanding profit. If you get $25 for a watch that cost you $11, you have a markup or *gross profit* of $14. Part of that $14 must go to pay those indirect expenses, that overhead. The question now is how much you must mark up the price. Is $14 enough to cover all those costs? How do you determine how much you must add to the $11 direct cost to determine the true, full cost of the item? That is, how do you discover your overhead rate?

In practice, most systems would divide indirect costs into several classes (e.g., overhead, fringe benefits, and general and administrative costs). Different kinds of business handle the accounting differently. Some even have different kinds of overhead, such as labor overhead and materials overhead. However, for convenience of explanation here, I lump all indirect costs together and call it "overhead." That explains the principles, and it is easy enough to understand the more sophisticated systems once you master the principles.

Overhead as a Rate

The most practical way of assigning overhead costs to sales is to establish a *rate* of overhead in percentage terms. That is, find the ratio between the direct costs and the indirect costs. For example, if all the merchandise you sold last year cost you $100,000, and all your indirect expenses for the year came to $75,000, your overhead rate is 100,000/75,000 or 0.75, which is 75 percent. (The first year, having no history and thus no historical data, you generally have to estimate your overhead rate and set it high enough to be safe.) So the watch that cost you $11 in direct cost must be assigned an additional cost of $11 x .75 or $8.25. The watch therefore cost you $19.25 in total, giving you a pretax profit of $5.75, which is 23 percent of the selling price.

You can now decide whether you can afford to discount that $25 price a bit. If you were to apply 20 percent as your necessary profit margin, you would charge $23.10 ($19.25 + [19.25 x 0.20]) for the watch. If you felt forced by competition to cut the price further, you have little left to cut, since your profit margin is not that great. That illustrates why it is so important to keep overhead as low as possible. If you manage to reduce overhead to 60 percent, for example, you need add only $6.60 in overhead to the $11 cost of the watch for a total of $17.60, reducing your total cost by another $1.65, giving you more profit and more marketing leverage.

Another factor influencing your profits is your volume of sales. Suppose that the watch in question is a big seller. That is a factor you consider when deciding what to charge for it. The important question is not what percentage of profit you can make on the watch but what produces the greatest total number of dollars in profit. If you sell 1,000 of these watches at a $5 profit, the total is $5,000, of course. Suppose, however, that you could sell 2,000 by cutting the profit to $4 per watch. Would that pay you? Or suppose you can sell the watch at a $7.50 profit, but orders fall off about 20 percent to 800, instead of 1,000. That would still produce greater profit.

On the other hand, you may have some items that sell poorly at any price; not many of your customers seem to care for them under any circumstances. You find, however, that the number sold does not vary greatly even when you raise the price. Perhaps it does not pay to carry them at all, but it may pay to carry them at a large markup. That is, discounting the items does not help the sale of them, but taking a large profit on the item makes it worthwhile to carry it. You must experiment and test, but you need reliable and prompt accounting data to make the judgments and reach a wise decision.

Again, suppose you are looking for a loss leader, an item that will help bring in inquiries, furnishing new names and addresses to whom to send catalogs and literature. What kind of item makes a good loss leader? It must be something a great many people are likely to find useful enough to order, so slow-moving items do not make good loss leaders. It must also be something that can be "popularly priced": It must cost only a little and be highly competitive in price—lower than others offer it. It must also be something you can price competitively and yet not lose your shirt. Again, this demonstrates the value of a good accounting system to help you find what you need.

DO YOU NEED AN ACCOUNTANT?

With the modern desktop computer in almost all offices, even the smallest ones, it is easy enough to install your own computer-based accounting system, and you need not be an expert to run a system designed for a small business.

The programs will usually guide you with menus and print out any reports you need to study. However, if you feel the need for a professional accountant, it's easy enough to buy services from a local CPA. I recommend, however, that you do so only after you have mastered a few basics of accounting so that you can communicate with the accountant, ask the right questions, and not be intimidated by what appears to be frighteningly arcane knowledge.

Above all, it is important to use a system that is highly visible—that is, one that keeps you posted on how things are going, rather than one that requires you to wait until June to get reports on March or April operations. In short, you want a system appropriate to the size and nature of your business. Unfortunately, the accountant you retain will probably know little of the catalog business and so may try to urge a much larger and more complex system on you than you need, whereas you want a system that is as simple as possible, consistent with your business needs.

10

What It Takes to Succeed

Success in business is no accident, nor does it result from a simple formula. It is compounded of many ingredients cemented together by patience and perseverance. But a little luck does not hurt!

THE HIGH FAILURE RATE OF BUSINESS

Bankruptcies of small, young businesses have been increasingly common in the United States in recent years. The U.S. Small Business Administration, the U.S. Chamber of Commerce, Dun & Bradstreet, and various economists writing books and newspaper columns have reported and commented on this. In fact, a wide assortment of business experts have observed, speculated, and expressed opinions on this aspect of the business world. On one thing at least they are in general agreement, if not on most things: The number of failures of businesses in their first year or two of existence is large. On the causes of most such failures, they rarely agree. Here are just a few of the most popular reasons advanced for such failures:

Undercapitalization (or underfinancing, if you prefer)
Inadequate accounting
Lack of advance planning
Poor management generally
Lack of business experience

I believe that these experts tend to overlook at least one obvious factor when they make these observations: marketing. Before discussing marketing, however, it's valuable to consider the other factors named here. They are valid

213

and important enough to merit their own discussions, especially the matter of inexperience in business. Every beginning entrepreneur ought to know and consider several of these business fundamentals.

A FEW FUNDAMENTAL DISCUSSIONS

Cataloging is essentially a mail-order or direct-mail business, and subject to the influences that affect direct-mail success. As mentioned previously, mail order, direct mail, and cataloging are not different in basic business principles than any other business: The verities of business in general apply here as they do elsewhere. To avoid the several causes of business failure, you should consider a few questions about how businesses work. If you are newly in business or now contemplating a venture into business, it may be particularly helpful to explore several basic factors that apply to all business ventures. (Some of these are among the most-asked questions at small-business seminars.)

What Form of Business Organization Should You Use?

To incorporate or not to incorporate? That appears to be almost eternally burning brightly as a question. (It is one of the most frequently asked questions at my seminars.) Many starting out in business believe it to be a must or at least a highly desirable move to be able to add "Inc." after their business name, whatever that is.

First, it may help to clear up some misunderstandings about incorporation. In most states, it is neither difficult nor expensive to incorporate yourself and your venture today. Also, in most states, you do not absolutely require the services of a qualified lawyer in order to incorporate, although you may wish to discuss the question with a lawyer and get legal definitions that are well beyond the scope of this book. That is because there are several forms of incorporation, and what is best for one individual and his or her enterprise is not necessarily best for the next one.

I chose to incorporate as a simple, closely held or "close" corporation. That means that I do not offer stock to the public; all stock is held by the founders of the corporation. Taxes are levied both on corporate profits and on stockholders' salaries or other income from the corporation. Some people believe that a "Subchapter S corporation" is the way to go because it offers tax advantages, in that individuals getting income from the corporation are taxed, but the corporation itself is not taxed. There are also a number of other forms of incorporation, such as nonprofit incorporation, which has its own pros and cons. In general, however, the main benefit of doing business as a corporation is that it shields you from personal liabilities for the business liabilities of the corporation, although there are also a few tax benefits and possibly other advantages and benefits.

You can incorporate quite easily in most states by inquiring of your state's attorney general, although you can probably get the information at your own city hall or county government office. In Maryland, my own state, the State Department of Assessment and Taxation in Baltimore handles the matter, issuing a one-page form, which you fill out and return with the required fee (it was $40 when I incorporated here a few years ago).

When the officials check and verify that no one has already registered a corporation in the name you have chosen, you are advised that your corporation now exists. You need a set of bylaws, stock certificates, resolution forms, and a seal. (The seal is not a must item, however, because your signature is a "seal," technically, and it satisfies legal requirements; also, even a rubber stamp will serve.) You can buy a complete package of those things from people who specialize in such matters, and you can generally find several such suppliers listed in the yellow pages of any sizable community. At the time I chose to incorporate my own modest venture, the entire package, incorporation and appurtenances thereto, cost me slightly less than $100. There has been a little more inflation since then, and the cost may have risen a bit, but it is still easily affordable for most people in most states.

You can also form a partnership as a way of doing business or you can be a sole proprietorship if you have no other principals in your venture. It is a much simpler way of doing business, but you are then personally responsible for every liability of the business. You certainly should be aware of that. Incorporation imposes some additional accounting and tax burdens on you, but they are not especially onerous as additions to the basic burdens for such things. Incorporation does afford you some protection that is worth having for a catalog business—even essential, in my opinion.

If you trade under your personal name (e.g., Harry Jones or Harry Jones and Company), you need nothing except whatever business licenses your local jurisdiction requires. If you have incorporated, you have discharged your legal obligation to register properly and need do no more, except perhaps for local licensing that may apply. If you use a trade name, however, such as HJ Associates, you are Harry Jones doing business as (DBA) HJ Associates, and you must register that DBA name. Such registration is likely to be a requirement of both your state and your county governments. It is usually a simple procedure of making out forms, paying the fees, and advertising the fact that Harry Jones is doing business as HJ Associates at such and such location. You can hire a lawyer to handle this for you, or you can do it yourself.

Do You Need Consulting and Other Specialist Help?

In this age of increasingly complex taxes and laws—not to mention computers and their effect on business—fewer and fewer business owners are willing to face these complexities alone. Most turn to accountants, attorneys, and other consultants for help. That is as it should be.

However, you should also understand what your relationships with all these experts ought to be and what you should expect and require of them. Don't make the all-too-common mistake of expecting—or allowing—these individuals to make your decisions. That is not their role. They are advisers only. Sensing your uncertainty or fears, a well-meaning lawyer, accountant, or other expert may make such strong recommendations and present only that strong recommendation so that you unthinkingly accept it. Stop and think about that: Should you permit a stranger to make your business decisions?

The answer is "no," of course, but unless you specifically ask for it, you may not get a complete pro-and-con accounting and appraisal, as you should have. The role of an expert consultant is to analyze your problem or need, to explain it to you, to present alternatives, to make a recommendation (when you ask for it), and to explain the rationale for the recommendation. A well-trained and completely honest consultant will make it clear that he or she presents only findings, conclusions, and recommendations; the final decision is yours and yours alone.

Decisions are always your sole responsibility. Effective decisions, however, are based on information, and that is why you turn to consultants—when you need information. Be sure that you get that information, all of it, and that you make your decision based on that information.

What Initial Plans, Estimates, Investments, and Commitments Should You Make?

One of the other basic mistakes newcomers to business make is to overinvest and to overcommit themselves initially. They rent expensive suites of offices, buy costly furniture and equipment, and order huge supplies of expensive stationery and other office supplies. Unfortunately, the optimism radiated by this is rarely justified. Most businesses require a lot of time (two to four years, usually) to get really well established, and many find success eventually doing something different than they had planned originally to do—sometimes radically different, in fact. Many of the prominent companies of today bear that out. Sears and Montgomery Ward were both mail-order businesses originally, before they became catalog businesses and finally retail department stores. Volt Information Sciences was originally a small-contract technical writing service before it grew into the leading supplier of professional–technical temporary workers and typesetting services, a $500 million per year corporation that is still growing rapidly. The huge Marriott hotel and restaurant chain started life as a root beer stand. And Milton Hershey never started out to be the king of chocolate.

Thus, it would not be an unprecedented event of business if it were to happen to you, too. You may very well start out to sell a line of cosmetics, for example. You stock merchandise, print brochures and stationery, have signs made, and otherwise commit yourself firmly to your cosmetic line. Six months or a year later, however, you may be forced to admit that your cosmetics are not selling nearly as well as you had hoped and be thus forced to look about you for another line of products or another route to success.

Also, despite initial success, some modern development may force the change by making obsolete the line you have been selling. Forced change was the case for Fingerhut, when the introduction of vinyl upholstery in automobiles brought an almost complete and sudden end to the automobile seat-cover business. (Fingerhut now sells a wide line of general merchandise.)

On the other hand, that sideline of perfumed soaps and candles that you more or less stumbled into may be doing remarkably well, and you then consider selling out that line of cosmetics and switching over to soaps and candles. It's not unusual. In fact, the changeover usually involves a more dramatic change than this, as Marriott and Sears illustrated.

Don't be surprised by this. Many large and successful companies started out on the wrong foot and became large and successful because the entrepreneur was not only *willing* to make any necessary changes but also deliberately *watchful* for alternative or ancillary opportunities. Consider your opening venture experimental and tentative, and probe constantly for improvements or better alternatives. Beware of emotional attachments that deaden your business judgment and instincts.

Overall, the moral is simple: Start as modestly as possible. If you can start at home, do so; many large corporations started in the home or garage of the founder. (Volt Information Sciences and Quill® Corporation are two such.) Buy only what you need immediately; you'll have time enough to expand later. Put your money into whatever brings income to you. You can live without the frills, and you don't need to impress anyone with anything except that you are a good businessperson.

What Are the Causes of Exceptions?

Many of those who venture into independent businesses are totally unpre-pared in all the areas of concern and should logically fail rather quickly—but they don't. Many untutored, inexperienced, underfinanced entrepreneurs manage to make huge successes of their endeavors, even with informal and thoroughly unprofessional accounting and bookkeeping systems and casual or improvised management. The economists do not remark on or acknowl-edge the existence of those exceptions to the rules they have postulated. How do these novice entrepreneurs manage to do everything "all wrong" and have it turn out all right—to succeed, often on a grand scale? Can it be that there are so many exceptions to the rule, yet the exceptions signify nothing?

There is no doubt that the deficiencies indicated by the experts do contribute to the downfall of many new ventures by eager new entrepreneurs; these deficiencies may even be the proximate causes of disaster in some cases. Business is not so simple, especially in this modern age, that simplistic answers can be found for problems. Still, causes must be related to effects if business problems are to be solved. Therefore, are the expertly indicated faults more than occasionally the primary fatal weaknesses of new ventures that do not succeed? Are they, that is, the weaknesses most directly responsible for disaster? There is ample evidence that such a conclusion is by no means certain. There are other considerations.

MARKETING *IS* BUSINESS

What appears rarely to be considered in the survey and analysis of business failures is the impact of marketing. How often does a business fail when its marketing is highly effective (i.e., when sales are being made in satisfying volume)? Rarely. In most cases, the decline of a business that was once successful or that appeared to be headed for success is first apparent as a decline in sales, a decline that the ever-hopeful proprietor dismisses as a temporary slump. (In some cases, on the other hand, a new business never achieves an ample sales volume to begin with, but the entrepreneur and the experts monitoring do not always regard this as directly symptomatic in itself.)

Bear in mind that *marketing* and *business* are almost synonymous terms in a very real sense. Business-management guru Peter Drucker has stated plainly that the primary objective of business is to create customers. That has been echoed many times over by others, as if such an obvious truth requires confirmation. What other reason does a business have for existence than to make sales? What function other than making those sales—marketing—is more important? What, therefore, is more important than sales and customers?

It is difficult to avoid the conclusion that marketing is much more likely to be the primary influence in success and failure than is any other activity of a business. Even the business that is very well managed by experienced people, with ample financing and an excellent accounting system, cannot succeed without ample sales—without marketing success.

The converse is also true: That business which achieves and maintains an adequate volume of sales can tolerate a great deal of inefficiency, even incompetence, and a great many do. Even some rather large and successful corporations are poorly managed in every department except marketing. But when marketing falters, however, as in the case of Robert Hall, W. T. Grant, E. J. Korvette, and others, the other virtues do not save the day. Giants and even long-established businesses succumb to deficiencies in marketing just as pygmies and newcomers do. The failure of marketing is always a thrust to the heart.

Marketing Must Produce Profits

None of the foregoing is to say that marketing alone is the beginning and the end: Primary though it is, just making sales is not enough. Sales must be profitable. Goods must be sold at a profit—a price in excess of the cost of the goods that is large enough to cover all costs of making the sale, including salaries and overhead expenses at least. Those other expenses—overhead, especially—must be controlled so that they do not wipe out profits; excessive overhead—"runaway" overhead costs, as some refer to it—has damaged some businesses beyond repair. It is possible to make sales at what ought to be a proper markup over the cost of the merchandise, but with such high overhead costs that they nullify the benefits of the sales. Poor management generally and specific management weaknesses such as poor inventory control and poor purchasing practices can also contribute to business disaster.

Still, marketing is the one area where effective functioning is an absolute requisite and ineffective functioning is certain death. It is almost futile to discuss all the other functions and factors that enter into making a success of business unless it is accepted first that no business function is more unforgiving of shortcomings than is marketing.

How Much of a Success Does Marketing Have to Be?

Many successful businesses sell merchandise at a small markup, a markup that produces a very small gross profit on each sale. Such businesses are based on the principle of doing a large volume of sales and keeping all costs shaved to the bone. They are based on ROI—return (profit) on investment or net worth of the company—rather than on profit margins or gross sales. That is, you can operate on a tiny margin—as little as 1 percent, for example—if your total volume is great enough. Suppose that your venture reflects an investment of $200,000, produces $2 million in sales, and shows a net (after tax) profit of 1 percent. The 1 percent may be regarded by some as pitifully small, but it is a 10 percent ROI (aside from the fact that you presumably have drawn an ample salary for yourself). Your ROI is thus quite acceptable. Dollars are, in the end, the real measures. The success of business is achieved and measured by the success of marketing—doing that large sales volume—as well as by keeping costs low. Even then, the success lasts only as long as the marketing succeeds in maintaining that large volume of sales. Many successful discount houses attest to that, just as do unsuccessful ones.

That means that there is no absolute standard for the degree of success required of marketing. The sales volume (i.e., the income) required is linked to the other factors: to the markups, the overhead, and the other costs. (However, the reverse is true also, to the extent that costs are controllable.)

Many businesses have it both ways. Even businesses selling merchandise generally at comfortable or what might be referred to as "normal" markups often have sales that offer certain items at exceptionally low prices. Retail booksellers often have a table or two of "remaindered" books (books that did not sell well enough to keep them in print at their original prices) selling at about one fourth the normal cover price, for example. One well-known bookstore chain that sells all books at discount prices carries a large assortment of such remaindered books. Some observers who know the retail book business have speculated that this entrepreneur's profits come largely and perhaps even primarily from the sale of these bargain books.

BASIC MARKETING MISTAKES

Marketing is far from an exact science, for it depends on public reaction, which is rarely predictable; it is as unpredictable as "show biz," for who knows what personality the public will come to love? Thus, mistakes in marketing are made by experienced, large organizations spending large amounts of money, just as they are made by inexperienced, small organizations spending small amounts of money. It's easy to identify the campaigns that are mistakes because they vanish as soon as the organization finds that the campaign is not producing results. Of course, the inverse is also true: Successful campaigns can be easily identified by their continued life.

Despite the element of luck in marketing, there are certain principles that can enhance or diminish the likelihood of success. It is thus sometimes not at all difficult to identify basic mistakes that major advertisers often make, although it is difficult to understand why or how they have made them. One outstanding example was the Ford car company's TV campaign of a few years ago, when the popular Bill Cosby delivered a pitch for Ford's marvelous new ideas. The pitch concluded that it was easy to see "why" to buy a Ford: because Ford "wants to be your car company." It was also easy to see that whoever was responsible for that advertising of Ford did not understand the basic concept that the buyer does not give a damn about what the seller wants. Ford could not have found a bigger turnoff than trying to thrust its own desires down the buyers' throats! It is truly incredible that they did not see the fundamental mistake they were making. The only explanation might be that all too often corporate executives dismiss their own staff specialists and impose their own uninformed choices on the advertising agencies. (If only the advertising agencies had the integrity and the courage to refuse to implement a campaign that they know is all wrong!)

Alka Seltzer goofed equally with its now-famous "stomach" commercials. Beautifully done—they were very artistic and entertaining—they were too subtle for the general public: Hardly anyone got the message. The campaign was a Clio (advertising industry award) winner and a marketing/advertising loser, a true tragedy for both the agency and the company.

Though some mistakes of marketing and advertising become famous, most mistakes are whatever did not work. You usually don't know what is a mistake until you discover whether it worked. Even when you defy tradition or conventional wisdom and do what others say will not work, you may be right because conventional wisdom is not always right. An approach that failed a dozen times may succeed the next time it is tried because conditions are different, the "time is right," or some other variation makes the difference. Conventional wisdom is so often wrong that turning it on its head and doing the opposite often works quite well, as I and others have often found.

Still, business must learn from experience and must set some guidelines based on logical probability rather than on exceptions. Many "rules" or guidelines have developed based on experience and logic (although the logic is often merely rationalization). Use these as guidance, but be aware that they are guiding principles only, not absolute truth.

The "Me Too" Mistake

One mistake many make in marketing is to employ imitation instead of innovation. Too often, the entrepreneur compounds the error by imitating the largest and most successful competitors in the field. Most of the time, what works for the large and successful competitor does not and cannot work for you because (a) you do not have their resources, or (b) your conditions and situation differ from theirs in other ways. For example, the marketing tactics of a large competitor may be based on a strategy of saturating the market with its campaign and thus depends on a large marketing budget. You could not hope to compete with your minuscule budget. Or perhaps your competitor is so well known that the name alone makes the difference: No one would notice you if you were advertising "Me, too." Before you try to base advertising on what some competitor has done, be sure that you understand—*fully*—what that competitor's strategy was and can therefore appraise your own chances of competing against it.

Another mistake newcomers often make is basing their advertising on comparison, trying to prove that their products are better than those of the competitor, instead of working to present the merits of their product based on its own attributes. To resort to a military analogy, this is again trying to attack the enemy (your competitor) where he or she is strong and you are weak, always a tactical error. Message: Never apologize or work overtime at compensating for your weaknesses, or for what you conceive them as being, or for what you think your prospects perceive them as being; you are probably wrong. In any case, it is far better simply to ignore such ideas and to concentrate on your strengths or what you can offer and make appear to be strengths.

Military analogies apply in many ways. For example, even the strongest competitor has weaknesses—or, if not truly weaknesses, at least areas of vulnerability. You can find and attack areas that the competitor has not anticipated and is not prepared to defend. That is how inferior forces beat superior ones, and how newcomers and upstarts unseat entrenched organizations. In marketing, it is often far more effective to focus on differences than on similarities.

There was a time when Bromo Seltzer dominated the market for antacids. Then along came Alka Seltzer, the undisputed champion today (stomach ads and all). In fact, in its early days, when Alka Seltzer and Bromo Seltzer were dispensed at drug store fountains, Alka Seltzer provided a little machine that would grind the Alka Seltzer tablets into a coarse powder that resembled Bromo Seltzer. Eventually, Alka Seltzer's marketers realized that they were trying to imitate Bromo Seltzer and did not have to say "me too" to sell their product. Accordingly, those Alka Seltzer machines disappeared a long time ago. It was, or at least could be made to appear to be, much easier to simply drop two Alka Seltzer tablets into a glass of water than to measure out a capful of Bromo Seltzer powder and use two glasses to pour the water and powder mixture back and forth in what was then the classic gesture and action for dispensing Bromo Seltzer.

Alka Seltzer still features that "plop plop, fizz fizz" of two tablets in water to represent the difference and the superiority of Alka Seltzer. Again, the difference was more important than the similarity, and the alleged simplicity and ease of dropping two tablets into a glass of water became the advantage of Alka Seltzer over Bromo Seltzer. Remember always the Elmer Wheeler philosophy: When someone hands you a lemon, make lemonade! Turn around all apparent disadvantages and problems, for the flip side of a problem is the solution, and the flip side of a disadvantage is an advantage.

Exclusivity

You must make two kinds of sales or persuasions in marketing: One is to persuade prospects to buy what you are offering; the other is to persuade them to buy it from you. If you have an exclusive product of some kind you must make that exclusivity apparent so that the prospect knows that it is available only from you. (Note how advertisers of proprietary and unique items are at great pains to make prospects aware of that exclusivity.) However, if you are selling some item that is available elsewhere, you must guard against selling for your competitors. Carelessness or thoughtlessness in advertising can sometimes result in doing just that.

If your product line is not exclusive with you, you must make something about your offer exclusive. It may be your guarantee, your price, your terms, a free gift or bonus item, a rebate plan, a different medium or method for advertising, a contest, or any other feature that makes your offer stand out and attract buyers. Study what your competitors are doing and find some strategy that is not used by others in their appeals and offers. There are many possible ways of making your own offer exclusive or "different" in some manner.

Don't overlook the possibility of attracting customers by indirect benefits, such as a free newsletter or a helpful column of ideas and information included in your catalog. (Quill uses both these ideas, and the use of helpful information in catalogs is an increasingly popular method of inducing prospects to read and save catalogs.) See what other services you can come up with. Always *do* for your customer. He or she is as concerned with his or her own interests as you are for yours. Whether framed consciously or not by every prospective buyer, there is always the question, "What's in it for me?" Anticipate that question when you prepare your literature. What's more, in the catalog sales business, you must answer not only "What's in it for me?" to buy from this merchant, but also "What's in it for me?" to spend my time reading this catalog instead of dropping it in the trash can.

A Central Concept

Try to market in a positive way by finding claims you can make that are different and innovative instead of imitative. Montgomery Ward did it with an innovative guarantee. Alka Seltzer does it with "Oh, what a relief it is!" Sears became noted for its outstanding catalog, which became *the* stereotypical catalog, the catalog without peers, overshadowing all others. All State Insurance does it with the cupped hands, signifying its protection, as Prudential does with its "Rock" (Gibraltar), signifying dependable and unyielding reliability, and General Electric Company does with its slogans of the moment, currently "We bring good things to life."

"GROWTH": WHAT IS IT?

It is often said that a business cannot stand still. It must "grow," or it dies. Just what is meant by the term *grow?* Does it mean, as many interpret it, to grow larger in size . . . in sales? Or does it mean something else?

Whatever you sell, a tightly defined line or a broad assortment of goods or services, marketing ought to be based on a concept, as in the examples of Sears, Prudential, and General Electric. K-Mart, formerly Kresge's, then a direct competitor of the Woolworth dime stores, is an outstanding example of growth. The evolution of K-Mart was no accident. It was the result of two years' study of retailing trends, which had changed considerably over the years. (Business cannot stand still and survive; business graveyards are full of the bones of businesses that stood still, a few of which have been mentioned in this book, as object lessons.)

The venerable A&P chain of neighborhood stores grew similarly as the automobile inspired a migration to the suburbs and the rise of the supermarkets, and A&P became a chain of supermarkets. In recent years, they began to falter, and they became revitalized with a new concept and a new name: Super Fresh, a name that sends its own message.

In fact, if these examples have not already delivered the message, recognize now that growth has nothing to do with size or sales volume changes. It has to do with keeping up with what is happening in society generally. It has to do with recognizing that change is at least as inevitable as death (a big change) and taxes. If history teaches us nothing else, it teaches us that change is continuous and inevitable and that those who will not change are the dinosaurs of the modern age.

Growth is change. The U.S. Pressed Steel Car Company grew and today it is U.S. Industries. Volt Technical Corporation grew and today it is Volt Information Sciences. Hot Shoppes grew and today is Marriott Corporation. Kresge grew and today it is K-Mart. Of course, mere name change is not growth, and name change is not always necessary. International Business Machines— IBM—did not change its name when it became the leading computer company, nor did the Parker Pen Company when it turned to the manufacture and sale of ballpoint and felt-tip pens, in place of metal nibs, sold with ink bladders and ink cartridges.

Growth involves keeping up and changing with the trends and the times, and change is required at an ever-greater frequency, but it is the price of success in business and in many other things. You can never rest on yesterday's successes or even today's victories. Tomorrow demands more.

SPECIAL SALES AND PROMOTIONS

Perpetual Special Sales

Most business organizations occasionally have special sales. The sales are usually held because they have some remainder odd lots, because certain items in inventory are moving slowly and they want to clear them out, or because business is slow generally and needs some stimulus. However, many business organizations constantly have "special sales," as their routine or standard way of doing business. Some even claim that everything in their line is on sale every week. That is one way of doing business regularly because the buying public never gets tired of pursuing bargains to save money, and the word *sale* never wears out.

Many marketers make the notion of a special sale more credible by offering a special reason for each sale. A few of the "kinds" of sales you are likely to find advertised were presented in Chapter 4. Despite the length of that list, you can surely think up a few of your own. It somehow helps when the customer can associate a sale with some special reason or occasion.

Special Promotions

Many of the extra services you provide are permanent features of the way you do business, while others are temporary or "special promotions." A newsletter or business-tips column in your catalog may be a permanent feature, whereas a contest may be a temporary promotion—sometimes happening only once, sometimes periodically or even on a more or less regular basis, as in the case of the well-known Publishers Clearinghouse contests. A few other types of special promotions are these:

One-cent sales

Two-for-one sales (or "Buy two, get one free")

Discount coupons

Free seminars with door prizes

Special prize for the first 50 customers

Special loss leaders (mentioned in Chapters 3 and 7)

CONVERSION

In connection with leaders and loss leaders, consider what you are trying to do with your marketing. First of all, there is a difference between making sales and making customers. If you sell an item that the typical customer is likely to need or want to buy only once or, at best, only once in many years—an automobile or exercise bike—and you sell nothing else, you must obviously be out to make sales more than to make customers. You have little probability of repeat sales, at least not in the near future, and you must thus turn a profit on each sale if you are to survive. In the catalog business, however, you are obviously out to create customers—buyers who will return to buy again. (It is implicit in cataloging.) Therefore, that first sale to a new buyer is critical, *whether or not that sale is profitable.* You can afford to make that first sale to a new buyer at a break-even price or even at a slight loss, in such cases, because that first sale is *part of your marketing cost.* You must regard it that way. Even if you make that first sale at a cost less than the cost of the merchandise and getting the order, you did not actually lose money; you invested some money in marketing, in creating customers for future profits.

The conventional rules of mail order dictate a need for selling items at several times their direct cost to you, but those rules do not apply to your first sales. You can sell some items at three or more times their cost to you, but you can't sell all items that way. Most nationally advertised "name brands" and their equivalents are sold at 10 to 40 percent markup over their cost to you, and there is no way that you can sell them at three or four times—300 to 400 percent—their cost. In catalog sales of general merchandise (i.e., selling a variety of items people use regularly), your discount usually is going to be from 25 to 40 percent of the list price, and competition is often going to force you to sell the items at markups of only 10 to 20 percent. The only way you can survive in most cataloging ventures is by creating customers—repeat business, that is. The first sale costs you a lot of money. Sales to established customers cost you little. Recognition of that immutable—or almost immutable—truth is essential to your success.

The problem created by this immutable truth is that the first sale to a new buyer does not necessarily mean that you have made a customer. You must *convert* that first-time buyer into a customer through treatment that persuades the buyer to buy again. Not before you have made at least one follow-up sale to that first-time buyer can you believe that you have indeed made a customer, rather than merely a sale.

For that reason, it's worth making extra efforts to ensure that you satisfied the customer in the first sale (as well as in each succeeding sale). In most cases it is good business and sound marketing economics to adjust the buyer's complaints, even when you do not believe that they are entirely justified. It costs money to get customers, and it is usually cheaper to keep them than to replace them! Sometimes, that lesson is unfortunately lost to many entrepreneurs. But it is a lesson worth learning.

11

Financing Your Venture

Financing, especially initial financing for launching a venture, is by no means the least important business problem, or even the least complex one that you must face and solve.

HOW MUCH MONEY WILL YOU NEED?

Financing refers primarily to (a) investment capital, for the initiation of the venture ("front-end money" or "start-up capital"); (b) operating capital for covering day-to-day expenses; and (c) capital required for expansion once success increases the size of the business. How much financing your catalog venture will require for start-up will vary widely with the nature of what you sell (e.g., the cost of merchandise, the inventory you choose to carry, the trade credit you can win, and how you fulfill orders—from inventory or via drop-shipping— among many other factors).

The additional financing needed for operating your business also varies. For example, it is possible to conduct a catalog business with very little capital, by beginning in your own home, as many others have. You might enroll in some multilevel marketing system, or you might mail some distributor's catalog with your own name imprinted on the catalog and order forms, and you have the distributor fill all orders by drop-shipping for you. In addition to minimal operating costs, your principal start-up costs in this mode of operation are usually only for advertising, printing, and postage, unless the distributor requires you to buy a starting inventory or pay some kind of franchise fee.

These low-investment, low-cost approaches limit you in more than one way. First of all, you are limited to the products and terms of those distributors or manufacturers who offer arrangements of various kinds—multilevel marketing, trade credit, drop-shipping, or other aids to getting started. Not all offer aids by any means. Many offer ready-made catalogs of their merchandise and will imprint your own name and address in them, for example, but not all of those will drop-ship for you. In fact, many insist that you stock some minimum inventory as a first condition to selling their lines of merchandise, thus requiring an investment for merchandise. Also, they may insist on including in that inventory all items that appear in their catalog, even those that sell slowly. Some will offer terms—credit on your first order, provided you pay for the first order when you place the second order. (This is a fairly common arrangement with companies who market door-to-door.)

Having merchandise drop-shipped for you is not without its real costs to you. It normally means taking a much smaller profit as a price for the service. For example, an item that you can buy for your own inventory at 40 percent of its list price will be discounted to you by some lesser amount—perhaps only 25 percent—if you have it drop-shipped. Your risk and initial investment are greatly reduced, but so is your profit margin and your probability of success.

Although it is a practical possibility to start your catalog business this way, it is certainly more desirable to start with enough capital to create your own inventory and thus have complete control over profit margins, fulfillment, and other aspects of the venture. (One disadvantage of drop-shipping is that you have no control over fulfillment, and orders may not be filled as promptly as you and your customers wish.) In any case, the discussions that follow here are based on the assumption that you will wish to maintain a full capability, including inventory and whatever else is needed to establish yourself as a truly independent cataloger.

How much capital you will require to do this will vary, depending on what you wish to sell, on what scale you wish to begin, how self-sufficient you wish to be, and how wide a market you wish to pursue. It is possible to start in your own home with a tiny inventory, but for the purposes of this discussion, I will assume that you are going to start on a more ambitious scale and will need a substantial amount of money, at least some significant number of thousands of dollars, for a proper start.

A FEW BASIC FACTS ABOUT FINANCING

First of all, be aware that there are two basic methods for financing: debt financing and equity financing. The concepts are quite simple: *Debt financing* refers to borrowing money, money that must be repaid, usually with interest.

Equity financing refers to inducing others to invest in your enterprise, thereby acquiring for themselves an interest in or a share of ownership in your venture, from which they hope to gain a financial benefit. You do not have an obligation to repay the money when you succeed in getting equity financing, but you do surrender some part of your ownership in the venture.

Neither method is easy. The high rate of business failures makes both lenders and investors cautious, which is probably why lenders gain a reputation, merited or not, for lending money only to those who demonstrate that they do not need it: Lenders are far more ready to make secured loans, loans in which the borrower has furnished some collateral to reduce the risk the lender experiences. Similarly, of course, investors are equally concerned about risking their own capital. There are a number of ways for raising capital via either general method. Equity financing is discussed at the close of this chapter; debt financing is more commonly used by small start-up businesses.

DEBT FINANCING

Bank Loans

The best-known source of loans, and the one most of us approach with the greatest fear, is the bank. Banks and smiling bankers can inundate you with TV commercials and mail that explain how much they want to help you, urging you to apply for loans that are so easy to get. Then they turn down your application coldly, with an evasive explanation that leaves you in the dark as to why the loan was denied. Perhaps the requested loan was too small to interest the bankers: Oddly enough, many banks tend strongly to reject an application for a small loan for a business much more quickly than an application for a large loan. (It is because of this that the Small Business Administration often makes small business loans directly with government funds, although their financial assistance generally is based on guaranteeing loans made by lending institutions, just as the FHA [Federal Housing Administration], FmHA [Farmers Home Administration], and VA [Department of Veteran Affairs] guarantee mortgages.)

On the other hand, perhaps your application did not satisfy their ideas of what justifies a loan or what represents adequate collateral. Also, perhaps the bank favors one kind of loan over another, for whatever reason. That is, your description of the loan may be all wrong from the banker's point of view. Bankers have their own trade or professional jargon and their own standards for judging the qualifications of an applicant, and you must use their jargon and understand their standards to communicate effectively with and persuade them.

Despite the banker's preference for large loans, banks do make many small loans, even personal loans that are not secured by anything other than the individual's earning power and apparent honesty and trustworthiness—so-called signature loans. Many small businesses have been launched on the basis of personal loans as start-up capital. It is generally easier to obtain such loans while maintaining regular employment, so this should be obtained "before you quit your day job."

Loan Categories

A great deal of business financing is of a short-term nature. Even the largest corporations depend on the lending institutions to finance various facets of business, such as inventory, to name just one category that bankers tend to recognize.

Inventory Loans.   An automobile dealer probably has the inventory of automobiles on a "floor plan," which simply means that the dealer has borrowed money to pay for the automobiles and is paying interest while the automobiles stand unsold. Of course, these loans are secured by the automobiles, so the risk to the lender is relatively small. An inventory loan, if the inventory appears to be readily salable, is usually relatively easy to get because of the (usually) low risk. Inventory loans are therefore a specific category that most bankers recognize and are favorably disposed toward.

Line of Credit.   A line of credit, in general terms, is something like overdraft protection: In overdraft protection, the bank credits overdrafts of your checking account as a personal loan instead of bouncing your check. In a line-of-credit arrangement, you have a guaranteed line against which you can finance your operations, to the maximum established by your bank. There are several variations of this basic arrangement so that many businesses use it in various ways, which your banker can explain to you.

Commercial Loans.   One significant feature of this type of loan is that whereas many kinds of loans require periodic repayments, commercial loans are repaid in full at the end of the term, whether that is three months, six months, one year, or longer. (In some cases, interest payments are made at specified intervals, and you pay the principal at the end of the term, or you make payments on principal regularly. However, sometimes, if you cannot make payments on the principal when due, the bank will permit you to make payments on the interest and postpone making the payment on the principal.)

Accounts Receivable. Unless you deal on a strictly cash basis, which is not always possible (especially in business-to-business cataloging), you will find yourself with an increasing total of accounts receivable. It is difficult—almost suicidal, in a business sense—to deny good customers terms for payment—credit, that is. However, in doing so, your own cash reserves are likely to be badly strained. Ironically, the more business you do, the more severe the problem becomes. So you turn to the banks once again for help. You ask the bank to advance you money against your accounts receivable; they are your collateral.

In accounts receivable loans, banks often prefer to handle the accounts. That is, they will advance you perhaps about 75 percent of the face value of each account receivable if you have established the creditworthiness of the account, and you will forward the payment to the bank when the customer pays. The bank will then balance the account and credit your own account with the difference. (Actually, the bank is keeping books for you on these accounts and thereby providing a valuable and additional service!)

Factoring. In an extension of the accounts-receivable idea, a bank may actually buy your accounts receivable and be entirely responsible for collection. You may have experienced this personally when you bought a house, signed papers with a mortgage company, and a few weeks later received a notice from a bank that you were henceforth to send your house payments to them. (They probably sent you a payment book also.) The mortgage company simply sold your account to a bank, who took it over.

Medium- and Long-Term Loans. The foregoing are all short-term loans, and most are secured in one way or another, so they are relatively easy loans to arrange. Medium- and long-term loans are more difficult to arrange, especially if and when they are basic loans to launch a new venture. To a large degree, success in getting such loans depends on the quality of your application or loan proposal. That is often the most decisive factor in the process.

HOW TO WRITE A LOAN PROPOSAL

The heart of a loan proposal is the *business plan*. A well-written business plan is a firm underpinning for both debt financing and equity financing. Bankers want to know what the security is for their loans, and if you can demonstrate that the loan increases the value of your company, you have made a major step forward already. In fact, only relatively minor change is required to convert a good business plan into a sound loan proposal. There are, in fact, eight parts to a proper proposal, along the following lines:

1. Summary
2. Top management personnel
3. Nature of the business
4. Projections of sales and profits
5. Financial statements
6. Proposed use of loan money
7. Size of loan
8. Payback plans

However, the following caveat should be made clear here: The following notes and discussions are based on the premise of a loan proposal seeking start-up funding. This must be adapted to other situations and other needs. For example, if you are a well-established business seeking financing for expansion, you will *report* sales and financial *history*, rather than *project estimates*.

Components of a Proposal

Summary.   The summary, a first element in a business plan or loan proposal, is perhaps more important than you may believe; it can be decisive. It need not be long; it can be as little as one page, rarely more than two or three pages. It should be highly specific, identifying products to be marketed, and where and how things will be done. Will you manufacture, or will you have products manufactured under contract? To whom will you sell? What markets? How will you reach your markets? Avoid generalizations here. Shun hyperbole. Facts are impressive and convincing. Use nouns and verbs; avoid superlatives. Trim your language. Verbose plans are a liability, not an asset. Write it out and edit thoroughly.

Top Management People.   Bankers want to know with whom they are dealing. Introduce yourself and your other principals, if any, with résumés or written profiles of some sort. In these, give your bankers assurance that you are all experienced businesspeople who will manage efficiently and wisely. Set their minds at rest and win their confidence.

Nature of the Business.   This is one of the more important areas. Tell the reader just what this venture is all about. What will you sell? What will your inventory turnover rate be? Bankers would like to know the answers to these and similar questions. Describe the business as accurately as you can, and note here that bankers tend to be conservative. That means that they are usually much more optimistic about your chances of selling conventional merchandise than new items of unknown market appeal. The market prospects for innovative items are not likely to arouse their enthusiastic endorsement.

Projections.   Bankers are especially interested in what you estimate you can and will do in sales and profits, provided you can offer a convincing argument for the projections you make. Offer your targets and your rationales for them, and back up those projections and rationales with sound figures for their basis. Describe also your alternatives and fall-back plans to be initiated immediately should a hazard to your primary plans appear.

The alternative or fall-back plans are important here. Explain them in enough detail to make it clear that they are concrete, thought-out plans and not blue smoke. Be sure in explaining both these and your basic plans that you cover every source of income made possible by your plans.

Provide as much information as you can about your anticipated cash flow. If you are planning to sell consumer goods at retail via catalogs, your charge accounts will presumably be covered by established credit cards. However, if you are going to sell to other business firms, you will almost surely be forced to carry a few accounts. In such case, provide information here on the terms you offer, how you verify creditworthiness when a firm applies for an open account, and what you do to collect overdue accounts. Bankers usually are bearish about accounts more than 60 days old; the shorter the term of the accounts, the better. Bankers are also likely to react far more favorably to a large spread of small accounts than to a small spread of large accounts. They usually regard the latter as a higher risk.

Financial Statements.   You must present financial statements, as relevant. If you are already an operating company, provide the statements of current and prior years (up to three years prior), and your best projections for three years yet to come. If at all possible, make these audited statements. Bankers would prefer that verification and would be much more impressed if your statements are so verified by a certified public accountant. Your own net worth, credit rating, and general reputation are also important factors, especially for start-up loans, and documentation of your earnings and tax returns for the same period is often required. Any specific names of both business and personal acquaintances who can vouch for you will help your case, in this respect.

It is helpful to present two projections, one showing estimated operations and business without the requested loan, the other with it. That is to show what you expect the loan to do for you in increasing business and the value of the enterprise, adding weight and credibility to your proposed plan for repayment.

If this is to be a start-up loan, by all means, be down to earth in your projections. To estimate that a new business is going to be immediately profitable is unrealistic, and brands you a novice. That will cause an immediate loss of faith in all your representations. It is far better to be bearish than bullish in your estimates. It can and does sometimes happen, of course, that a business venture is an immediate success, but it's a rare banker or experienced businessperson who would gamble on that premise. In fact, you ordinarily do very well if you break even the first year in a new venture, and it is certainly not at all unusual to require two or three years for a venture to start becoming profitable. Be honest in your projections, and seek help in making them if you tend to be overly optimistic.

Specific Details of Proposed Use.   Although what you plan to use the money for may be apparent to the lender by now, the purpose has been expressed only in general terms, such as "for inventory expansion" or "working capital." It is necessary to be more precise. If it is to add another line of merchandise, for example, explain what the line is, how much you need to buy, and other details that make your need and use of the money crystal clear. Be sure that it agrees with other, related matters.

Size of Loan.   Obviously, you must state the amount of money you are seeking. Be sure that the amount of money you ask for is appropriate to what you say you are going to use the money for. Break down your planned expenditures in enough detail to support everything you have said earlier— what you will use the money for and what you expect it to do for business. Be as accurate as you can in making this set of estimates. It is likely to prove a mistake, costing you a loss of credibility, to ask for more or less than you need. Be sure to do your homework by making careful analyses of what you need and how you will invest the money. Otherwise, you will be unable to answer many of the questions you will almost surely be asked. You must "know the numbers."

Payback Plans.   Your proposed repayment plan is perhaps the most critical part of the loan proposal, and it is probably the most complex and difficult part to develop and write. There are certain principles that most bankers believe to be more or less sacred in establishing the acceptability of a payback plan. You will plan payback over some specific time period, of course, and your plan will present financial data showing the payment of interest as a business cost and payments of principal made out of your net profits, which should have increased as a result of the loan and generated the money to repay it. The money should cut costs, increase sales, and/or raise efficiency so as to result in added net profits sufficient to repay the loan. That is, show the effects of the loan as creating an asset that will last at least for the life of the repayment period. (Your financial statements, especially your projections of the effects of infusing capital into your business, should support this plan and verify its viability.)

Getting Help

This is not an easy task, and you may find it advisable to get some professional help, perhaps from your accountants or from a specialist in this field, at least for developing the payback plans. There are consultants and other specialists who are experienced in preparing loan proposals and in guiding businesspeople through the shoals. In fact, many such specialists operate as loan brokers who undertake the entire job of helping you get a bank loan by helping you with the application or loan proposal and otherwise advising and guiding you, while they act as intermediaries. Such individuals advertise these services, and they work for fees, usually a small percentage of the loan, the actual percentage varying with the size of the loan. You can find their advertising notices in the classified columns of many small business and "opportunity" periodicals that are listed in the "References" section. Typical advertisements appear under such headings as "Loans by Mail," "Business Services," and "Financial Services."

Unfortunately, some advertisers charge substantial fees for their services or claimed services, but they do not guarantee results. If you hire someone for a specific service, such as writing or helping with the writing of the proposal, be sure that the individual is well qualified to give you substantial help with it. Otherwise, you will be well advised to do business only with loan brokers who work in exchange for a percentage of the loan. They get paid only if you get the loan, so you are protected against being victimized.

The bank's own loan officer will give you some help, especially with the payback plan, if you ask and you are prepared with all the figures required. Be sure that you are so prepared. Go with a draft and ask him or her to critique it and advise you as to what else you need.

General Observations

Be sure that you are not asking the bank for 100 percent financing when you are seeking a start-up loan. Lenders are decidedly unsympathetic to entrepreneurs who can't or won't invest a significant portion of their own money or other assets in the venture. Be sure that you specify what you are personally investing.

In general, don't cover things up. If you hide some fact that you think will harm your chances for approval and the bank learns of this, your application is likely to die right there. Don't inflate the claimed value of your assets or conceal your liabilities; bankers are in a good position to judge the value of your claimed assets, and they will judge them conservatively, you can be sure. They are also likely to learn the truth about your liabilities. It is far less risky to be frank about everything, including the bad news as well as the good news. In fact, what the banker thinks about your personal character and trustworthiness—and they will check with credit-reporting services and any other source of information available to them—is highly important.

It is a good idea to make it easier for the banker to check your creditworthiness by furnishing the names of suppliers and others in a good position to verify it. For this and other reasons generally, validate and verify your figures by any means possible, including written statements or estimates from suppliers, industry estimates, statements from your accounting firm, and anything else that supports what you say in your proposal or is the basis for what your proposal says. The more of this kind of validation you can supply, the more *credible* your proposal will be, and credibility is always a critical need for a proposal of any kind, but especially for a loan proposal.

It is generally agreed that the best time to get acquainted with your banker is when you do not need a loan. Undoubtedly, the best time to take a banker to lunch is when business is good and everything is going well. It helps greatly when your banker has a good opinion of how well your business is doing. He or she is then much more likely to be sympathetic to your cause when the time arrives that makes it necessary for you to apply for a loan.

A good time to borrow money is when a bank or its local branch office is new. Get yourself established there, meet the officers, become known to them. You may also find that a small bank or small branch office will be more receptive to you than a large bank for the obvious reason that you may be a big fish in a small pond, rather than the reverse.

The equity in your home or in any property you own is an excellent asset that is easily convertible to cash, especially in these days of escalating real estate values. If you have owned your home or some other property for a few years, it has almost surely appreciated in market value. Even if it has been a relatively short time since you bought it, you probably have a significant amount of equity you can trade for cash (i.e., borrow against).

Many entrepreneurs, especially those starting out without prior experience and without much money of their own, run into a stone wall in trying to make a commercial loan. Their best bet is a personal loan, if they are employed, have some personal assets they can pledge, or have a cosigner. Many small businesses are launched on the strength of a personal or "signature" loan, as many banks call it. However, even that is not the only resource available.

One other resource that can at least ease the burden of front-end financing is trade credit. That is, credit extended by suppliers. Frequently, you can buy an inventory on credit, with 30 or more days allowed before payment is due. In some cases, it is even possible to get inventory on consignment; that is, you don't pay for the goods until they are sold.

Use these methods, plus drop-shipping for some of your items, and you have at least reduced the amount of capital you need to get started. Although it is often hardest to get loans for start-ups approved (because you are trying to borrow for an unproved venture), in some respects, financing a start-up is easier than financing expansion by using these and some other methods. Many other resources are available.

FINANCING WITH CREDIT CARDS

In today's economy, if your personal credit is good, you can build an almost unlimited line of credit with plastic—with credit cards, especially the gold cards. Because of the drawbacks of high interest rates and large monthly payments, this is a method that you should resort to only if you cannot get a conventional bank loan. However, many entrepreneurs have used this approach: It is possible, if you are willing to accept the disadvantages.

Most Visa and MasterCharge credit cards will give you a line of credit up to two or three thousand dollars, and gold cards usually go to $5,000. Some even offer a line of credit several times that amount. They also offer cash advances against the line of credit, and some even provide you with checks so that you can write bank drafts against the credit card account.

You can easily get several gold cards, as many as you want, in fact; they need not be from local banks but may be issued to you from any bank in the country. Many people carry several of these bank cards, as well as others, such as American Express and Discover. In one case, reported in *Entrepreneur* magazine (June 1989, "Charge it!," by Kenneth Shropshire), a man funded a $150,000 start-up with 37 credit cards. However, many small businesspeople use plastic credit everyday for small expenses—entertaining a client, travel, and other such incidentals—almost automatically.

Not many entrepreneurs will want to use three dozen credit cards to finance a six-figure start-up; that is a bit extreme, although it is not unknown. But plastic credit is a useful ancillary line of credit when you can get a bank loan but need a bit more than the bank will approve. Conversely, you may want only a small loan because you know that you can turn to your credit cards if necessary.

The more one researches the problems and opportunities in connection with raising capital for business, the more apparent it becomes that there is an abundance of capital available and that difficult as it may seem at times to raise the necessary capital, nothing succeeds as well as persistence does. There is simply an almost endless reservoir of avenues to explore. Those who persevere almost invariably find the money they need eventually. Above all, don't give up.

HELP FROM THE GOVERNMENT

There are many kinds of help offered by government agencies of many kinds, including aid in getting loans and even some direct loans from the government itself. The number and diversity of programs is far greater than you can imagine, and while the federal government leads the way, it is not the sole dispenser of government aid.

Federal Programs

The federal government long ago established a pattern of assisting certain classes of individuals in many ways, and one of these ways is in getting financing for business ventures. The VA has long administered the G.I. Bill, which includes helping veterans (especially those who are disabled) finance business ventures by guaranteeing their loans. Similar programs to help small business generally have long been operated by the Small Business Administration (SBA). The Department of Commerce, through its Minority Business Development Administration has aided minority entrepreneurs, as has the SBA (through its 8a and other programs). Too, women have sometimes qualified as members of a minority and been eligible for such aid.

In addition to loan programs, there are many other kinds of assistance offered by the federal government through more than a thousand programs listed and described in the annual *Catalog of Federal Domestic Assistance*, published each year by the government's Office of Management and Budget (OMB) and available from the Government Printing Office (Address: Superintendent of Documents, U.S. Government Printing Office, Washington, DC 20402) currently at $32. Even if you do not qualify under any of the special provisions for the $700 billion worth of federal programs, you still probably will find it useful to investigate them. The SBA, for example, publishes many helpful reports and other documents, many of them free, others available at small cost. Too, there are programs of free consulting and other help of various kinds, such as with writing a loan proposal, and even help in doing business with government agencies.

One of the major problems with all government programs is that the government does a poor job of making the programs known to the public generally. Partly, at least, this is due to political considerations, such as reluctance to do anything that makes the government appear to be in competition with private interests. In any case, it is necessary to pursue information aggressively. When you do, you may find that your problems are lessened by orders of magnitude. You are probably going to get a few surprises. For example, you may find that your best bet lies with the U.S. Department of Agriculture (USDA). No, you do not have to be a farmer to qualify. The USDA's FmHA has programs quite similar to those of the SBA and others, and many of the business loans made are to individuals living in cities.

State Programs

Most state governments have followed suit in providing similar programs to help veterans, minorities, and small businesses generally, but they have the same problem in disseminating information about them: It is not always easy to learn about the programs and services, which include such things as loans, loan guarantees, marketing studies, consulting services, information, training programs, literature, marketing help, and help in writing business plans.

GRANTS

Many organizations, including governments and foundations, make many grants—gifts of money for what the grantor believes to be a worthy cause. The various federal grant programs are listed in the *Catalog of Federal Domestic Assistance*, referred to earlier.

Winning grant money usually requires the writing of a grant proposal, which is not very different from a loan proposal. It must explain the proposed use of the money in detail, following the guidelines laid down by the grantor.

There is help available for writing grant proposals. Federal agencies and sometimes state agencies will often help. In fact, in some federal programs, the agency will actually assign someone to help you with the proposal. Other than federal and state governments, there are at least two private-sector sources:

Grantsmanship Center
1030 S. Grand Avenue
Los Angeles, CA 90015
(213) 749-4721
(800) 421-9512

Foundation Center
888 Seventh Avenue
New York, NY 10019
(212) 975-1120
(202) 331-1400
(216) 861-1933
(415) 397-0902
(800) 424-9836

EQUITY FINANCING

Many people finance start-ups and/or expansions by selling stock in their ventures. That is what the stock market is all about: corporations selling stock—shares of ownership—in their ventures. Even a small, upstart corporation can do it. James Ling, ultimately head of a multibillion dollar conglomerate of many prominent companies, owned a small contracting business when he incorporated as a public corporation and offered stock to the public, even personally going out and knocking on doors to do so. It was from his success in that small beginning that LTV—Ling Temco Vought—ultimately resulted, along with a meat packing company, a pharmaceuticals company, and a sporting goods company, among others.

It is not necessary to go public, however, to raise venture capital. There are many venture capitalists around, individuals and organizations with capital, seeking sound investments. There are hundreds of small business investment companies (SBICs) and minority small business investment companies (MESBICs), for example, whose sole purpose is to invest in companies, often new start-ups. The "References" section lists many sources of aid and additional details of where to turn in the quest for money.

12

Miscellaneous Aids
to Success

*There are more roads to success than there are to failure. Here are a few
guideposts to help you find the right roads.*

MARKETING WITHOUT MONEY: USING PR
(PUBLIC RELATIONS)

PR Basics

Marketing is an absolute necessity of business, as pointed out many times in the
foregoing pages; no business venture can hope to succeed without marketing.
It is difficult to even guess how many business ventures fail because the
marketing effort fails to produce enough sales. That inadequacy is not always
due to poor judgment or poor execution in marketing; it is often due to the most
common weakness of fledgling businesses: shortage of capital. Marketing can
be and usually is quite expensive.

There are at least three major expenses in most marketing campaigns:
advertising, printing, and postage. However, when a business fails because
there was not enough capital available for proper marketing, it is often a
tragedy of sorts because there are often effective ways to market with extremely
little capital. In general terms this is called "public relations" or "PR," its more
well-known abbreviation. PR is free—nominally, at least. The cost of a well-
planned and well-executed PR is almost insignificant, compared with what it
can produce in marketing results.

The real objective of PR is publicity. That is what PR is designed to get for the individual and the organization—coverage in the media, both print and broadcast. Public relations is a euphemism for activities designed to get publicity. *Publicity* is free advertising, which is often far more powerful and more effective than paid advertising. It is what all those personal appearances by entertainment stars and others on talk shows are about. They are there to plug—publicize—their newest movies, TV shows, plays, or books, or their own careers in general. That scandalous scene (or alleged scene) in a famous Hollywood or New York City restaurant that is reported in the tabloids is there to plug the restaurant and/or the individuals involved in the incident reported. Many of the apparent scoops made by intrepid reporters are actually handouts by PR specialists. That is why you can find stories that are virtual carbon copies of each other in more than one periodical and reported on more than one radio and TV station: The stories were written by PR specialists and planted simultaneously in all the media by the wide distribution of the handouts (also known as "releases"). In fact, many prominent figures in entertainment and many organizations either employ PR specialists directly or keep freelance PR specialists on permanent retainer.

Few small businesses use PR with enough frequency or skill to derive even a fraction of the possible benefit. Perhaps this is because the marketers for these businesses are totally unfamiliar with the truth about PR and have an image of PR based entirely on the imaginative and false images of PR that they have seen portrayed (i.e., caricatured) in Hollywood movies—high-risk stunts by irrepressible and irresponsible characters. Perhaps they believe other nonsense about PR. Following are a few of the most frequently asked questions:

Q: Do I need a special consultant, a PR expert?

A: You may very well get the best results by hiring an experienced PR specialist, but many people run their own PR quite effectively. Read on and find out what it takes to mount an effective PR campaign, and then you can answer this question for yourself.

Q: Is PR expensive?

A: That is like asking whether an automobile or a wrist watch is expensive. It can be and often is, as conducted by large organizations, but it doesn't have to be. There are many inexpensive ways to conduct PR campaigns. Again, you will find the answer to that question in the discussions to follow.

Q: Do I need to "know somebody" to get publicity?

A: A great many people believe that "inside contacts" are necessary to plant stories with reporters, editors, columnists, talk-show hosts, and commentators. It doesn't hurt to know a few such people, and experienced PR specialists certainly do know some of these people, but it is definitely not a requirement, nor is it the answer. No matter who you do or do not know, you are not likely to get publicity if you do not have something the other party finds worth using. The reverse is also true: Give the other party something useful, and he or she will run it whether you are an acquaintance or a stranger.

Q: Is PR really effective? Will it really help me in my marketing?

A: Indeed PR can be extremely effective, often even more effective than the expensive paid advertising. Once again, read on, and judge for yourself.

PR Tools

The main or most widely used tool of PR is the press release, also referred to as a "news release," "publicity release," or simply "release." There are also many other inexpensive PR tools that you can use.

Write and Mail Press Releases

Usage.　You can get lots of free advertising with press releases. Find an angle that makes them worthwhile for editors and publishers to use, while presenting plugs for your catalogs and offerings. This is a major opportunity for PR, probably the most widely used tool of PR, the classic tool. Use it freely; it is inexpensive, versatile, and extremely flexible.

As in the case of the newsletter, however, you must play fair with releases and use them to make news announcements, rather than pure and unabashed advertising, or they will be discarded immediately. Editors and others who receive releases are quite aware that their publications or broadcast studios are businesses that depend on selling space or time for advertising, and they are not going to give that space or time away free. They are also quite aware of what PR and publicity mean and why they are being sent releases. Therefore, it must be a trade: You will get the space or time if what you have sent is of some value to the other in what might be called "newsworthiness." That is, your release must include information that would be of interest to the readers or viewers or listeners.

Format.　Figure 12–1 is an example of such a release prepared on a regular letterhead. (Those who issue releases frequently usually have a special form with "News" or "Release" printed prominently on it.) Note that the copy

& ASSOCIATES

NEWS RELEASE

Contact:

Richard Bruno
415-239-6162

FOR IMMEDIATE RELEASE
September 7, 1989

NATIONAL ELECTRONIC FOR-SALE-BY-OWNER MULTIPLE LISTING

SERVICE LAUNCHES 'FIZZBO' DEALER NETWORK

SAN FRANCISCO, CA -- Dial Direct Response Marketing,
Inc. (DDRM) today announced it will offer a limited number of
local Dealerships for 'Fizzbo Real Estate MLS' (FIZZBO),
a recently launched computerized for-sale-by-owner
advertising service that matches buyers and sellers of real
estate.

"More and more homeowners are opting for Do-It-Yourself
home sales", said DDRM President Jane Shapiro, "and FIZZBO
offers a cost effective way for home sellers to compete for a
prospective buyer's attention. For a flat, one time fee of
$99.95, property owners can list their real estate until it's
sold, and save thousands of dollars in real estate brokerage
commissions."

FIZZBO, the first interactive service of its type, is
available domestically to users of Minitel Service Company's
popular interactive electronic communications service, as

44 Monterey Boulevard · Suite 1400 · San Francisco, California 94131   415 239-6162

Figure 12–1. Typical publicity release.

is double-spaced for the convenience of editors and lists a "contact" for any editor or other reader who wishes to follow up with inquiries. Although the writer of this release did not do so, most who write such releases use a notation "more" or "end" at the bottom of the page to guide the reader with information as to whether there is another page following. (### and -30- are also used frequently to signify the end of the copy.)

A headline helps alert the reader immediately as to the main content, just as a headline does in straight advertising. Send copies to editors and columnists of relevant periodicals—newspapers, magazines, and newsletters—and use copies also as general marketing literature in your mailings.

Some people use both sides of a sheet when issuing releases, but I believe that to be a poor practice because it is inconvenient to handle copy that is written on both sides of a sheet. It is best to prepare a release as you would any manuscript copy—double spaced, typed on one side only, with generous margins for the editor's use.

Two Styles.   There are two styles you can use for releases. Probably the style most favored and most often recommended by the professionals in the field is the well-known journalistic one, the inverted pyramid that is taught in all journalism courses and used for straight reporting. (This is represented in Figure 12–2.)

In the inverted pyramid, the lead, an introductory sentence or paragraph, presents the essence of the story, as exemplified in the lead of the release in Figure 12–1. *Who, what, when, where, why,* and *how* are all there in the lead. Each succeeding paragraph adds details, but if an editor chopped the story at any point after the lead, it would still be a complete account in answering those questions. That is the reason for using this format: It enables an editor to fit the item into whatever space or time is available. The conclusion (not included in the example because there is an additional page not shown in the figure) sums the story up, perhaps adds an interesting fillip to it, such as a surprise to act as a "snapper."

Not all releases are written this way. Some are written as features, which do not necessarily follow that standard style of traditional journalism. Unfortunately, this may give the editor problems in fitting the item into available space or time, which may force the editor to kill the release, so it is a format that is less favored by writers of releases.

With a little imagination, it is not difficult to find news pegs or angles on which to base releases so as to make them newsworthy in the sense that the term is used here. Here are a few ideas to help you do this:

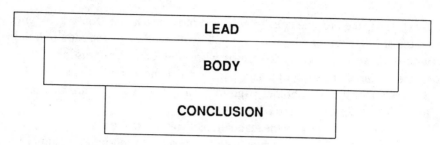

Figure 12–2. Journalistic inverted pyramid.

What product do you have in your line that is different or novel in any way? Try to find one that has an intriguing angle, and write a release around it, being sure to include your own business identity. For example, you might base a story on a new kitchen gadget, using an approach such as the following:

NOW YOU CAN HAVE SQUARE HARD-BOILED EGGS!

A resourceful independent inventor has invented a little plastic mold to make your hard-boiled eggs square so that they can't roll off the plate, and this novel gadget is being distributed exclusively by Peter Petrillo Gifts, Inc., a mail order catalog firm.

What products do you carry that have a romantic background? For example, if you sell spices that come from India or some other exotic place, do a little research into the story behind the item. (The public library is an excellent resource for this.) Who discovered this spice? Who grows it? How is it gathered and processed? How does it get here? What are the relevant statistics? And so on.

What about the history of cataloging? Who were the pioneers? How did they get the idea? How did they get started? How big is the catalog business? Who/what is the smallest cataloger? The largest?

Not every product has to have an exotic background to be interesting. There are many interesting stories behind domestic products. Suppose you sell items made of brass or copper. Dig up the interesting stories behind the history of copper and its alloys. Come up with some statistics. Find out what the experts say about the future of the metal.

Releases can stand on their own as independent and self-sufficient PR tools, or they can be used in conjunction with other PR tools and activities, as in some of the following cases.

Prepare Free Brochures

In many cases, a small brochure on the subject of the release can be both a wide expansion of the effort and an added inducement to editors to publish your release. That is, you can invite readers to send a stamped, self-addressed envelope for the free brochure that offers more details on the subject. You can also distribute the brochure in other ways, too, offering to supply them to schools and libraries, for example, and enclosing them with each order filled. In fact, the release can be addressed specifically to announce the availability of the free brochure.

Write Product Releases

Many publications carry a "new products" section and will describe your product without cost if you send a news release (some call it a "product release"). Figure 12–3 illustrates how the text of one of those notices might appear in a magazine. Where appropriate, as in this case, a photograph of the product ought to be sent along. Usually, a 4" x 5" black-and-white glossy will do. (The square egg mold would have been perfect for this.) You can find many examples of catalogers using the introduction of new products as opportunities to publicize their catalogs through such product releases.

Publish a Free Newsletter

This has been mentioned already. It's a good medium, much cheaper than paid advertising and often more effective. Give it some serious thought. Make it simple—a page or two—and publish on an easy schedule—quarterly, for example; you can always publish more frequently or expand it in size later. It is much easier and much more practicable to start small and expand than to start big and contract, of course. Caution: Use this PR tool only indirectly or partially for straight advertising. If your newsletter is complete and unabashed advertis-

---

THREE-WAY UTENSIL: Fork-like in appearance, this eating utensil also serves as a knife and spoon. The knife along both edges cannot cut your mouth (claims the maker) and the fork tines and spoon contour are said to allow comfort and ease of handling. Set of six: 9.95 ppd. *NEAA Sales Co., Dept PP, 6770 Crampton Court, Box 19389, San Diego, CA 92119.*

Figure 12–3. Typical product release.

ing, it will soon be discarded unread and will do you no good. You can include direct advertising, but that must be in addition to material that is useful to the reader and constitutes the main theme of the newsletter.

And, as in the case of the free brochure, you can use releases in conjunction with the newsletter to announce it and to invite readers to send for a sample copy or a free subscription.

Write Articles

Make time to write articles for the trade journals that are read by those who are good prospects for what you sell. Editors of those journals are so eager for new material that many pay (modestly) for articles. In fact, even "Letters to the Editor" offer useful PR. Sometimes, when they get to know you, editors will even ask you to write letters to them for publication in those columns! In a way, an article is a greatly expanded release because you can use several thousand words in an article, whereas that would usually be far too many for a release.

Do Radio and TV Guest Shots

Not all the talk shows are headed by Johnny Carson or Pat Sajak. You would be surprised at how many not-so-prominent radio and TV talk show hosts there are and how eagerly their producers will welcome your appearance on their shows, in person or by telephone. To get on such a show, don't call or talk to the host of the show; talk to the producer. Call and find out who the producer is, for that is who will arrange to get you on if you have something interesting to offer. A good idea is to call ahead and advise the producer that you are sending a release or an outline of what you would like to talk about, and then follow up with another call later. If you can be available on short notice, be sure to emphasize that because producers run into no-shows and other last-minute emergencies, and that multiplies your probability for getting on.

Arrange Newspaper and Magazine Interviews

The print media, especially the trade journals, newsletters, and other specialty publications, are as eager as the not-so-prominent talk-show hosts to get interviewees. Find some interesting things to say and pursue the editors of those publications. I have had some telephone interviews that resulted in quite good articles in such media as these. I have also written to reporters, especially those writing for the business section of newspapers, to seek and get permission from their editors to interview me, resulting in very helpful PR. However, you can also pursue editors and writers in other sections of the newspaper.

Many large newspapers carry special sections on food, health, entertainment, travel, local businesses, and other special interests. Many newspapers also have thick Sunday editions with even more special sections and entire magazines.

Do Guest Shots on Others' Seminars

Many individuals offer seminars of many kinds, and more than a few organizations make a business of offering seminars on various subjects. They often welcome guest speakers and may even offer you a contract to present an entire seminar.

GETTING LEADS

Hardly a day passes that I do not find a catalog or two in my post office box. The majority of them are from sellers of computer equipment and supplies, and the runner-up category is that of sellers of office equipment and supplies. How do they get my name and address? They get it from others, usually via list brokers. Through those brokers, they get my name and address from publishers of periodicals to which I subscribe, from other mail-order dealers from whom I have bought items, from associations to which I belong, from publishers for whom I have written, from advertising copy I have run, and probably from some other sources of which I am not even aware. Never underestimate the resourcefulness of the list brokers; they are almost incredibly able at what they do.

You, too, can find lists of periodicals, TV and radio stations, talk show hosts and producers, and other such resources. You can also use some of the publications listed in the "References" section.

TESTING

Having considered the need for detailed data to make diagnostic analyses and wise decisions, how do you get this data? Does the accounting system spill it forth automatically? Of course it does not. Consider first that you are dealing with a large number of items, perhaps several hundred, in fact. Consider, too, that the accounting system can only report what has happened in fact; it cannot project what would happen if you tried advertising a different price, using a loss leader, or otherwise experimenting with alternative marketing strategies. There are spreadsheet programs designed to do this, but you must first know the factors to supply to the programs, and you may not yet know what the factors are (e.g., what happens to sales figures of a given item when you raise or lower the price?). To learn that, you must do some testing, a function of mail order that I consider to be the most important one of all.

Verifying the Conventional Wisdom

There is a great deal of conventional wisdom in the mail-order business, as there is in all businesses. Others who have relevant experience will tell you what works and what does not work. There is no way, however, to be sure that others' experiences, *their* conventional wisdom, will be appropriate for you. There is abundant evidence that each case is individual, and you must learn your own truths every day. You do this by testing. As expert direct-mail writer Herschell Gordon Lewis says in his book, *Direct Mail Copy That Sells!* (Prentice Hall 1984), "We learn something each time we test, but what we learn seems to apply only to that one case; the results may very well be completely reversed the next time, even when the next case seems to be a parallel one."

Moreover, tests refute conventional wisdom again and again. Everyone in direct mail "knows" that two- and three-color printing pulls better than black-and-white printing—until a test proves the opposite for a given campaign. Everyone "knows" that "the more you tell, the more you sell"— until a test demonstrates a one-page letter performing better than a three-page letter. So there is never a time when you should launch a campaign without testing. There is no other way to really know what works and what doesn't work, or what works well and what does not work well—for *this* campaign.

Basically, testing is sound science. Scientists advance human knowledge by speculating, theorizing, and testing. In mail order, you theorize that a certain approach will produce better results than others, and you try it out in a test mailing. You then measure the results to determine whether your theory both was sound and worked. To be even more efficient about it, you speculate on several possible variants that might produce the best results, and you test them all simultaneously. You then compare the results to see which approach did work best. A proper accounting system will provide the figures, but a good test design is required.

Testing is one area where direct mail is demonstrably superior to media advertising. Because you must usually place your orders for media advertising in periodicals weeks and even months in advance, it usually requires unacceptably long lag times for testing via media advertising. However, you can mail a thousand or two pieces for each alternative approach within days and have enough results back in two or three weeks to form your judgments. So, although many entrepreneurs do use media advertising for testing their offers, I believe that direct mail is *the* way to test your offers. In any case, although you may use some media advertising to develop leads and to build mailing lists, the main medium for catalog sales is direct mail.

Even with rented lists, however, you may wish to use the lists to elicit inquiries or expressions of interest before you mail catalogs to everyone on a list. At an earlier time, catalogers simply mailed catalogs to everyone on whatever lists they used. That was when printing, paper, and postage were relatively cheap. Today, the cost of manufacturing all but the simplest catalogs is so great that many catalogers will supply catalogs only on specific request, some will supply them free of charge only to established customers, and some charge a dollar or two for their catalogs, although many will refund or credit that charge on the first order. If your own catalog is too expensive to mail to a cold list, you may wish to mail a package of sales literature, offering a loss leader or special of some sort, or you may wish to mail an inexpensive, abbreviated catalog, as Quill and others do. In such case, you should test your copy as well as your lists.

The Right Forms Help

Following are a few suggested forms for monitoring test mailings and recording the results. First is Figure 12–4, which illustrates the basic idea of logging in the daily orders. The "key" column refers to the item being tested. If you are testing three different prices, for example, mailing perhaps 2,000 pieces out to three different lists, each offering a different bonus item, you key them in some manner so that you know to which list the buyer has responded—that is, which bonus item pulled the greatest number of responses.

Practically speaking, this form is a bit too basic to do the job you would want done in most instances. Figure 12–5 carries the idea a bit further and collects a great deal more data for analysis. Several other formats are suggested by Figures 12–6 and 12–7. These can all be varied, of course, to suit your own needs, whether it is to test mailing lists, copy, loss leaders, or any other element of a campaign. Note that in one of the forms, a column is headed "ROI %," referring to return on investment, which is more significant than response. Response is an indication of how well a mailing pulls orders, but it tells you nothing of whether the campaign is profitable or not. The ROI is thus a far more useful figure.

DAY & DATE _____

KEY	NO. ORDERS	SALES ($)
TOTALS:		

Figure 12–4. Basic data sought by test.

DAY, DATE	KEY	MAILING DATE	NO. PCS	COST	NO. ORDERS	SALES($)
TOTALS:						

Figure 12–5. More sophisticated data-gathering form.

KEY: _____   NO. PCS MAILED: _____   DATE: _____   COST: $ _____

NO. ORDERS	RESPONSE %	SALES($)	FULFIL. COST	ROI %	GROSS PROFIT

KEY: _____   DATE MAILED: _____   COST: $ _____

DATE	NO. CALLS	NO. CARDS/LTRS	NOTES
TOTALS:			COST PER INQUIRY: $ _____

Figure 12–6. Sheet 1, variations of data-collection forms.

KEY: _____   DATE OF MAILING: _____   COST PER LEAD _____

DATE	NO. SALES	SALES TOTAL ($)	REMARKS
TOTALS:			COST PER SALE: $ _____

Figure 12–7. Sheet 2, variations of data-collection forms.

MAIL-ORDER LAW

When young Montgomery Ward introduced his radical new idea of unconditional guarantees and prompt refunds for returned merchandise, he was
confronted with the incredulous dismay of other merchants. *Caveat emptor*
("let the buyer beware") had always been the order in commerce. The buyer
was responsible for his or her own buying decisions, and the seller's responsibility ended with delivery of the merchandise. The buyer had even more
reason to be wary of mail order because the buyer had only the advertised
claims for guidance and was thus gambling—presumably with eyes open—
with every order. That is, there was even greater abuse in mail-order selling
than in face-to-face or across-the-counter selling at that time.

Eventually, the new standards set by Montgomery Ward and others of
similar persuasion became the norm, but many mail-order merchants did not
conform with these new ethical standards for business. Instead, they took
advantage of the fact that the buyer had not seen the merchandise he or she was
ordering, so the abuses continued.

In recent years, this has changed. The widespread use of credit cards has given the consumer (the buyer, that is) a measure of control. Customers paying by credit cards can ask their credit card issuer to withhold payment if there is a dispute, so it is in your own interest to try to settle disputes or satisfy complaints as promptly as possible. In addition, some federal control has evolved, justified by the fact that mail-order trade is conducted across state lines and often with the use of the federal postal system.

The federal control of mail order, with authority to administer and enforce the law, is conferred on the Federal Trade Commission (FTC). Briefly, the main provisions of the law are these:

Unless you specifically advise the buyer to the contrary in advance, you are required to ship the order within 30 days after receiving it. If, for any reason, you are unable to do so, you must advise the buyer in writing of this, with a promised date for shipment (not more than 30 days additional), but you must also offer the buyer the option of canceling the order and getting a refund. Because you must have the buyer's consent to the postponement or delay in shipping, you must provide the buyer with a stamped, self-addressed card or envelope. That, however, is to your advantage, to avoid later problems if buyers claim that they were not advised or given the opportunity to cancel orders and get refunds. (Do keep careful records.) In any case, the customer has the right to cancel an order at any time before it has been shipped.

You must make refunds within seven business days if the original order was paid for by check or money order, or you must credit the account within one billing cycle if paid for by credit card.

APPENDIX A

Mailing List Managers and Brokers

The following is by no means the complete itemization of mailing-list sources, but it is representative, and it includes many of the leading list brokers.

Alvin B. Zeller, 475 Park Avenue S., New York, NY 10016, (212) 223-0814

American Bar Association, 750 N. Lake Shore Drive, Chicago, IL 60611, (312) 988-5435

American Church Lists, 1939 Stadium Oaks, No. 110, Arlington, TX 76004, (817) 261-6233

American Institute of Physics, 335 E. 45th Street, New York, NY 10017, (212) 661-9404

American List Counsel, 88 Orchard Road, Princeton, NJ 08540, (201) 874-4300, (800) 822-5478, Fax (201) 874-4433

American Management Systems, 9255 Sunset Blvd, Los Angeles, CA 90069, (213) 858-1520

AZ Marketing Services, Inc., 31 River Road, Cos Cob, CT 06807, (203) 629-8088

Best Mailing Lists, Inc., 34 W. 32nd Street, New York, NY 10001, (212) 868-1080, (800) 692-2378, Fax (212) 947-0136

CBS Magazines, 1515 Broadway, New York, NY 10036, (212) 719-6677 CompuName, Inc., 411 Theodore Fremd Avenue, Rye, NY 10580, (914) 925-2401

Dependable Lists, Inc., 950 S. 25th Avenue, Bellwood, IL 60104, (312) 544-1000

Direct Media List Management Group, Inc., 70 Riverdale Avenue, P.O. Box 4565, Greenwich, CT 06830, (203) 531-1091

D-J Associates, P.O. Box 2048, 77 Danbury Road, Ridgefield, CT 06877, (203) 431-8777

Donnelley Marketing Information Services, 1351 Washington Blvd, Stamford, CT 06902, (203) 965-5400

Dun & Bradstreet International, 99 Church Street, New York, NY 10007, (212) 265-7525

Ed Burnett Consultants, 99 W. Sheffield Avenue, Englewood, NJ 07631, (201) 871-1100, (800) 223-7777

Jammi Direct Marketing Services, 2 Executive Drive, Fort Lee, NJ 07024, (201) 461-8868

The Kaplan Agency, Inc., Creative List Services, 11 Forest Street, New Canaan, CT 06840, (203) 972-3600

The Kleid Company, Inc., 530 Fifth Avenue, New York, NY 10036, (212) 819-3400

List Services Corporation, 890 Ethan Allen Highway, Ridgefield, CT 06877, (203) 438-0327

Millard Group, Inc., 10 Vose Farm Road, Peterborough, NH 03458, (603) 924-9262

Mokrynski & Associates, Inc., 401 Hackensack Avenue, Hackensack, NJ 07601, (201) 488-5656

Qualified Lists Corporation, 135 Bedford Road, Armonk, NY 10504, (914) 273-6606

R. L. Polk & Co., 6400 Monroe Blvd, Taylor, MI 48180, (313) 292-3200

Roman Managed Lists, Inc., 101 West 31st Street, New York, NY 10001, (212) 695-3838

The SpeciaLists, Ltd., 120 East 16th Street, New York, NY 10003, (212) 677-6760

Standard Rate & Data Service, 3004 Glenview Road, Wilmette, IL 60091, (312) 441-2153, (800) 323-4601

Stevens Response Systems, 225 N. New Road, Waco, TX 76710, (817) 776-9000

Total Media Concepts, Inc., 222 Cedarlane, Teaneck, NJ 07666, (201) 692-0018

Woodruff-Stevens & Associates, 345 Park Avenue S., New York, NY 10010, (212) 685-4600

W. S. Ponton, 5149 Butler Street, Pittsburgh, PA 15201, (412) 782-2360

APPENDIX B

A Few Sources for Special Services

Even experts who know how to do it all cannot always handle it all alone and do not always have staff to help. That is why the mail-order and catalog industry relies on consultants and other specialists to help. Following are a few representative names of such specialists.

Consultants and Copywriters

Advanced Marketing Technologies
450 Overland Drive
Stratford, CT 06497
(203) 386-1002

Bob Bly
174 Holland Avenue
New Milford, NJ 07646
(201) 599-2277

Jeffrey P. Geibel
61 Sycamore Street, Suite 101
Belmont, MA 02178-1310

Rene Gnam
1 Response Road
Holiday, FL 33590
(813) 938-1555

Stan Greenfield
1220 Broadway
New York, NY 10001

(212) 736-0042
LCH Direct
348 Park Street West, #206
North Reading, MA 01864
(800) 233-6245
Galen Stilson
1442 Red Oak Drive
Tarpon Springs, FL 33589
(813) 937-3480

Associations

Advertising and Marketing International Network
One Bank Street
Stamford, CT 06901

Advertising Council
825 Third Avenue
New York, NY 10022

American Marketing Association
250 S. Wacker Drive
Chicago, IL 60606

Direct Marketing Association
6 East 43rd Street
New York, NY 10017

Direct Selling Association
1776 K Street, NW
Washington, DC 20005

Mail Advertising Service Association, International
7315 Wisconsin Avenue
Bethesda, MD 20814

References

Of course, you can't read everything ever written on the subject of mail order, cataloging, raising capital, getting publicity, and the many other topics discussed in these pages, but the following literature has all proved useful to me at one time or another, so I respectfully pass on the titles to you.

Books

Bly, Robert W., *Create the Perfect Sales Piece*, John Wiley, New York, 1985

Cohen, William A., *Building a Mail Order Business*, John Wiley, New York, 1985

Cohen, William A., *The Entrepreneur & Small Business Problem Solver*, John Wiley, New York, 1983

Goldstein, Arnold S., *Starting on a Shoestring*, John Wiley, New York, 1984

Gosden, Freeman F., Jr., *Direct Marketing Success*, John Wiley, New York, 1985

Hoge, Cecil C., Sr., *Mail Order Moonlighting*, Ten Speed Press, Berkeley, 1976

Holtz, Herman, *The Direct Marketer's Workbook*, John Wiley, New York, 1986

Holtz, Herman, *Great Promo Pieces*, John Wiley, New York, 1988

Lesko, Matthew, *Getting Yours* (Third Edition), Penguin Books, New York, 1989

Lewis, Herschell Gordon, *Direct Mail Copy That Sells*, Prentice Hall, Englewood Cliffs, NJ, 1984

Mancuso, Joseph R., *How to Write a Winning Business Plan*, Prentice Hall, Englewood Cliffs, NJ, 1985

O'Hara, Patrick, *SBA Loans*, John Wiley, New York, 1989

Palder, Edward, *The Catalog of Catalogs*, Woodbine House, Kensington, MD, 1987

Parkhurst, William, *How to Get Publicity*, Times Books, New York, 1985

Periodicals

Business Opportunities Digest, 301 Plymouth Drive, NE, Dalton, GA 30721

Catalog Business, Mill Hollow Corp., 19 W. 21st Street, New York, NY 10010

DM News, Mill Hollow Corp., 19 W. 21st Street, New York, NY 10010

Entrepreneur, 2392 Morse Avenue, Irvine, CA 92714

Home Office Computing, Scholastic, Inc., 730 Broadway, New York, NY 10003

Income Opportunities, 380 Lexington Avenue, New York, NY 10017

Money Making Opportunities, Success Publishing International, 11071 Ventura Blvd., Studio City, CA 91604

New Business Opportunities, 2392 Morse Avenue, Irvine, CA 92714

Small Business Opportunities, Harris Publications, Inc., 1115 Broadway, New York, NY 10010

Spare Time Money Making Opportunities, Kipen Publishing Corp., 5810 W. Oklahoma Avenue, Milwaukee, WI 53219

Target, North American Publishing Co., 401 N. Broad Street, Philadelphia, PA 19108

Index

A & P, 225
Accounting,
  costs, 208
  general considerations, 204
  need for, 205
  overhead, 209
  understanding the chief elements
    of, 207
Advantages and disadvantages of
  selling via catalogs, 7, 32
Alan Thomas Designs, 115
Alka Seltzer, 151, 221, 222, 224
All State Insurance, 224
American Drop Shippers Directory,
  19
American Parade of Catalogs, 6, 41
American Psychological Association,
  27
Anchor Specialties Co., 19
Anka Company, Inc., 19, 155
Appeal of catalogs, 7
Avon Fashions, 13, 19
Avon Products, 2, 22
AZ Marketing Services, 180

Beauty by Spector, 115

Bendah, David, 18
Best Mailing Lists, 1
Bloomingdale's, 114
Bluestocking Press, 14
Bly, Robert W., 165
Boardroom Lists, 184
Boardroom Reports, 184
Boettger, Frank, 53
Books 'n' Bears by Mail, 14
Bounceback orders, 11, 60
Brady, Diamond Jim, 71
Bromo Seltzer, 222
Burnett, Ed, 180
Burpee, 14
Business administration and
  organization,
  incorporation versus other forms,
    214
  help in organizing, 216

Capitalization requirements, 8
Carol's Creations, 17
Cars & Parts, 185
Carson, Johnny, 252
Catalog Business, 30, 121, 177
Catalog distribution, 5, 20

Cataloging,
    ideas, novel and innovative, 41
finding/choosing items for, 54
    generalization versus
        specialization, 47
    gift items, 57
    market analysis for, 50
Catalog marketing,
    advantages over store retailing,
        73, 76
    customer feedback, 85
    customer relations, 120
    discount pricing, customer
        expectations of, 202
    estimates, premises, and
        assumptions, 81
    general versus special catalogs,
        57
    guarantees, 88, 145
    niche markets, 114
    repetitive mailings, 146
    strategies, 38
Catalog of Catalogs, 1
*Catalog of Federal Domestic
    Assistance*, 241, 242
Chilcutt Direct Marketing, 184
Citibank, 143
Comer, Gary, 84
Comparison with selling single item,
    10, 12, 60
Computer Direct, 118
Computer Shopper, 6, 99, 127, 202
Cook Bros., Inc., 19
Copywriting,
    action, asking for, 141
    benefits, 150
    credibility, 143, 148
    communication, question of, 123

denotation and connotation, 124
    elements of sales copy, 126
    headlines, 128
    hook, the, 126
    myths, 149
    offer, the, 115, 139
    persuasion, means of, 124
    promise, the, 139, 142, 148, 151
    proof, 87, 137, 142, 148
Cossman, Joe, 12, 13, 68, 91
Cost burdens and analyses,
    general, 9,
    kinds of costs, 208
Cosby, Bill, 221
Create the Perfect Sales Piece, 165
Credit card use, 5
Crutchfield Corporation, 13, 14

Dahl, Gary, 12
Databases,
    adding to, 70
    definition, 193
    mailing lists as, 59, 179, 186
    versus mailing lists, 198
Database managers (computer
        software),
    comparison with mailing-list
        management software, 197
    flat-file, 197
    mailing list managers, use as, 197
    relational, 198
    types of, 66, 197
    uses of, 196
Definition of catalog sales business,
    17
Demographic considerations,
    elements of, 108
    mailing lists, in, 187

Department of Commerce, 241
Direct mail,
    basic elements of, 153
    strategies of, 164
    versus mail order, 4, 78
Direct Mail Copy That Sells, 169, 254
Direct Marketing Success, 29
Direct Media, 178
*Directory of Major Public
    Corporations*, 69
Direct response marketing, 78
DM News, 177, 185
Doubleday List Marketing, 184
Drucker, Peter, 53, 79, 218
Dun & Bradstreet, 184
Dun's Marketing Services, 184

Edgar B. Furniture Plantation, 64
Egghead Software, 30
8-Week Cholesterol Cure, The, 104
E.J.Korvette, 219
Electronics Boutique, 32
Entrepreneur, 240

Family Fashions, 2
Federal Express, 100
Federal Trade Commission, 145
Figis, 13
Financing the business,
    basic kinds of financing, 230
    credit card financing, 239
    Federal programs, 231, 240
    grants, 242
    loan proposals, 233
    loans, types of, 232
    Small Business Administration,
        231
Fingerhut, 2, 13, 119, 217

Flea markets, 21
Forum Publishing Co., 166, 169
Foundation Center, 242
Fuller Brush Company, 22, 71
Fund raising, 21

Gift catalogs, 57
General Electric (GE), 147, 224
General Motors (GM), 147
Girard, Joe, 53
Global Computer Supplies, 48
Gordon, Herschell Lewis, 169, 254
Gosden, Freeman F., Jr., 29
Government Marketing News, Inc.
    (GMNI), 147
Grantsmanship Center, 242
Gucci, 114

Hanover House, 1, 30
Harriet Carter Gifts, 13
Harry and David Holiday Book of
    Gifts, 57
Henry, Dee, 121
Hershey, Milton, 217
Horn & Hardart, 30
Hot Shoppes, 225
*How to Prosper in the Coming Bad
    Years*, 105

I. Magnin, 114
Inmac Personal Computer Catalog,
    30
Inquiry advertising, 11, 189
International Business Machines
    (IBM), 147, 225
Inventory management, 19
Item selection,
    building a line, 66

Item selection *(continued)*

   carrying a standard line, pros and
     cons, 65
   serendipity in, 68
   strategy of and criteria for
     choosing, 60
Items sold by catalog, diversity of, 6,
   30

Jack Hurshman Advertising, 160
JDR Microdevices, 120
J. Peterman Company, 41
J. Smith Winter Catalog, 59

Karbo, Joe, 68, 90, 149
Keillor, Garrison, 47
Kleid Company, Inc., 178
K-Mart, 224, 225
Kresge, 225
Krob, Carol, 17

*Ladies Home Journal,*27
Lands' End, 14, 84
Lazy Man's Way to Riches, The, 90,
   149
Leaders and loss leaders, 11, 63,
   192, 211
Lead generation, 5, 11, 79
L'eggs, 13
Lewis, Herschell Gordon, 169
Lillian Vernon, 13
Ling Temco Vought, 242
L. L. Bean, 3, 13, 59
Lord & Taylor, 114
Lotions & Lace Company, 18

Mailing lists,
   brokers for, 26

compiled lists, 27
computer software for managing,
   196
customer lists, 27, 199
databases, as, 179, 186, 193
demographics for, 107
general, 23
house, 199
importance of, 177
kinds of, 27, 188
quality of, defining/measuring,
   178, 187
related terms, 178
response lists, 27
who owns, 178
Mail Order Associates, 18
Mail order jargon, 86
Mail order,
   versus direct mail, 4, 78
Markets and marketing,
   customer feedback, 85
   database, 193
   estimates, premises, and
     assumptions, 81
   exclusivity strategy, 223
   expenses of, principal, 245
   "growth," meaning of, 224
   guarantees, 88
   mistakes, classic, 220
   offer, the, 87, 115, 139
   positioning, 113
   PR in, 192, 245
   proposition, 87
   segmentation, 110
   size of market, 113
   strategies, 38, 223
   timeliness of data, 112
Marriott, 217, 225
Mary Kay, 22

Mason Shoe Mfg. Co., 19
Meredith List Marketing, 180
Mission Orchards, 36
M&B Company, 38
Merlite Industries, 18
Miller, Jack, 22, 48, 95
Montgomery Ward, 2, 18, 29, 88,
    114, 143, 146, 217, 224, 258
Motivational appeals,
    customer relations, 120
    desire to win, 100
    fear and greed, 104
    "free" versus discount, 118
    gifts, 119
    perpetual sales, 118
    rebates versus discounts, 119
    snob appeal, 109

National Publications, Inc., 18
Neiman-Marcus, 114
New York Times, 160

Palder, Edward L., 1
Parker Pen Company, 225
Party sales, 21
Perfect mail order item, the, 64
PR—public relations/publicity,
    articles, 252
    general, as marketing and
        advertising, 245
    interviews, 252
    major expenses of, 245,
    newsletter, free, 251
    q & a—questions and answers—
        about, 246
    releases, news/publicity, 247
    radio and TV appearances, 252
    releases, product, 251
    seminar guesting, 253

Premier Publishers, Inc., 19
Pricing,
    competitive, 209
    customers versus sales, 203
    general considerations in, 201
Prudential, 224
Purchasing agents and catalogs, 49

Qualified Lists Corp., 185
Qualifying prospects, 78
Quill Business Tips, 166
Quill Corporation, 12, 13, 14, 22, 48,
    94, 95, 105, 144, 217
Radio Corporation of America
    (RCA), 147
Raleigh, 22
Rand McNally & Company, 154
Reader's Digest, 192
Reimers, Bob and Beverlee, 14
Repeated mailings, effects of, 12
Robert Hall, 219
Rosenfeld, Jack, 30
Ross Book Service, 14
Ross, Miriam D., 14
Route sales, 22

Sajak, Pat, 252
Schanzle, Gwenda and Pamela, 121
Sears, 2, 12, 14, 17, 18, 29, 59, 62,
    114, 143, 146, 217, 224
Sellers, Patricia, 84
Shropshire, Kenneth, 240
Simply Tops catalog, 102
Small Business Administration, 23,
    213, 241
Small Business Opportunities, 1
Specialty Merchandise Corporation,
    1, 18, 115, 155
Spector, Myer, 115

Spencer Gifts, 13
Spiegel, 2, 12, 14, 17,18, 59, 114,
    143, 146
Sroge, Maxwell, 114
Staples, 29
Super Fresh, 225
Swiss Colony, 13

Target Marketing, 177
Testing,
    economies of scale, significance
        of, 86
    general, 83, 85, 253
    items to test, importance and
        priorities of, 86
    measuring results, 121
Thomas Register, 70
Tiffany's, 99
Tiger Software catalog, 100
Tools of the Trade, 14

U.S.Industries, 225
U.S.Pressed Steel Car Company, 225

Visual Horizons, 38

Volt Information Sciences, 217, 225
Volt Technical Corporation, 225

Wagon jobbing, 22
Walter Drake, 164
Walters, Dottie, 53
Want Ad, The, 45
Washington Post, The, 202
Weinberg, Phyllis, 30
Wheeler, Elmer, 53, 223
Willet, Bill, 2, 19
Williams, Jane A., 14
Willow Creek catalog, 76
Wisconsin Cheeseman, 14
Woodbine House, 1
Woolworth, 224
Worldwide Bargain Hunters, 154
Writer's Market, 1
W.T. Grant, 219

Xerox, 67

Ziglar, Zig, 53